PUBLIC AFFAIRS

PUBLIC AFFAIRS

C. P. SNOW

CHARLES SCRIBNER'S SONS
New York

CONTENTS

ACKNOWLEDGMENTS

'THE Two Cultures and the Scientific Revolution' was delivered as the Rede Lecture at Cambridge in 1959, and published in the same year by the Cambridge University Press. 'A Second Look' was first printed in the *Times Literary Supplement* in 1963, and included in the second edition of 'The Two Cultures', under the title of *The Two Cultures and the Scientific Revolution: and a Second Look*, published by the Cambridge University Press in 1964. 'The Case of Leavis and the Serious Case' was first printed in the *Times Literary Supplement* in 1970.

'Science and Government' was delivered as the Godkin Lectures at Harvard in 1960, and published by the Harvard University Press. The 'Appendix' was published separately in 1962, also by the Harvard University Press.

'The Moral Un-neutrality of Science' was delivered in 1960 to the American Association for the Advancement of Science, and published in the Association's journal, *Science*, in 1961.

'The State of Siege' was delivered as the John Findley Green Foundation Lectures at Westminster College, Fulton, Missouri, in 1968. It was published by Charles Scribner's Sons in New York in 1969, and by Oxfam in London in 1970.

I wish to express my gratitude to all those who invited me to give these lectures in the first place, and to the various publishers who have now permitted me to collect them in this volume. I owe a special debt of gratitude to Mr Arthur Crook, the Editor of the *Times Literary Supplement*.

Mr Brian Coleman, of the Royal Roads Military College, Victoria, B.C., has been of great assistance in the preparation of the volume, editorially and in many other ways. To him also my grateful thanks.

12 March 1971   C.P.S.

PROLOGUE

THIS is a selection from the public statements that I have made from 1959 to the present day. I have made a good many others on various subjects, but these are concentrated on the same set of themes, or really one central theme. For reasons which I mention in the Epilogue, I am not likely to add much to them in the future, and it seemed that this might be a suitable time to make them available in one volume.

I had been thinking about this theme – which is the complex of dangers in front of us for the rest of the century – for a good many years before 1959, but I hadn't been free to express myself in public. This was because, ever since 1940, I had been a public servant in the pay of Her Majesty's Government. I had been a rather irregular public servant, for most of those two decades working on a part-time engagement, in order to give me some time to write my novels. But I was nevertheless bound by the obligations and conventions of the public service. It is an old, and on the whole valuable, convention that one doesn't make statements which bear directly on politics. Anything else is acceptable, if it comes within the category of 'imaginative' writing. Public servants, from long before Trollope's time down to our own, have published novels, poems, plays and no one has thought of objecting. In my own case, I was treated with great indulgence by my Treasury colleagues and successive First Civil Service Commissioners; I wrote my books and published them, and though sometimes, as in *The New Men*, they had perceptible political undertones, they were well within the rules. I shouldn't have thought it decent not to keep within the rules. Once or twice I wrote fairly innocuous pieces on direct public issues: one of these is mentioned in a note on pp. 45 and 147: these were published anonymously, for the sake of propriety, but had been discussed with my colleagues. I signed a few other even more harmless pieces, such as the first sketch, confined to the academic and unpolitical side, of the Two Cultures.

This arrangement suited me well enough. In fact, as I confessed in one of these addresses (cf. p. 196) it suited me too well. All that I most deeply wanted to write I could write. For the rest, there is much comfort in sheltering behind an institution. Men far better than I am find it a satisfactory moral solvent. Maybe there is something in-harmonious and suspect about those who can't. But still I couldn't. When I met Hammarskjöld, I felt a surreptitious sympathy for at least one of his gnomic utterances: and when I wrote about him I found myself saying – in our world, can a man feel even remotely reconciled to himself unless he has tried to do what little he can in action? Well, many men can, with better and bolder characters than mine. But again I couldn't. The only form of action open to me was speaking, attempting to influence and persuade. I committed myself to having a shot at it.

I don't think that, from the beginning, I expected to have much effect. In our present circumstances, there aren't many private voices which could produce much effect, certainly not mine. As I mention in the Epilogue, the dangers about which I have been talking remain entirely unaffected by anything which I and hundreds of others have been saying. To that extent, we have been a total failure. Yet, speaking for myself, I doubt whether that would have been an excuse for not trying.

I set out to say some very simple things, and to say them as simply as I could. All prescripts for action have to be simple. Action itself is simple, or else it doesn't happen. It is different in kind from what goes in the depth of our natures: anyone who wants to know what goes in mine has to read my novels, where the ambiguities, cowardices and irrationalities are clear enough. The person who gives public addresses has to put behind him a great mass of his own qualifications. But what he says ought to be, within its limits, what he believes to be true.

What I believed and still believe to be true, was, I repeat, very simple.

1. We – that is, most people in the world – are moving into great dangers. One of these is the possibility of thermonuclear war. This, though real, is less probable than the other two major dangers: the gap between the rich and poor countries of the world (which was the preoccupation from which I started) and the prospect of over-population and the suffering it will bring with it (which I didn't face completely until the end).

2. These dangers have been brought about by technology, or what we can now call applied science: that is, our ability to under-stand, control and use certain features of the natural world. Tech-nology has two faces, benign and threatening. All through history it has brought blessings and curses: I have reiterated that time and time again. It was true when men first made primitive tools and clambered out into the open savannah: one of the earliest uses of those tools seems to have been for homicide. It was true of the discovery of agriculture: which transformed social living, but also made some sort of organised armies practicable. It was true of the first industrial revolution. Perhaps the sharpest example of this two-faced nature of technology is the effect of medicine. Medicine is in human terms the most significant of all technologies. In the last two generations it has spread all round the world. It has reduced infantile mortality, even in the poorest countries, to an extent which would have seemed unbelievable in the most privileged families in England two hundred years ago. That is a positive good which no one – unless lost to the final relics of human feeling – would wish away. Yet it has led us straight into the flood of population which is the greatest danger of the next fifty years.

3. The only weapon we have to oppose the bad effects of technology is technology itself. There is no other. We can't retreat into a non-technological Eden which never existed. We can't look into ourselves, take comfort from any doctrine of individual salvation, and trust to our natural goodness to carry us through. Anyone who does that is afflicted by romantic illusions, in the worst sense, about what he sees within himself: he hasn't used reason to explore the irrational. The problems for humanity are altogether less innocent, more difficult and different in kind. It is only by the rational use of technology – to control and guide what technology is doing – that we

can keep any hopes of a social life more desirable than our own: or in fact of a social life which is not appalling to imagine.

4. That being so, people will have to understand what technology, applied science, science itself is like, and what it can and cannot do. Such understanding is a necessary part of late twentieth-century education. We require a common culture in which science is an essential component. Otherwise we shall never see the possibilities, either for evil or good.

5. As well as an educated population not totally ignorant of the scientific process (which is the most that we can realistically expect) we need something more. The scientific decisions inside government are, and will be increasingly, of critical importance. Often they have been taken by inadequate methods, or worse than that. There isn't a perfect solution of how to take scientific decisions, certainly not in parliamentary democracies and presumably not anywhere else. There isn't a perfect solution, but we now have enough experience to see how some follies can be avoided.

6. Even if we make all these adjustments, and have good fortune – on the whole, we have had good fortune over nuclear weapons – we are still faced with a black prospect. The rate of increase of world population is not slowing down: it will have doubled by the year 2000, and may double again in another generation. The world's natural resources – in the first instance in food, but then elsewhere – can't cope for long with such a rate of increase. To this danger there is as yet no answer.

Those were the simple things I have tried to say. Many of them are platitudinous: but platitudes have a regrettable knack of being true. In these lectures I have often repeated myself. That was in the nature of the exercise. The statement – there was really only one – I wanted to express in somewhat different forms, with different examples and different stresses. But the core is the same.

The four main pieces were designed as lectures, and I hope they will be read with that in mind. With minor textual corrections, I have left them as originally delivered. I have made some predictions which have turned out correct, some not so (for instance in 1959 I considerably over-estimated the material advance of the poor world). On one or two questions, mainly of local English interest, I have changed my mind. Over the years I have come to see more virtues in some features of our education than I did in 1959. But I don't think I have altered perceptibly on the major issues, except perhaps in mood.

All these addresses, except 'The State of Siege', involved me in a certain amount of trouble, not only argument but occasionally abuse. In the case of 'The Moral Un-neutrality of Science', the abuse was political. That was fair enough, for that speech was in essence a political exhortation about a political choice. I haven't thought it worth while to include here any of that debate on nuclear bombs. It was all settled years ago, and the arguments are now dead. On the other hand, the arguments about 'The Two Cultures and the Scientific Revolution' and 'Science and Government' continued for a long time, and crop up still. Some of them have been very interesting, both in essence and in detail. When I found myself engaged in them, I set myself as a model my old friend G. H. Hardy, who had his share of controversy, and tried to catch some faint echo of his tone. How far I succeeded, which isn't very far, can be judged from 'A Second Look' and the Appendix to 'Science and Government'. Neither of these, nor the third supplementary item, 'The Case of Leavis and the Serious Case', was intended to be given as lectures; they were written for the printed page.

The third of these arose from the fact that I remained dissatisfied with the purely academic formulation of 'The Two Cultures' concept. Then, early in 1970, I took part in a discussion at the University of Texas at Austin, tried a new exposition on Dirac and other colleagues, and felt that, as my final attempt, it was worth setting down on paper. During that month I learned of another attack mixed up with a personal accusation which was at the same time denigratory and utterly untrue. It was immediately demonstrated as being untrue by testimony independent of myself – though, as it happened, I had documentary proof in my own possession. Well, as a rule, I should pass this sort of thing over: but, after some thought, I decided that in this case it was probably wrong to do so. I have given my reason in the article itself.

'The State of Siege' hasn't evoked any denunciations at all, except for a mild one from a Soviet academic, written more in sorrow than in anger, regretting that 'a man who has tried his best according to his lights' should have become so faint-hearted.

Since 'The State of Siege' was delivered, I have had a couple of years to reflect. In the Epilogue, I shall add another word about my present position and what I am now inclined to think.

THE TWO CULTURES AND THE SCIENTIFIC REVOLUTION

I. THE TWO CULTURES

IT is about three years since I made a sketch in print of a problem which had been on my mind for some time.[1] It was a problem I could not avoid just because of the circumstances of my life. The only credentials I had to ruminate on the subject at all came through those circumstances, through nothing more than a set of chances. Anyone with similar experience would have seen much the same things and I think made very much the same comments about them. It just happened to be an unusual experience. By training I was a scientist: by vocation I was a writer. That was all. It was a piece of luck, if you like, that arose through coming from a poor home.

But my personal history isn't the point now. All that I need say is that I came to Cambridge and did a bit of research here at a time of major scientific activity. I was privileged to have a ringside view of one of the most wonderful creative periods in all physics. And it happened through the flukes of war – including meeting W. L. Bragg in the buffet on Kettering station on a very cold morning in 1939, which had a determining influence on my practical life – that I was able, and indeed morally forced, to keep that ringside view ever since. So for thirty years I have had to be in touch with scientists not only out of curiosity, but as part of a working existence. During the same thirty years I was trying to shape the books I wanted to write, which in due course took me among writers.

There have been plenty of days when I have spent the working hours with scientists and then gone off at night with some literary colleagues. I mean that literally. I have had, of course, intimate friends among both scientists and writers. It was through living among these groups and much more, I think, through moving regularly from one to the other and back again that I got occupied with the problem of what, long before I put it on paper, I christened to myself as the 'two cultures'. For constantly I felt I was moving among two groups – comparable in intelligence, identical in race, not grossly different in social origin, earning about the same incomes, who had almost ceased to communicate at all, who in intellectual, moral and psychological climate had so little in common that instead of going from Burlington House or South Kensington to Chelsea, one might have crossed an ocean.

In fact, one had travelled much further than across an ocean – because after a few thousand Atlantic miles, one found Greenwich Village talking precisely the same language as Chelsea, and both having about as much communication with M.I.T. as though the scientists spoke nothing but Tibetan. For this is not just our problem: owing to some of our educational and social idiosyncrasies, it is slightly exaggerated here, owing to another English social peculiarity it is slightly minimised; by and large this is a problem of the entire West.

By this I intend something serious. I am not thinking of the pleasant story of how one of the more convivial Oxford greats dons – I have heard the story attributed to A. L. Smith – came over to Cambridge to dine. The date is perhaps the 1890s. I think it must have been at St John's, or possibly Trinity. Anyway, Smith was sitting at the right hand of the President – or Vice-Master – and he was a man who liked to include all round him in the conversation, although he was not immediately encouraged by the expressions of his neighbours. He addressed some cheerful Oxonian chit-chat at the one opposite to him, and got a grunt. He then tried the man on his right hand and got another grunt. Then, rather to his surprise, one looked at the other and said, 'Do you know what he's talking about?' 'I haven't the least idea.' At this, even Smith was getting out of his depth. But the President, acting as a social emollient, put him at his ease, by saying, 'Oh, those are mathematicians! We never talk to *them*.'

No, I intend something serious. I believe the intellectual life of the whole of Western society is increasingly being split into two polar groups. When I say the intellectual life, I mean to include also a large part of our practical life, because I should be the last person to suggest the two can at the deepest level be distinguished. I shall come back to the practical life a little later. Two polar groups: at one pole we have the literary intellectuals, who incidentally while no one was looking took to referring to themselves as 'intellectuals' as though there were no others. I remember G. H. Hardy once remarking to me in mild puzzlement, some time in the 1930s: 'Have you noticed how the word "intellectual" is used nowadays? There seems to be a new definition which certainly doesn't include Rutherford or Eddington or Dirac or Adrian or me. It does seem rather odd, don't y' know.'[2]

Literary intellectuals at one pole – at the other scientists, and as the most representative, the physical scientists. Between the two a gulf of mutual incomprehension – sometimes (particularly among the young) hostility and dislike, but most of all lack of understanding. They have a curious distorted image of each other. Their attitudes are so different that, even on the level of emotion, they can't find much common ground. Non-scientists tend to think of scientists as brash and boastful. They hear Mr T. S. Eliot, who just for these illustrations we can take as an archetypal figure, saying about his attempts to revive verse-drama that we can hope for very little, but that he would feel content if he and his co-workers could prepare the ground for a new Kyd or a new Greene. That is the tone, restricted and constrained, with which literary intellectuals are at home: it is the subdued voice of their culture. Then they hear a much louder voice, that of another archetypal figure, Rutherford, trumpeting: 'This is the heroic age of science! This is the Elizabethan age!' Many of us heard that, and a good many other statements beside which that was mild; and we weren't left in any doubt whom Rutherford was casting for the role of Shakespeare. What is hard for the literary intellectuals to understand, imaginatively or intellectually, is that he was absolutely right.

And compare 'this is the way the world ends, not with a bang but a whimper' – incidentally, one of the least likely scientific prophecies ever made – compare that with Rutherford's famous repartee, 'Lucky fellow, Rutherford, always on the crest of the wave.' 'Well, I made the wave, didn't I?'

The non-scientists have a rooted impression that the scientists are shallowly optimistic, unaware of man's condition. On the other hand, the scientists believe that the literary intellectuals are totally lacking in foresight, peculiarly unconcerned with their brother men, in a deep sense anti-intellectual, anxious to restrict both art and thought to the existential moment. And so on. Anyone with a mild talent for invective could produce plenty of this kind of subterranean back-chat. On each side there is some of it which is not entirely baseless. It is all destructive. Much of it rests on misinterpretations which are dangerous. I should like to deal with two of the most profound of these now, one on each side.

First, about the scientists' optimism. This is an accusation which has been made so often that it has become a platitude. It has been made by some of the acutest non-scientific minds of the day. But it depends upon a confusion between the individual experience and the social experience, between the individual condition of man and his social condition. Most of the scientists I have known well have felt – just as deeply as the non-scientists I have known well – that the individual condition of each of us is tragic. Each of us is alone: sometimes we escape from solitariness, through love or affection or perhaps creative moments, but those triumphs of life are pools of light we make for ourselves while the edge of the road is black: each of us dies alone. Some scientists I have known have had faith in revealed religion. Perhaps with them the sense of the tragic condition is not so strong. I don't know. With most people of deep feeling, however high-spirited and happy they are, sometimes most of those who are happiest and most high-spirited, it seems to be right in the fibres, part of the weight of life. That is as true of the scientists I have known best as of anyone at all.

But nearly all of them – and this is where the colour of hope genuinely comes in – would see no reason why, just because the individual condition is tragic, so must the social condition be. Each of us is solitary: each of us dies alone: all right, that's a fate against which we can't struggle – but there is plenty of our condition which is not fate, and against which we are less than human unless we do struggle.

Most of our fellow human beings, for instance, are underfed and die before their time. In the crudest terms, *that* is the social condition. There is a moral trap which comes through the insight into man's loneliness: it tempts one to sit back, complacent in one's unique tragedy, and let the others go without a meal.

As a group, the scientists fall into that trap less than others. They are inclined to be impatient to see if something can be done: and inclined to think that it can be done, until it's proved otherwise. That is their real optimism, and it's an optimism that the rest of us badly need.

In reverse, the same spirit, tough and good and determined to fight it out at the side of their brother men, has made scientists regard the other culture's social attitudes as contemptible. That is too facile: some of them are, but they are a temporary phase and not to be taken as representative.

I remember being cross-examined by a scientist of distinction. 'Why do most writers take on social opinions which would have been thought distinctly uncivilised and démodé at the time of the Plantagenets? Wasn't that true of most of the famous twentieth-century writers? Yeats, Pound, Wyndham Lewis, nine out of ten of those who have dominated literary sensibility in our time – weren't they not only politically silly, but politically wicked? Didn't the influence of all they represent bring Auschwitz that much nearer?'

I thought at the time, and I still think, that the correct answer was not to defend the indefensible. It was no use saying that Yeats, according to friends whose judgment I trust, was a man of singular magnanimity of character, as well as a great poet. It was no use denying the facts, which are broadly true. The honest answer was that there is, in fact, a connection, which literary persons were culpably slow to see, between some kinds of early twentieth-century art and the most imbecile expressions of anti-social feeling.[3] That was one reason, among many, why some of us turned our backs on the arts and tried to hack out a new or different way for ourselves.[4]

But though many of those writers dominated literary sensibility for a generation, that is no longer so, or at least to nothing like the same extent. Literature changes more slowly than science. It hasn't the same automatic corrective, and so its misguided periods are longer. But it is ill-considered of scientists to judge writers on the evidence of the period 1914–50.

Those are two of the misunderstandings between the two cultures. I should say, since I began to talk about them – the two cultures, that is – I have had some criticism. Most of my scientific acquaintances think that there is something in it, and so do most of the practising artists I know. But I have been argued with by non-scientists of strong down-to-earth interests. Their view is that it is an over-simplification, and that if one is going to talk in these terms there ought to be at least three cultures. They argue that, though they are not scientists themselves, they would share a good deal of the scientific feeling. They would have as little use – perhaps, since they knew more about it, even less use – for the recent literary culture as the scientists themselves. J. H. Plumb, Alan Bullock and some of my American sociological friends have said that they vigorously refuse to be corralled in a cultural box with people they wouldn't be seen dead with, or to be regarded as helping to produce a climate which would not permit a social hope.

I respect those arguments. The number 2 is a very dangerous number: that is why the dialectic is a dangerous process. Attempts to divide anything into two ought to be regarded with much suspicion. I have thought a long time about going in for further refinements: but in the end I have decided against. I was searching for something a little more than a dashing metaphor, a good deal less than a cultural map: and for those purposes the two cultures is about right, and subtilising any more would bring more disadvantages than it's worth.

At one pole, the scientific culture really is a culture, not only in an intellectual but also in an anthropological sense. That is, its members need not, and of course often do not, always completely understand each other; biologists more often than not will have a pretty hazy idea of contemporary physics; but there are common attitudes, common standards and patterns of behaviour, common approaches and assumptions. This goes surprisingly wide and deep. It cuts across other mental patterns, such as those of religion or politics or class.

Statistically, I suppose slightly more scientists are in religious terms unbelievers, compared with the rest of the intellectual world – though there are plenty who are religious, and that seems to be increasingly so among the young. Statistically also, slightly more scientists are on the Left in open politics – though again, plenty always have called themselves conservatives, and that also seems to be more common among the young. Compared with the rest of the intellectual world, considerably more scientists in this country and probably in the U.S. come from poor families.[5] Yet over a whole range of thought and behaviour, none of that matters very much. In their working, and in much of their emotional life, their attitudes are closer to other scientists than to non-scientists who in religion or politics or class have the same labels as themselves. If I were to risk a piece of shorthand, I should say that naturally they had the future in their bones.

They may or may not like it, but they have it. That was as true of the conservatives J. J. Thomson and Lindemann as of the radicals Einstein or Blackett: as true of the Christian A. H. Compton as of the materialist Bernal: of the aristocrats de Broglie or Russell as of the proletarian Faraday: of those born rich, like Thomas Merton or Victor Rothschild, as of Rutherford, who was the son of an odd-job handyman. Without thinking about it, they respond alike. That is what a culture means.

At the other pole, the spread of attitudes is wider. It is obvious that between the two, as one moves through intellectual society from the physicists to the literary intellectuals, there are all kinds of tones of feeling on the way. But I believe the pole of total incomprehension of science radiates its influence on all the rest. That total incomprehension gives, much more pervasively than we realise, living in it, an unscientific flavour to the whole 'traditional' culture, and that unscientific flavour is often, much more than we admit, on the point of turning anti-scientific. The feelings of one pole become the anti-feelings of the other. If the scientists have the future in their bones, then the traditional culture responds by wishing the future did not exist.[6] It is the traditional culture, to an extent remarkably little diminished by the emergence of the scientific one, which manages the Western world.

This polarisation is sheer loss to us all. To us as people, and to our society. It is at the same time practical and intellectual and creative loss, and I repeat that it is false to imagine that those three considerations are clearly separable. But for a moment I want to concentrate on the intellectual loss.

The degree of incomprehension on both sides is the kind of joke which has gone sour. There are about fifty thousand working scientists in the country and about eighty thousand professional engineers or applied scientists. During the war and in the years since, my colleagues and I have had to interview somewhere between thirty to forty thousand of these – that is, about 25 per cent. The number is large enough to give us a fair sample, though of the men we talked to most would still be under forty. We were able to find out a certain amount of what they read and thought about. I confess that even I, who am fond of them and respect them, was a bit shaken. We hadn't quite expected that the links with the traditional culture should be so tenuous, nothing more than a formal touch of the cap.

As one would expect, some of the very best scientists had and have plenty of energy and interest to spare, and we came across several who had read everything that literary people talk about. But that's very rare. Most of the rest, when one tried to probe for what books they had read, would modestly confess, 'Well, I've *tried* a bit of Dickens', rather as though Dickens were an extraordinarily esoteric, tangled and dubiously rewarding writer, something like Rainer Maria Rilke. In fact that is exactly how they do regard him: we thought that discovery, that Dickens had been transformed into the type-specimen of literary incomprehensibility, was one of the oddest results of the whole exercise.

But of course, in reading him, in reading almost any writer whom we should value, they are just touching their caps to the traditional culture. They have their own culture, intensive, rigorous, and constantly in action. This culture contains a great deal of argument, usually much more rigorous, and almost always at a higher conceptual level, than literary persons' arguments; even though the scientists do cheerfully use words in senses which literary persons don't recognise, the senses are exact ones, and when they talk about 'subjective', 'objective', 'philosophy' or 'progressive',[7] they know what they mean, even though it isn't what one is accustomed to expect.

Remember, these are very intelligent men. Their culture is in many ways an exacting and admirable one. It doesn't contain much art, with the exception, an important exception, of music. Verbal exchange, insistent argument. Long-playing records. Colour-photography. The ear, to some extent the eye. Books, very little, though perhaps not many would go so far as one hero, who perhaps I should admit was further down the scientific ladder than the people I've been talking about – who, when asked what books he read, replied firmly and confidently: 'Books? I prefer to use my books as tools.' It was very hard not to let the mind wander – what sort of tool would a book make? Perhaps a hammer? A primitive digging instrument?

Of books, though, very little. And of the books which to most literary persons are bread and butter, novels, history, poetry, plays, almost nothing at all. It isn't that they're not interested in the psychological or moral or social life. In the social life, they certainly are, more than most of us. In the moral, they are by and large the soundest group of intellectuals we have; there is a moral component right in the grain of science itself, and almost all scientists form their own judgments of the moral life. In the psychological they have as much interest as most of us, though occasionally I fancy they come to it rather late. It isn't that they lack the interests. It is much more that the whole literature of the traditional culture doesn't seem to them relevant to those interests. They are, of course, dead wrong. As a result, their imaginative understanding is less than it could be. They are self-impoverished.

But what about the other side? They are impoverished too – perhaps more seriously, because they are vainer about it. They still like to pretend that the traditional culture is the whole of 'culture', as though the natural order didn't exist. As though the exploration of the natural order was of no interest in either its own value or its consequences. As though the scientific edifice of the physical world was not, in its intellectual depth, complexity and articulation, the most beautiful and wonderful collective work of the mind of man. Yet most non-scientists have no conception of that edifice at all. Even if they want to have it, they can't. It is rather as though, over an immense range of intellectual experience, a whole group was tone-deaf. Except that this tone-deafness doesn't come by nature, but by training, or rather the absence of training.

As with the tone-deaf, they don't know what they miss. They give a pitying chuckle at the news of scientists who have never read a major work of English literature. They dismiss them as ignorant specialists. Yet their own ignorance and their own specialisation is just as startling. A good many times I have been present at gatherings of people who, by the standards of the traditional culture, are thought highly educated and who have with considerable gusto been expressing their incredulity at the illiteracy of scientists. Once or twice I have been provoked and have asked the company how many of them could describe the Second Law of Thermodynamics. The response was cold: it was also negative. Yet I was asking something which is about the scientific equivalent of: *Have you read a work of Shakespeare's?*

I now believe that if I had asked an even simpler question – such as, What do you mean by mass, or acceleration, which is the scientific equivalent of saying, *Can you read?* – not more than one in ten of the highly educated would have felt that I was speaking the same language. So the great edifice of modern physics goes up, and the majority of the cleverest people in the Western world have about as much insight into it as their neolithic ancestors would have had.

Just one more of those questions, that my non-scientific friends regard as being in the worst of taste. Cambridge is a university where scientists and non-scientists meet every night at dinner.[8] About two years ago, one of the most astonishing discoveries in the whole history of science was brought off. I don't mean the sputnik – that was admirable for quite different reasons, as a feat of organisation and a triumphant use of existing knowledge. No, I mean the discovery at Columbia by Yang and Lee. It is a piece of work of the greatest beauty and originality, but the result is so startling that one forgets how beautiful the thinking is. It makes us think again about some of the fundamentals of the physical world. Intuition, common sense – they are neatly stood on their heads. The result is usually known as the non-conservation of parity. If there were any serious communication between the two cultures, this experiment would have been talked about at every High Table in Cambridge. Was it? I wasn't here: but I should like to ask the question.

There seems then to be no place where the cultures meet. I am not going to waste time saying that this is a pity. It is much worse than that. Soon I shall come to some practical consequences. But at the heart of thought and creation we are letting some of our best chances go by default. The clashing point of two subjects, two disciplines, two cultures – of two galaxies, so far as that goes – ought to produce creative chances. In the history of mental activity that has been where some of the break-throughs came. The chances are there now. But they are there, as it were, in a vacuum, because those in the two cultures can't talk to each other. It is bizarre how very little of twentieth-century science has been assimilated into twentieth-century art. Now and then one used to find poets conscientiously using scientific expressions, and getting them wrong – there was a time when 'refraction' kept cropping up in verse in a mystifying fashion, and when 'polarised light' was used as though writers were under the illusion that it was a specially admirable kind of light.

Of course, that isn't the way that science could be any good to art. It has got to be assimilated along with, and as part and parcel of, the whole of our mental experience, and used as naturally as the rest.

I said earlier that this cultural divide is not just an English phenomenon: it exists all over the Western world. But it probably seems at its sharpest in England, for two reasons. One is our fanatical belief in educational specialisation, which is much more deeply ingrained in us than in any country in the world, West or East. The other is our tendency to let our social forms crystallise. This tendency appears to get stronger, not weaker, the more we iron out economic inequalities: and this is specially true in education. It means that once anything like a cultural divide gets established, all the social forces operate to make it not less rigid, but more so.

The two cultures were already dangerously separate sixty years ago; but a prime minister like Lord Salisbury could have his own laboratory at Hatfield, and Arthur Balfour had a somewhat more than amateur interest in natural science. John Anderson did some research in inorganic chemistry in Leipzig before passing first into the Civil Service, and incidentally took a spread of subjects which is now impossible.[9] None of that degree of interchange at the top of the Establishment is likely, or indeed thinkable, now.[10]

In fact, the separation between the scientists and non-scientists is much less bridgeable among the young than it was even thirty years ago. Thirty years ago the cultures had long ceased to speak to each other: but at least they managed a kind of frozen smile across the gulf. Now the politeness has gone, and they just make faces. It is not only that the young scientists now feel that they are part of a culture on the rise while the other is in retreat. It is also, to be brutal, that the young scientists know that with an indifferent degree they'll get a comfortable job, while their contemporaries and counterparts in English or History will be lucky to earn 60 per cent as much. No young scientist of any talent would feel that he isn't wanted or that his work is ridiculous, as did the hero of *Lucky Jim*, and in fact, some of the disgruntlement of Amis and his associates is the disgruntlement of the under-employed arts graduate.

There is only one way out of all this: it is, of course, by rethinking our education. In this country, for the two reasons I have given, that is more difficult than in any other. Nearly everyone will agree that our school education is too specialised. But nearly everyone feels that it is outside the will of man to alter it. Other countries are as dissatisfied with their education as we are, but are not so resigned.

The U.S. teach out of proportion more children up to eighteen than we do: they teach them far more widely, but nothing like so rigorously. They know that: they are hoping to take the problem in hand within ten years, though they may not have all that time to spare. The U.S.S.R. also teach out of proportion more children than we do: they also teach far more widely than we do (it is an absurd Western myth that their school education is specialised) but much too rigorously.[11] They know that – and they are beating about to get it right. The Scandinavians, in particular the Swedes, who would make a more sensible job of it than any of us, are handicapped by their practical need to devote an inordinate amount of time to foreign languages. But they too are seized of the problem.

Are we? Have we crystallised so far that we are no longer flexible at all?

Talk to schoolmasters, and they say that our intense specialisation, like nothing else on earth, is dictated by the Oxford and Cambridge scholarship examinations. If that is so, one would have thought it not utterly impracticable to change the Oxford and Cambridge scholarship examinations. Yet one would underestimate the national capacity for the intricate defensive to believe that that was easy. All the lessons of our educational history suggest we are only capable of increasing specialisation, not decreasing it.

Somehow we have set ourselves the task of producing a tiny *élite* – far smaller proportionately than in any comparable country – educated in one academic skill. For a hundred and fifty years in Cambridge it was mathematics: then it was mathematics or classics: then natural science was allowed in. But still the choice had to be a single one.

It may well be that this process has gone too far to be reversible. I have given reasons why I think it is a disastrous process, for the purpose of a living culture. I am going on to give reasons why I think it is fatal, if we're to perform our practical tasks in the world. But I can think of only one example, in the whole of English educational history, where our pursuit of specialised mental exercises was resisted with success.

It was done here in Cambridge, fifty years ago, when the old order-of-merit in the Mathematical Tripos was abolished. For over a hundred years, the nature of the Tripos had been crystallising. The competition for the top places had got fiercer, and careers hung on them. In most colleges, certainly in my own, if one managed to come out as Senior or Second Wrangler, one was elected a Fellow out of hand. A whole apparatus of coaching had grown up. Men of the quality of Hardy, Littlewood, Russell, Eddington, Jeans, Keynes, went in for two or three years' training for an examination which was intensely competitive and intensely difficult. Most people in Cambridge were very proud of it, with a similar pride to that which almost anyone in England always has for our existing educational institutions, whatever they happen to be. If you study the fly-sheets of the time, you will find the passionate arguments for keeping the examination precisely as it was to all eternity: it was the only way to keep up standards, it was the only fair test of merit, indeed, the only seriously objective test in the world. The arguments, in fact, were almost exactly those which are used today with precisely the same passionate sincerity if anyone suggests that the scholarship examinations might conceivably not be immune from change.

In every respect but one, in fact, the old Mathematical Tripos seemed perfect. The one exception, however, appeared to some to be rather important. It was simply – so the young creative mathematicians, such as Hardy and Littlewood, kept saying – that the training had no intellectual merit at all. They went a little further, and said that the Tripos had killed serious mathematics in England stone dead for a hundred years. Well, even in academic controversy, that took some skirting round, and they got their way. But I have an impression that Cambridge was a good deal more flexible between 1850 and 1914 than it has been in our time. If we had had the old Mathematical Tripos firmly planted among us, should we ever have managed to abolish it?

II. INTELLECTUALS AS NATURAL LUDDITES

The reasons for the existence of the two cultures are many, deep, and complex, some rooted in social histories, some in personal histories, and some in the inner dynamic of the different kinds of mental activity themselves. But I want to isolate one which is not so much a reason as a correlative, something which winds in and out of any of these discussions. It can be said simply, and it is this. If we forget the scientific culture, then the rest of Western intellectuals have never tried, wanted, or been able to understand the industrial revolution, much less accept it. Intellectuals, in particular literary intellectuals, are natural Luddites.

That is specially true of this country, where the industrial revolution happened to us earlier than elsewhere, during a long spell of absentmindedness. Perhaps that helps explain our present degree of crystallisation. But, with a little qualification, it is also true, and surprisingly true, of the United States.

In both countries, and indeed all over the West, the first wave of the industrial revolution crept on, without anyone noticing what was happening. It was, of course – or at least it was destined to become, under our own eyes, and in our own time – by far the biggest transformation in society since the discovery of agriculture. In fact, those two revolutions, the agricultural and the industrial–scientific, are the only qualitative changes in social living that men have ever known. But the traditional culture didn't notice: or when it did notice, didn't like what it saw. Not that the traditional culture wasn't doing extremely well out of the revolution; the English educational institutions took their slice of the English nineteenth-century wealth, and perversely, it helped crystallise them in the forms we know.

Almost none of the talent, almost none of the imaginative energy, went back into the revolution which was producing the wealth. The traditional culture became more abstracted from it as it became more wealthy, trained its young men for administration, for the Indian Empire, for the purpose of perpetuating the culture itself, but never in any circumstances to equip them to understand the revolution or take part in it. Far-sighted men were beginning to see, before the middle of the nineteenth century, that in order to go on producing wealth, the country needed to train some of its bright minds in science, particularly in applied science. No one listened. The traditional culture didn't listen at all: and the pure scientists, such as there were, didn't listen very eagerly. You will find the story, which in spirit continues down to the present day, in Eric Ashby's *Technology and the Academics*.[12]

The academics had nothing to do with the industrial revolution; as Corrie, the old Master of Jesus, said about trains running into Cambridge on Sunday, 'It is equally displeasing to God and to myself.' So far as there was any thinking in nineteenth-century industry, it was left to cranks and clever workmen. American social historians have told me that much the same was true of the U.S. The industrial revolution, which began developing in New England fifty years or so later than ours,[13] apparently received very little educated talent, either then or later in the nineteenth century. It had to make do with the guidance handymen could give it – sometimes, of course, handymen like Henry Ford, with a dash of genius.

The curious thing was that in Germany, in the 1830s and 1840s, long before serious industrialisation had started there, it was possible to get a good university education in applied science, better than anything England or the U.S. could offer for a couple of generations. I don't begin to understand this: it doesn't make social sense: but it was so. With the result that Ludwig Mond, the son of a court purveyor, went to Heidelberg and learnt some sound applied chemistry. Siemens, a Prussian signals officer, at military academy and university went through what for their time were excellent courses in electrical engineering. Then they came to England, met no competition at all, brought in other educated Germans, and made fortunes exactly as though they were dealing with a rich, illiterate colonial territory. Similar fortunes were made by German techno-logists in the United States.

Almost everywhere, though, intellectual persons didn't compre-hend what was happening. Certainly the writers didn't. Plenty of them shuddered away, as though the right course for a man of feeling was to contract out; some, like Ruskin and William Morris and Thoreau and Emerson and Lawrence, tried various kinds of fancies which were not in effect more than screams of horror. It is hard to think of a writer of high class who really stretched his imaginative sympathy, who could see at once the hideous back-streets, the smoking chimneys, the internal price – and also the prospects of life that were opening out for the poor, the intimations, up to now un-known except to the lucky, which were just coming within reach of the remaining 99 per cent of his brother men. Some of the nineteenth-century Russian novelists might have done; their natures were broad enough; but they were living in a pre-industrial society and didn't have the opportunity. The only writer of world class who seems to have had an understanding of the industrial revolution was Ibsen in his old age: and there wasn't much that old man didn't under-stand.

For, of course, one truth is straightforward. Industrialisation is the only hope of the poor. I use the word 'hope' in a crude and prosaic sense. I have not much use for the moral sensibility of anyone who is too refined to use it so. It is all very well for us, sitting pretty, to think that material standards of living don't matter all that much. It is all very well for one, as a personal choice, to reject industrialisa-tion – do a modern Walden, if you like, and if you go without much food, see most of your children die in infancy, despise the comforts of literacy, accept twenty years off your own life, then I respect you for the strength of your aesthetic revulsion.[14] But I don't respect you in the slightest if, even passively, you try to impose the same choice on others who are not free to choose. In fact, we know what their choice would be. For, with singular unanimity, in any country where they have had the chance, the poor have walked off the land into the factories as fast as the factories could take them.

I remember talking to my grandfather when I was a child. He was a good specimen of a nineteenth-century artisan. He was highly intelligent, and he had a great deal of character. He had left school at the age of ten, and had educated himself intensely until he was an old man. He had all his class's passionate faith in education. Yet, he had never had the luck – or, as I now suspect, the worldly force and dexterity – to go very far. In fact, he never went further than maintenance foreman in a tramway depot. His life would seem to his grandchildren laborious and unrewarding almost beyond belief. But it didn't seem to him quite like that. He was much too sensible a man not to know that he hadn't been adequately used: he had too much pride not to feel a proper rancour: he was disappointed that he had not done more – and yet, compared with *his* grandfather, he felt he had done a lot. His grandfather must have been an agricultural labourer. I don't so much as know his Christian name. He was one of the 'dark people', as the old Russian liberals used to call them, completely lost in the great anonymous sludge of history. So far as my grandfather knew, he could not read or write. He was a man of ability, my grandfather thought; my grandfather was pretty unforgiving about what society had done, or not done, to his ancestors, and did not romanticise their state. It was no fun being an agricultural labourer in the mid to late eighteenth century, in the time that we, snobs that we are, think of only as the time of the Enlightenment and Jane Austen.

The industrial revolution looked very different according to whether one saw it from above or below. It looks very different today according to whether one sees it from Chelsea or from a village in Asia. To people like my grandfather, there was no question that the industrial revolution was less bad than what had gone before. The only question was, how to make it better.

In a more sophisticated sense, that is still the question. In the advanced countries, we have realised in a rough and ready way what the old industrial revolution brought with it. A great increase of population, because applied science went hand in hand with medical science and medical care. Enough to eat, for a similar reason. Everyone able to read and write, because an industrial society can't work without. Health, food, education; nothing but the industrial revolution could have spread them right down to the very poor. Those are primary gains – there are losses[15] too, of course, one of which is that organising a society for industry makes it easy to organise it for all-out war. But the gains remain. They are the base of our social hope.

And yet: do we understand how they have happened? Have we begun to comprehend even the old industrial revolution? Much less the new scientific revolution in which we stand? There never was anything more necessary to comprehend.

III. THE SCIENTIFIC REVOLUTION

I have just mentioned a distinction between the industrial revolution and the scientific revolution. The distinction is not clear-edged, but it is a useful one, and I ought to try to define it now. By the industrial revolution, I mean the gradual use of machines, the employment of men and women in factories, the change in this country from a population mainly of agricultural labourers to a population mainly engaged in making things in factories and distributing them when they were made. That change, as I have said, crept on us unawares, untouched by academics, hated by Luddites, practical Luddites and intellectual ones. It is connected, so it seems to me, with many of the attitudes to science and aesthetics which have crystallised among us. One can date it roughly from the middle of the eighteenth century to the early twentieth. Out of it grew another change, closely related to the first, but far more deeply scientific, far quicker, and probably far more prodigious in its result. This change comes from the application of real science to industry, no longer hit and miss, no longer the ideas of odd 'inventors', but the real stuff.

Dating this second change is very largely a matter of taste. Some would prefer to go back to the first large-scale chemical or engineering industries, round about sixty years ago. For myself, I should put it much further on, not earlier than thirty to forty years ago – and as a rough definition, I should take the time when atomic particles were first made industrial use of. I believe the industrial society of electronics, atomic energy, automation, is in cardinal respects different in kind from any that has gone before, and will change the world much more. It is this transformation that, in my view, is entitled to the name of 'scientific revolution'.

This is the material basis for our lives: or more exactly, the social plasma of which we are a part. And we know almost nothing about it. I remarked earlier that the highly educated members of the non-scientific culture couldn't cope with the simplest concepts of pure science: it is unexpected, but they would be even less happy with applied science. How many educated people know anything about productive industry, old-style or new? What is a machine-tool? I once asked a literary party; and they looked shifty. Unless one knows, industrial production is as mysterious as witch-doctoring. Or take buttons. Buttons aren't very complicated things: they are being made in millions every day: one has to be a reasonably ferocious Luddite not to think that that is, on the whole, an estimable activity. Yet I would bet that out of men getting firsts in arts subjects at Cambridge this year, not one in ten could give the loosest analysis of the human organisation which it needs.

In the United States, perhaps, there is a wider nodding acquaintance with industry, but, now I come to think of it, no American novelist of any class has ever been able to assume that his audience had it. He can assume, and only too often does, an acquaintance with a pseudo-feudal society, like the fag-end of the Old South – but not with industrial society. Certainly an English novelist couldn't.

Yet the personal relations in a productive organisation are of the greatest subtlety and interest. They are very deceptive. They look as though they ought to be the personal relations that one gets in any hierarchical structure with a chain of command, like a division in the army or a department in the Civil Service. In practice they are much more complex than that, and anyone used to the straight chain of command gets lost the instant he sets foot in an industrial organisation. No one in any country, incidentally, knows yet what these personal relations ought to be. That is a problem almost independent of large-scale politics, a problem springing straight out of the industrial life.

I think it is only fair to say that most pure scientists have themselves been devastatingly ignorant of productive industry, and many still are. It is permissible to lump pure and applied scientists into the same scientific culture, but the gaps are wide. Pure scientists and engineers often totally misunderstand each other. Their behaviour tends to be very different: engineers have to live their lives in an organised community, and however odd they are underneath they manage to present a disciplined face to the world. Not so pure scientists. In the same way pure scientists still, though less than twenty years ago, have statistically a higher proportion in politics left of centre than any other profession: not so engineers, who are conservative almost to a man. Not reactionary in the extreme literary sense, but just conservative. They are absorbed in making things, and the present social order is good enough for them.

Pure scientists have by and large been dim-witted about engineers and applied science. They couldn't get interested. They wouldn't recognise that many of the problems were as intellectually exacting as pure problems, and that many of the solutions were as satisfying and beautiful. Their instinct – perhaps sharpened in this country by the passion to find a new snobbism wherever possible, and to invent one if it doesn't exist – was to take it for granted that applied science was an occupation for second-rate minds. I say this more sharply because thirty years ago I took precisely that line myself. The climate of thought of young research workers in Cambridge then was not to our credit. We prided ourselves that the science we were doing could not, in any conceivable circumstances, have any practical use. The more firmly one could make that claim, the more superior one felt.

Rutherford himself had little feeling for engineering. He was amazed – he used to relate the story with incredulous admiration – that Kapitza had actually sent an engineering drawing to Metrovick, and that those magicians had duly studied the drawing, *made the machine*, and delivered it in Kapitza's laboratory! Rutherford was so impressed by Cockcroft's engineering skill that he secured for him a special capital grant for machinery – the grant was as much as six hundred pounds! In 1933, four years before his death, Rutherford said, firmly and explicitly, that he didn't believe the energy of the nucleus would ever be released – nine years later, at Chicago, the first pile began to run. That was the only major bloomer in scientific judgment Rutherford ever made. It is interesting that it should be at the point where pure science turned into applied.

No, pure scientists did not show much understanding or display much sense of social fact. The best that can be said for them is that, given the necessity, they found it fairly easy to learn. In the war, a great many scientists had to learn, for the good Johnsonian reason that sharpens one's wits, something about productive industry. It opened their eyes. In my own job, I had to try to get some insight into industry. It was one of the most valuable pieces of education in my life. But it started when I was thirty-five, and I ought to have had it much earlier.

That brings me back to education. Why aren't we coping with the scientific revolution? Why are other countries doing better? How are we going to meet our future, both our cultural and our practical future? It should be obvious by now that I believe both lines of argument lead to the same end. If one begins by thinking only of the intellectual life, or only of the social life, one comes to a point where it becomes manifest that our education has gone wrong, and gone wrong in the same way.

I don't pretend that any country has got its education perfect. In some ways, as I said before, the Russians and Americans are both more actively dissatisfied with theirs than we are: that is, they are taking more drastic steps to change it. But that is because they are more sensitive to the world they are living in. For myself, I have no doubt that, though neither of them has got the answer right, they are a good deal nearer than we are. We do some things much better than either of them. In educational tactics, we are often more gifted than they are. In educational strategy, by their side we are only playing at it.

The differences between the three systems are revelatory. We teach, of course, a far smaller proportion of our children up to the age of eighteen: and we take a far smaller proportion even of those we do teach up to the level of a university degree. The old pattern of training a small *élite* has never been broken, though it has been slightly bent. Within that pattern, we have kept the national passion for specialisation: and we work our clever young up to the age of twenty-one far harder than the Americans, though no harder than the Russians. At eighteen, our science specialists know more science than their contemporaries anywhere, though they know less of any-thing else. At twenty-one, when they take their first degree they are probably still a year or so ahead.

The American strategy is different in kind. They take everyone, the entire population,[16] up to eighteen in high schools, and educate them very loosely and generally. Their problem is to inject some rigour – in particular some fundamental mathematics and science – into this loose education. A very large proportion of the eighteen-year-olds then go to college: and this college education is, like the school education, much more diffuse and less professional than ours.[17] At the end of four years, the young men and women are usually not so well trained professionally as we are: though I think it is fair comment to say that a higher proportion of the best of them, having been run on a looser rein, retain their creative zest. Real severity enters with the Ph.D. At that level the Americans suddenly begin to work their students much harder than we do. It is worth remembering that they find enough talent to turn out nearly as many Ph.D.s in science and engineering each year as we contrive to get through our first degrees.

The Russian high school education is much less specialised than ours, much more arduous than the American. It is so arduous that for the non-academic it seems to have proved too tough, and they are trying other methods from fifteen to seventeen. The general method has been to put everyone through a kind of continental Lycée course, with a sizeable component, more than 40 per cent, of science and mathematics. Everyone has to do all subjects. At the university this general education ceases abruptly: and for the last three years of the five-year course the specialisation is more intensive even than ours. That is, at most English universities a young man can take an honours degree in mechanical engineering. In Russia he can take, and an enormous number do take, a corresponding degree in one bit of mechanical engineering, as it might be aerodynamics or machine-tool design or diesel engine production.

They won't listen to me, but I believe they have overdone this, just as I believe they have slightly overdone the number of engineers they are training. It is now much larger than in the rest of the world put together – getting on for fifty per cent larger.[18] Pure scientists they are training only slightly more than the United States, though in physics and mathematics the balance is heavily in the Russian direction.

Our population is small by the side of either the U.S.A. or the U.S.S.R. Roughly, if we compare like with like, and put scientists and engineers together, we are training at a professional level per head of the population one Englishman to every one and a half Americans to every two and a half Russians.[19] Someone is wrong.

With some qualifications, I believe the Russians have judged the situation sensibly. They have a deeper insight into the scientific revolution than we have, or than the Americans have. The gap between the cultures doesn't seem to be anything like so wide as with us. If one reads contemporary Soviet novels, for example, one finds that their novelists can assume in their audience – as we cannot – at least a rudimentary acquaintance with what industry is all about. Pure science doesn't often come in, and they don't appear much happier with it than literary intellectuals are here. But engineering does come in. An engineer in a Soviet novel is as acceptable, so it seems, as a psychiatrist in an American one. They are as ready to cope in art with the processes of production as Balzac was with the processes of craft manufacture. I don't want to overstress this, but it may be significant. It may also be significant that, in these novels, one is constantly coming up against a passionate belief in education. The people in them believe in education exactly as my grandfather did, and for the same mixture of idealistic and bread-and-butter reasons.

Anyway, the Russians have judged what kind and number of educated men and women[20] a country needs to come out top in the scientific revolution. I am going to oversimplify, but their estimate, and I believe it's pretty near right, is this. First of all, as many alpha-plus scientists as the country can throw up. No country has many of them. Provided the schools and universities are there, it doesn't matter all that much what you teach them. They will look after themselves.[21] We probably have at least as many pro rata as the Russians and Americans; that is the least of our worries. Second, a much larger stratum of alpha professions – these are the people who are going to do the supporting research, the high class design and development. In quality, England compares well in this stratum with the U.S.A. or U.S.S.R.: this is what our education is specially geared to produce. In quantity, though, we are not discovering (again per head of the population) half as many as the Russians think necessary and are able to find. Third, another stratum, educated to about the level of Part I of the Natural Sciences or Mechanical Sciences Tripos, or perhaps slightly below that. Some of these will do the secondary technical jobs, but some will take major responsibility, particularly in the human jobs. The proper use of such men depends upon a different distribution of ability from the one that has grown up here. As the scientific revolution goes on, the call for these men will be something we haven't imagined, though the Russians have. They will be required in thousands upon thousands, and they will need all the human development that university education can give them.[22] It is here, perhaps, most of all that our insight has been fogged. Fourthly and last, politicians, administrators, an entire community, who know enough science to have a sense of what the scientists are talking about.

That, or something like that, is the specification for the scientific revolution.[23] I wish I were certain that in this country we were adaptable enough to meet it. In a moment I want to go on to an issue which will, in the world view, count more: but perhaps I can be forgiven for taking a sideways look at our own fate. It happens that of all the advanced countries, our position is by a long way the most precarious. That is the result of history and accident, and isn't to be laid to the blame of any Englishman now living. If our ancestors had invested talent in the industrial revolution instead of the Indian Empire, we might be more soundly based now. But they didn't.

We are left with a population twice as large as we can grow food for, so that we are always going to be *au fond* more anxious than France or Sweden:[24] and with very little in the way of natural resources – by the standard of the great world powers, with nothing. The only real assets we have, in fact, are our wits. Those have served us pretty well, in two ways. We have a good deal of cunning, native or acquired, in the arts of getting on among ourselves: that is a strength. And we have been inventive and creative, possibly out of proportion to our numbers. I don't believe much in national differences in cleverness, but compared with other countries we are certainly no stupider.

Given these two assets, and they are our only ones, it should have been for us to understand the scientific revolution first, to educate ourselves to the limit and give a lead. Well, we have done something. In some fields, like atomic energy, we have done better than anyone could have predicted. Within the pattern, the rigid and crystallised pattern of our education and of the two cultures, we have been trying moderately hard to adjust ourselves.

The bitterness is, it is nothing like enough. To say we have to educate ourselves or perish, is a little more melodramatic than the facts warrant. To say, we have to educate ourselves or watch a steep decline in our own lifetime, is about right. We can't do it, I am now convinced, without breaking the existing pattern. I know how difficult this is. It goes against the emotional grain of nearly all of us. In many ways, it goes against my own, standing uneasily with one foot in a dead or dying world and the other in a world that at all costs we must see born. I wish I could be certain that we shall have the courage of what our minds tell us.

More often than I like, I am saddened by a historical myth. Whether the myth is good history or not, doesn't matter; it is pressing enough for me. I can't help thinking of the Venetian Republic in their last half-century. Like us, they had once been fabulously lucky. They had become rich, as we did, by accident. They had acquired immense political skill, just as we have. A good many of them were tough-minded, realistic, patriotic men. They knew, just as clearly as we know, that the current of history had begun to flow against them. Many of them gave their minds to working out ways to keep going. It would have meant breaking the pattern into which they had crystallised. They were fond of the pattern, just as we are fond of ours. They never found the will to break it.

IV. THE RICH AND THE POOR

But that is our local problem, and it is for us to struggle with it. Sometimes, it is true, I have felt that the Venetian shadow falls over the entire West. I have felt that on the other side of the Mississippi. In more resilient moments, I comfort myself that Americans are much more like us between 1850 and 1914: whatever they don't do, they do react. It's going to take them a long and violent pull to be as well prepared for the scientific revolution as the Russians are, but there are good chances that they will do it.

Nevertheless, that isn't the main issue of the scientific revolution. The main issue is that the people in the industrialised countries are getting richer, and those in the non-industrialised countries are at best standing still: so that the gap between the industrialised countries and the rest is widening every day. On the world scale this is the gap between the rich and the poor.

Among the rich are the U.S., the white Commonwealth countries, Great Britain, most of Europe, and the U.S.S.R. China is betwixt and between, not yet over the industrial hump, but probably getting there. The poor are all the rest. In the rich countries people are living longer, eating better, working less. In a poor country like India, the expectation of life is less than half what it is in England. There is some evidence that Indians and other Asians are eating less, in absolute quantities, than they were a generation ago. The statistics are not reliable, and informants in the F.A.O. have told me not to put much trust in them. But it is accepted that, in all non-industrialised countries, people are not eating better than at the subsistence level. And they are working as people have always had to work, from Neolithic times until our own. Life for the overwhelming majority of mankind has always been nasty, brutish and short. It is so in the poor countries still.

This disparity between the rich and the poor has been noticed. It has been noticed, most acutely and not unnaturally, by the poor. Just because they have noticed it, it won't last for long. Whatever else in the world we know survives to the year 2000, that won't. Once the trick of getting rich is known, as it now is, the world can't survive half rich and half poor. It's just not on.

The West has got to help in this transformation. The trouble is, the West with its divided culture finds it hard to grasp just how big, and above all just how fast, the transformation must be.

Earlier I said that few non-scientists really understand the scientific concept of acceleration. I meant that as a gibe. But in social terms, it is a little more than a gibe. During all human history until this century, the rate of social change has been very slow. So slow, that it would pass unnoticed in one person's lifetime. That is no longer so. The rate of change has increased so much that our imagination can't keep up. There is *bound* to be more social change, affecting more people, in the next decade than in any before. There is *bound* to be more change again, in the 1970s. In the poor countries, people have caught on to this simple concept. Men there are no longer prepared to wait for periods longer than one person's lifetime.

The comforting assurances, given *de haut en bas*, that maybe in a hundred or two hundred years things may be slightly better for them – they only madden. Pronouncements such as one still hears from old Asia or old Africa hands – Why, it will take those people five hundred years to get up to our standard! – they are both suicidal and technologically illiterate. Particularly when said, as they always seem to be said, by someone looking as though it wouldn't take Neanderthal Man five years to catch up with *him*.

The fact is, the rate of change has already been proved possible. Someone said, when the first atomic bomb went off, that the only important secret is now let out – the thing works. After that, any determined country could make the bomb, given a few years. In the same way, the only secret of the Russian and Chinese industrialisation is that they've brought it off. That is what Asians and Africans have noticed. It took the Russians about forty years, starting with something of an industrial base – Tsarist industry wasn't negligible – but interrupted by a civil war and then the greatest war of all. The Chinese started with much less of an industrial base, but haven't been interrupted, and it looks like taking them not much over half the time.

These transformations were made with inordinate effort and with great suffering. Much of the suffering was unnecessary: the horror is hard to look at straight, standing in the same decades. Yet they've proved that common men can show astonishing fortitude in chasing jam tomorrow. Jam today, and men aren't at their most exciting: jam tomorrow, and one often sees them at their noblest. The transformations have also proved something which only the scientific culture can take in its stride. Yet, when we don't take it in our stride, it makes us look silly.

It is simply that technology is rather easy. Or more exactly, technology is the branch of human experience that people can learn with predictable results. For a long time, the West misjudged this very badly. After all, a good many Englishmen have been skilled in mechanical crafts for half a dozen generations. Somehow we've made ourselves believe that the whole of technology was a more or less incommunicable art. It's true enough, we start with a certain advantage. Not so much because of tradition, I think, as because all our children play with mechanical toys. They are picking up pieces of applied science before they can read. That is an advantage we haven't made the most of. Just as the Americans have the advantage that nine out of ten adults can drive a car and are to some extent mechanics. In the last war, which was a war of small machines, that was a real military asset. Russia is catching up with the U.S. in major industry – but it will be a long time before Russia is as convenient a country as the U.S. in which to have one's car break down.[25]

The curious thing is, none of that seems to matter much. For the task of totally industrialising a major country, as in China today, it only takes will to train enough scientists and engineers and technicians. Will, and quite a small number of years. There is no evidence that any country or race is better than any other in scientific teachability: there is a good deal of evidence that all are much alike. Tradition and technical background seem to count for surprisingly little.

We've all seen this with our own eyes. I myself have found Sicilian girls taking the top places in the Honours Physics course – a very exacting course – at the University of Rome: they'd have been in something like purdah thirty years ago. And I remember John Cockcroft coming back from Moscow some time in the early 1930s. The news got round that he had been able to have a look, not only at laboratories, but at factories and the mechanics in them. What we expected to hear, I don't know: but there were certainly some who had pleasurable expectations of those stories precious to the hearts of Western man, about moujiks prostrating themselves before a milling machine, or breaking a vertical borer with their bare hands. Someone asked Cockcroft what the skilled workmen were like. Well, he has never been a man to waste words. A fact is a fact is a fact. 'Oh,' he said, 'they're just about the same as the ones at Metrovick.' That was all. He was, as usual, right.

There is no getting away from it. It is technically possible to carry out the scientific revolution in India, Africa, South-East Asia, Latin America, the Middle East, within fifty years. There is no excuse for Western man not to know this. And not to know that this is the one way out through the three menaces which stand in our way – H-bomb war, over-population, the gap between the rich and the poor. This is one of the situations where the worst crime is innocence.

Since the gap between the rich countries and the poor can be removed, it will be. If we are short-sighted, inept, incapable either of good-will or enlightened self-interest, then it may be removed to the accompaniment of war and starvation: but removed it will be. The questions are, how, and by whom. To those questions, one can only give partial answers: but that may be enough to set us thinking. The scientific revolution on the world-scale needs, first and foremost, capital: capital in all forms, including capital machinery. The poor countries, until they have got beyond a certain point on the industrial curve, cannot accumulate that capital. That is why the gap between rich and poor is widening. The capital must come from outside.

There are only two possible sources. One is the West, which means mainly the U.S., the other is the U.S.S.R. Even the United States hasn't infinite resources of such capital. If they or Russia tried to do it alone, it would mean an effort greater than either had to make industrially in the war. If they both took part, it wouldn't mean that order of sacrifice – though in my view it's optimistic to think, as some wise men do, that it would mean no sacrifice at all. The scale of the operation requires that it would have to be a national one. Private industry, even the biggest private industry, can't touch it, and in no sense is it a fair business risk. It's a bit like asking Duponts or I.C.I. back in 1940 to finance the entire development of the atomic bomb.

The second requirement, after capital, as important as capital, is men. That is, trained scientists and engineers adaptable enough to devote themselves to a foreign country's industrialisation for at least ten years out of their lives. Here, unless and until the Americans and we educate ourselves both sensibly and imaginatively, the Russians have a clear edge. This is where their educational policy has already paid big dividends. They have such men to spare if they are needed. We just haven't, and the Americans aren't much better off. Imagine, for example, that the U.S. government and ours had agreed to help the Indians to carry out a major industrialisation, similar in scale to the Chinese. Imagine that the capital could be found. It would then require something like ten thousand to twenty thousand engineers from the U.S. and here to help get the thing going. At present, we couldn't find them.

These men, whom we don't yet possess, need to be trained not only in scientific but in human terms. They could not do their job if they did not shrug off every trace of paternalism. Plenty of Europeans, from St Francis Xavier to Schweitzer, have devoted their lives to Asians and Africans, nobly but paternally. These are not the Europeans whom Asians and Africans are going to welcome now. They want men who will muck in as colleagues, who will pass on what they know, do an honest technical job, and get out. Fortunately, this is an attitude which comes easily to scientists. They are freer than most people from racial feeling; their own culture is in its human relations a democratic one. In their own internal climate, the breeze of the equality of man hits you in the face, sometimes rather roughly, just as it does in Norway.

That is why scientists would do us good all over Asia and Africa. And they would do their part too in the third essential of the scientific revolution – which, in a country like India, would have to run in parallel with the capital investment and the initial foreign help. That is, an educational programme as complete as that of the Chinese, who appear in ten years to have transformed their universities and built so many new ones that they are now nearly independent of scientists and engineers from outside. Ten years. With scientific teachers from this country and the U.S., and what is also necessary, with teachers of English, other poor countries could do the same in twenty.

That is the size of the problem. An immense capital outlay, an immense investment in men, both scientists and linguists, most of whom the West does not yet possess. With rewards negligible in the short term, apart from doing the job: and in the long term most uncertain.

People will ask me, in fact in private they have already asked me – 'This is all very fine and large. But you are supposed to be a realistic man. You are interested in the fine structure of politics; you have spent some time studying how men behave in the pursuit of their own ends. Can you possibly believe that men will behave as you say they ought to? Can you imagine a political technique, in parliamentary societies like the U.S. or our own, by which any such plan could become real? Do you really believe that there is one chance in ten that any of this will happen?'

That is fair comment. I can only reply that I don't know. On the one hand, it is a mistake, and it is a mistake, of course, which anyone who is called realistic is specially liable to fall into, to think that when we have said something about the egotisms, the weaknesses, the vanities, the power-seekings of men, that we have said everything. Yes, they are like that. They are the bricks with which we have got to build, and one can judge them through the extent of one's own selfishness. But they are sometimes capable of more, and any 'realism' which doesn't admit of that isn't serious.

On the other hand, I confess, and I should be less than honest if I didn't, that I can't see the political techniques through which the good human capabilities of the West can get into action. The best one can do, and it is a poor best, is to nag away. That is perhaps too easy a palliative for one's disquiet. For, though I don't know how we can do what we need to do, or whether we shall do anything at all, I do know this: that, if we don't do it, the Communist countries will in time. They will do it at great cost to themselves and others, but they will do it. If that is how it turns out, we shall have failed, both practically and morally. At best, the West will have become an enclave in a different world – and this country will be the enclave of an enclave. Are we resigning ourselves to that? History is merciless to failure. In any case, if that happens, we shall not be writing the history.

Meanwhile, there are steps to be taken which aren't outside the powers of reflective people. Education isn't the total solution to this problem: but without education the West can't even begin to cope. All the arrows point the same way. Closing the gap between our cultures is a necessity in the most abstract intellectual sense, as well as in the most practical. When those two senses have grown apart, then no society is going to be able to think with wisdom. For the sake of the intellectual life, for the sake of this country's special danger, for the sake of the Western society living precariously rich among the poor, for the sake of the poor who needn't be poor if there is intelligence in the world, it is obligatory for us and the Americans and the whole West to look at our education with fresh eyes. This is one of the cases where we and the Americans have the most to learn from each other. We have each a good deal to learn from the Russians, if we are not too proud. Incidentally, the Russians have a good deal to learn from us, too.

Isn't it time we began? The danger is, we have been brought up to think as though we had all the time in the world. We have very little time. So little that I dare not guess at it.

NOTES

1. 'The Two Cultures', *New Statesman*, 6 October 1956.
2. This lecture was delivered to a Cambridge audience, and so I used some points of reference which I did not need to explain. G. H. Hardy (1877–1947) was one of the most distinguished pure mathematicians of his time, and a picturesque figure in Cambridge both as a young don and on his return in 1931 to the Sadleirian Chair of Mathematics.
3. I said a little more about this connection in 'Challenge to the Intellect', *Times Literary Supplement*, 15 August 1958. I hope some day to carry the analysis further.
4. It would be more accurate to say that, for literary reasons, we felt the prevailing literary modes were useless to us. We were, however, reinforced in that feeling when it occurred to us that those prevailing modes went hand in hand with social attitudes either wicked, or absurd, or both.
5. An analysis of the schools from which Fellows of the Royal Society come tells its own story. The distribution is markedly different from that of, for example, members of the Foreign Service or Queen's Counsel.

6. Compare George Orwell's *1984* (1949), which is the strongest possible wish that the future should not exist, with J. D. Bernal's *World Without War* (1958).

7. *Subjective*, in contemporary technological jargon, means 'divided according to subjects'. *Objective* means 'directed towards an object'. *Philosophy* means 'general intellectual approach or attitude' (for example, a scientist's 'philosophy of guided weapons' might lead him to propose certain kinds of 'objective research'). A 'progressive' job means one with possibilities of promotion.

8. Almost all college High Tables contain Fellows in both scientific and non-scientific subjects.

9. He took the examination in 1905.

10. It is, however, true to say that the compact nature of the managerial layers of English society – the fact that 'everyone knows everyone else' – means that scientists and non-scientists do in fact know each other as people more easily than in most countries. It is also true that a good many leading politicians and administrators keep up lively intellectual and artistic interests to a much greater extent, so far as I can judge, than in the United States. These are both among our assets.

11. I tried to compare American, Soviet and English education in 'New Minds for the New World', *New Statesman*, 6 September 1956.

12. The best, and almost the only, book on the subject.

13. It developed very fast. An English commission of inquiry into industrial productivity went over to the United States as early as 1865.

14. It is reasonable for intellectuals to prefer to live in the eighteenth-century streets of Stockholm rather than in Vallingby. I should myself. But it is not reasonable for them to obstruct other Vallingbys being built.

15. It is worth remembering that there must have been similar losses – spread over a much longer period – when men changed from the hunting and food-gathering life to agriculture. For some, it must have been a genuine spiritual impoverishment.

16. This is not quite exact. In the states where higher education is most completely developed, for example, Wisconsin, about 95 per cent of children attend High School up to eighteen.

17. The United States is a complex and plural society, and the standards of colleges vary very much more than those of our universities. Some college standards are very high. Broadly, I think the generalisation is fair.

18. The number of engineers graduating per year in the United States is declining very sharply. I have not heard an adequate explanation for this.

19. The latest figures of graduates trained per year (scientists and engineers combined) are roughly U.K. 13,000, U.S.A. 65,000, U.S.S.R. 130,000.

20. One-third of Russian graduate engineers are women. It is one of our major follies that, whatever we say, we don't in reality regard women as suitable for scientific careers. We thus neatly divide our pool of potential talent by two.

21. It might repay investigation to examine precisely what education a hundred alpha-plus creative persons in science this century have received. I have a feeling that a surprising proportion have not gone over the strictest orthodox hurdles, such as Part II Physics at Cambridge and the like.

22. The English temptation is to educate such men in sub-university institutions, which carry an inferior class-label. Nothing could be more ill-judged. One often meets American engineers who, in a narrow professional sense, are less rigorously trained than English products from technical colleges; but the Americans have the confidence, both social and individual, that is helped through having mixed with their equals at universities.

23. I have confined myself to the University population. The kind and number of technicians is another and a very interesting problem.

24. The concentration of our population makes us, of course, more vulnerable also in military terms.

25. There is one curious result in all major industrialised societies. The amount of talent one requires for the primary tasks is greater than any country can comfortably produce, and this will become increasingly obvious. The consequence is that there are no people left, clever, competent and resigned to a humble job, to keep the wheels of social amenities going smoothly round. Postal services, railway services, are likely slowly to deteriorate just because the people who once ran them are now being educated for different things. This is already clear in the United States, and is becoming clear in England.

THE TWO CULTURES:
A SECOND LOOK

IT is over four years since (in May 1959) I gave the Rede Lecture at Cambridge. I chose a subject which several of us had been discussing for some time past. I hoped at most to act as a goad to action, first in education and second – in my own mind the latter part of the lecture was always the more pressing – in sharpening the concern of rich and privileged societies for those less lucky. I did not expect much. Plenty of people were saying similar things. It seemed to me to be a time when one should add one's voice. I thought I might be listened to in some restricted circles. Then the effect would soon die down: and in due course, since I was deeply committed, I should feel obliged to have another go.

For a while that appeared to be a reasonable prognosis. According to precedent, the lecture was published, as a paper-covered pamphlet,[1] the day after it was delivered. It received some editorial attention, but, in the first months, not many reviews. There was not, and could not be, any advertising. *Encounter* published long extracts, and these drew some comment.[2] I had a number of interesting private letters. That, I thought, was the end of it.

It did not turn out quite like that. By the end of the first year I began to feel uncomfortably like the sorcerer's apprentice. Articles, references, letters, blame, praise, were floating in – often from countries where I was otherwise unknown. The whole phenomenon, in fact, as I shall shortly explain, hadn't much connection with me. It was a curious, rather than a pleasurable, experience. The literature has gone on accumulating at an accelerating pace: I suppose I must, by the nature of things, have seen more of it than anyone else; but I have not seen anything like the whole. And it is frustrating to be told that some of the more valuable discussions have been taking place in languages not accessible to most Englishmen, such as Hungarian, Polish and Japanese.

As the flood of literature mounted, two deductions became self-evident. The first was that if a nerve had been touched almost simultaneously in different intellectual societies, in different parts of the world, the ideas which produced this response couldn't possibly be original. Original ideas don't carry at that speed. Very occasionally one thinks or hopes that one has said something new: and waits a little bleakly for years, in the hope that it will strike a spark of recognition somewhere. This was quite different. It was clear that many people had been thinking on this assembly of topics. The ideas were in the air. Anyone, anywhere, had only to choose a form of words. Then – click, the trigger was pressed. The words need not be the right words: but the time, which no one could predict before-hand, had to be the right time. When that happened, the sorcerer's apprentice was left to look at the water rushing in.

It seems to be pure chance that others had not found themselves, some time earlier, in the same apprentice-like position. Jacob Bronowski had, at various times in the fifties,[3] dealt imaginatively with many aspects of these problems. Merle Kling in 1957 published an article[4] – unknown to me until much later – which closely anticipated the first half of my lecture. Professional educators such as A. D. C. Peterson had done much the same. In 1956[5] and 1957[6] I myself wrote two pieces which, though shorter than the Rede Lecture, contained much of its substance. Yet none of us got much response. Two years later the time was right; and any one of us could have produced a hubbub. It is a reminder of the mysterious operation of what, in the nineteenth century, was reverently referred to as the *Zeitgeist*.

The first deduction, then, is that these ideas were not at all original, but were waiting in the air. The second deduction is, I think, equally obvious. It is, that there must be something in them. I don't mean that they are necessarily right; I don't mean that they couldn't have been expressed in many different or better forms: but contained in them or hidden beneath them, there is something which people, all over the world, suspect is relevant to present actions. It would not have mattered whether these things were said by me or

Bronowski or Kling, or A or B or C. A complex argument started, and will go on. This could not have happened adventitiously. It certainly could not have happened through any personal impact. On these issues our personalities mean nothing: but the issues themselves mean a good deal.

The sheer volume of comment has been formidable, some of it agreeing with me, some cross-bench, and some disagreeing. Many of the criticisms I respect. I have not replied to them piecemeal, since I have been following a rule which I have set myself in other controversies. It seems to me that engaging in immediate debate on each specific point closes one's own mind for good and all. Debating gives most of us much more psychological satisfaction than thinking does: but it deprives us of whatever chance there is of getting closer to the truth. It seems preferable to me to sit back and let what has been said sink in – I don't pretend this is altogether easy – and then, after a longish interval, with the advantage of what I have heard and of new knowledge, see what modifications I should make if I were going to give the lecture again. This is what I am doing now. I intend to continue the same practice in the future. If I think I have anything further to add, I shall leave it for some time.

During the arguments so far, there has been one unusual manifestation, which I shall mention just to get it out of the way. A few, a very few, of the criticisms have been loaded with personal abuse to an abnormal extent: to such an extent in one case, in fact, that the persons responsible for its publication in two different media[7] made separate approaches to me, in order to obtain my consent. I had to assure them that I did not propose to take legal action. All this seemed to me distinctly odd. In any dispute acrimonious words are likely to fly about, but it is not common, at least in my experience, for them to come anywhere near the limit of defamation.

However, the problem of behaviour in these circumstances is very easily solved. Let us imagine that I am called, in print, a kleptomaniac necrophilist (I have selected with some care two allegations which have not, so far as I know, been made). I have exactly two courses of action. The first, and the one which in general I should choose to follow, is to do precisely nothing. The second is, if the nuisance becomes intolerable, to sue. There is one course of action which no one can expect of a sane man: that is, solemnly to argue the points, to produce certificates from Saks and Harrods to say he has never, to the best of their belief, stolen a single article, to obtain testimonials signed by sixteen Fellows of the Royal Society, the Head of the Civil Service, a Lord Justice of Appeal and the Secretary of the M.C.C., testifying that they have known him for half a lifetime, and that even after a convivial evening they have not once seen him lurking in the vicinity of a tomb.

Such a reply is not on. It puts one in the same psychological compartment as one's traducer. That is a condition from which one has a right to be excused.

The argument, fortunately, will suffer no loss if we ignore criticisms of this particular spirit, and any associated with them: for such intellectual contributions as they contain have been made, with civility and seriousness, by others.

There will need to be some cleaning up in due course. Textbook examples of the effects of some psychological states are not always conveniently come by: but a good many exist in this section of the literature. Do certain kinds of animosity lead to an inability to perform the physical act of reading? The evidence suggests so. The original lecture was quite short. The text is very simple. Most people, more particularly when attacking with virulence, would take pains to get straightforward quotations right. Yet this has not happened. There are various examples which, like the whole episode, seem to me somewhat bizarre. I will just select the crudest. One of my outrages in the Rede Lecture has been said to be the use of a phrase – 'We die alone'. This phrase has been quoted and brandished, not only in a piece for which the publishers obtained my indemnification,[8] but in others which followed suit.[9] When I lost count, the number of times this quotation had been repeated was, I think, ten.

But where does the quotation come from? Cast your eye over the Rede Lecture with modest textual attentiveness. You will not find the phrase. It occurs nowhere. Indeed it would be surprising if it did. For I was trying to make a statement of the extremest singularity. No one would elect to make such a statement in plural form. Oddly enough, the English language does not meet the requirements comfortably. 'One dies alone' is not right. I finally had to use a phrase which was clumsy but said what I meant – 'Each of us dies alone'.

This concept, by the way, like so much else in the whole argument, is not original. It has been used in introspective thought, and particularly in introspective religious thought, for centuries. So far as I know, it was said first by Blaise Pascal: *On mourra seul.*

There will be scope for investigations of this kind later: but, I hope, not now. The important thing is to take the personalities, so far as we are able, out of the discussion. In what I am going to write myself I shall try to aim at this.

As I have already said, I think the most useful thing I can now do is to have another look at what I originally wrote: to look at it in the light of what has been said about it, for, against, and at right angles; and to do so with the help of new scientific, sociological and historical knowledge which, as research proceeds, should help, at least on a part of the problem, to provide not an opinion but an answer.

II

The statements in the lecture were as simple as I could make them. Any statements which have any reference to action must be simple. There is always something wrong, if one is straining to make the commonplace incomprehensible. I hedged the statements round with qualifications and I tried to illustrate some of them. I will now remove the qualifications and the pictures and rephrase the essence of the lecture as quietly as I can.

It is something like this. In our society (that is, advanced Western society) we have lost even the pretence of a common culture. Persons educated with the greatest intensity we know can no longer communicate with each other on the plane of their major intellectual concern. This is serious for our creative, intellectual and, above all, our moral life. It is leading us to interpret the past wrongly, to misjudge the present, and to deny our hopes of the future. It is making it difficult or impossible for us to take good action.

I gave the most pointed example of this lack of communication in the shape of two groups of people, representing what I have christened 'the two cultures'. One of these contained the scientists, whose weight, achievement and influence did not need stressing. The other contained the literary intellectuals. I did not mean that literary intellectuals act as the main decision-makers of the Western world. I meant that literary intellectuals represent, vocalise, and to some extent shape and predict the mood of the non-scientific culture: they do not make the decisions, but their words seep into the minds of those who do. Between these two groups – the scientists and the literary intellectuals – there is little communication and, instead of fellow-feeling, something like hostility.

This was intended as a description of, or a very crude first approximation to, our existing state of affairs. That it was a state of affairs I passionately disliked, I thought was made fairly clear. Curiously enough, some commentators have assumed that I approved of it; but at this I confess myself defeated, and take refuge in muttering Schiller's helpful line.[10]

To finish this précis. There is, of course, no complete solution. In the conditions of our age, or any age which we can foresee, Renaissance man is not possible. But we can do something. The chief means open to us is education – education mainly in primary and secondary schools, but also in colleges and universities. There is no excuse for letting another generation be as vastly ignorant, or as devoid of understanding and sympathy, as we are ourselves.

III

From the beginning, the phrase 'the two cultures' evoked some protests. The word 'culture' or 'cultures' has been objected to: so, with much more substance, has the number two. (No one, I think, has yet complained about the definite article.)

I must have a word about these verbal points before I come to the more wide-reaching arguments. The term 'culture' in my title has two meanings, both of which are precisely applicable to the theme. First, 'culture' has the sense of the dictionary definition, 'intellectual development, development of the mind'. For many years this definition has carried overtones, often of a deep and ambiguous sort.

It happens that few of us can help searching for a refined use of the word: if anyone asks, What is culture? Who is cultured? the needle points, by an extraordinary coincidence, in the direction of ourselves.

But that, though a pleasing example of human frailty, doesn't matter: what does matter is that any refined definition, from Coleridge onwards, applies at least as well (and also as imperfectly) to the development a scientist achieves *in the course of his professional vocation* as to the 'traditional' mental development or any of its offshoots. Coleridge said 'cultivation' where we should say 'culture' – and qualified it as 'the harmonious development of those qualities and faculties which characterise our humanity'.[11] Well, none of us manages that; in plain truth, either of our cultures, whether literary or scientific, only deserves the name of sub-culture. *'Qualities and faculties which characterise our humanity.'* Curiosity about the natural world, the use of symbolic systems of thought, are two of the most precious and the most specifically human of all human qualities. The traditional methods of mental development left them to be starved. So, in reverse, does scientific education starve our verbal faculties – the language of symbols is given splendid play, the language of words is not. On both sides we underestimate the spread of a human being's gifts.

But, if we are to use 'culture' in its refined sense at all, it is only lack of imagination, or possibly blank ignorance, which could deny it to scientists. There is no excuse for such ignorance. A whole body of literature has been built up over a generation, written, incidentally, in some of the most beautiful prose of our time, to demonstrate the intellectual, aesthetic and moral values inherent in the pursuit of science (compare A. N. Whitehead's *Science and the Modern World*, G. H. Hardy's *A Mathematician's Apology*, J. Bronowski's *Science and Human Values*). There are valuable insights scattered all over American and English writing of the last decade – Needham, Toulmin, Price, Piel, Newman, are only a few of the names that come to mind.

In the most lively of all contributions to this subject, a Third Programme feature not yet published, Bronowski deliberately avoided the word 'culture' for either side and chose as his title 'Dialogue between Two World Systems'. For myself, I believe the word is still appropriate and carries its proper meaning to sensible persons. But, while sticking to that word, I want to repeat what was intended to be my main message, but which has somehow got over-laid: that neither the scientific system of mental development, nor the traditional, is adequate for our potentialities, for the work we have in front of us, for the world in which we ought to begin to live.

The word 'culture' has a second and technical meaning, which I pointed out explicitly in the original lecture. It is used by anthro-pologists to denote a group of persons living in the same environ-ment, linked by common habits, common assumptions, a common way of life. Thus one talks of a Neanderthal culture, a La Tène culture, a Trobriand Island culture: the term, which is a very useful one, has been applied to groups within our own societies. For me this was a very strong additional reason for selecting the word; it isn't often one gets a word which can be used in two senses, both of which one explicitly intends. For scientists on the one side, literary intellectuals on the other, do in fact exist as cultures within the anthropological scope. There are, as I said before, common attitudes, common standards and patterns of behaviour, common approaches and assumptions. This does not mean that a person within a culture loses his individuality and free will. It does mean that, without knowing it, we are more than we think children of our time, place and training. Let me take two trivial and non-controversial examples. The overwhelming majority of the scientific culture (that is, the group of scientists observed through anthropological eyes) would feel certain, without needing to cogitate or examine their souls, that research was the primary function of a university. This attitude is automatic, it is part of their culture: but it would not be the attitude of such a proportion in the literary culture. On the other hand, the overwhelming majority of the literary culture would feel just as certain that not the slightest censorship of the printed word is, in any circumstances, permissible. This position doesn't have to be reached by individual thought: again it is part of the culture. It is such an un-questioned part, in fact, that the literary intellectuals have got their way more absolutely than, thirty years ago, would have seemed conceivable.

That is enough on 'cultures'. Now for the number Two. Whether this was the best choice, I am much less certain. Right from the start I introduced some qualifying doubts. I will repeat what I said, near the beginning of the lecture.

The number 2 is a very dangerous number; that is why the dialectic is a dangerous process. Attempts to divide anything into two ought to be regarded with much suspicion. I have thought a long time about going in for further refinements: but in the end I have decided against. I was searching for something a little more than a dashing metaphor, a good deal less than a cultural map: and for those purposes the two cultures is about right, and subtilising any more would bring more disadvantages than it's worth.

That still seems to me fairly sensible. But I am open to correction, and I have been much impressed by a new feature in the situation, which I will come to in a moment. Before that, however, I ought to mention two lines of argument; one goes happily away into nullity, the other, which I should once have followed myself, can be misleading. The first says, no, there aren't two cultures, there are a hundred and two, or two thousand and two, or any number you like to name. In a sense this is true: but it is also meaningless. Words are always simpler than the brute reality from which they make patterns: if they weren't, discussion and collective action would both be impossible. *Of course* there is sub-division after sub-division within, say, the scientific culture. Theoretical physicists tend to talk only to each other, and, like so many Cabots, to God. Either in scientific politics or open politics, organic chemists much more often than not turn out to be conservative: the reverse is true of biochemists. And so on. Hardy used to say that one could see all these diversities in action round the council table of the Royal Society. But Hardy, who was no respecter either of labels or institutions, would not on that account have said that the Royal Society represented nothing. In fact, its existence is a supreme manifestation or symbol of the scientific culture.[12] This attempt at excessive unsimplicity, the 'two thousand and two cultures' school of thought, crops up whenever anyone makes a proposal which opens up a prospect, however distant, of new action. It involves a skill which all conservative functionaries are masters of, as they ingeniously protect the status quo: it is called 'the technique of the intricate defensive'.

The second line of argument draws, or attempts to draw, a clear line between pure science and technology (which is tending to become a pejorative word). This is a line that once I tried to draw myself:[13] but, though I can still see the reasons, I shouldn't now. The more I have seen of technologists at work, the more untenable the distinction has come to look. If you actually see someone design an aircraft, you find him going through the same experience – aesthetic, intellectual, moral – as though he were setting up an experiment in particle physics.

The scientific process has two motives: one is to understand the natural world, the other is to control it. Either of these motives may be dominant in any individual scientist; fields of science may draw their original impulses from one or the other. Cosmogony for example – the study of the origin and nature of the cosmos – is a pretty pure example of the first class. Medicine is the type specimen of the second. Yet, in all scientific fields, however the work originated, one motive becomes implicit in the other. From medicine, which is a classical technology, men have worked back to 'pure' scientific problems – such as, say, the structure of the haemoglobin molecule. From cosmogony, which seems the most unpractical of all subjects, have come insights into nuclear fission – which, for evil and potentially for good, no one could call an unpractical activity.

This complex dialectic between pure and applied science is one of the deepest problems in scientific history. At present there is much of it which we don't begin to understand. Sometimes the practical need which inspires a wave of invention is brutally obvious. No one has to be told why British, American, German scientists suddenly – at first unknown to each other – made great advances in electronics between 1935 and 1945. It was equally plain that this immensely powerful technological weapon would soon be used in the purest of scientific researches, from astronomy to cybernetics. But what conceivable external stimulus or social correlative set Bolyai, Gauss and Lobachewski – also, in the beginning, unknown to each other – working at the same point in time on non-Euclidean geometry, apparently one of the most abstract of all fields of the conceptual imagination? It is going to be difficult to find a satisfying answer. But we may make it impossible, if we start by assuming a difference in kind between pure science and applied.

IV

So the phrase 'the two cultures' still seems appropriate for the purpose I had in mind. I now think, however, that I should have stressed more heavily that I was speaking as an Englishman, from experience drawn mainly from English society. I did in fact say this, and I said also that this cultural divide seems at its sharpest in England. I now realise that I did not emphasise it enough.

In the United States, for example, the divide is nothing like so unbridgeable. There are pockets of the literary culture, influenced by the similar culture in England, which are as extreme in resisting communication and in ceasing to communicate: but that isn't generally true over the literary culture as a whole, much less over the entire intellectual society. And, just because the divide is not so deep, just because the situation is not accepted as a fact of life, far more active steps are being taken to improve it. This is an interesting example of one of the laws of social change: change doesn't happen when things are at their worst, but when they are looking up. So it is at Yale and Princeton and Michigan and California, that scientists of world standing are talking to non-specialised classes; at M.I.T. and Cal. Tech. where students of the sciences are receiving a serious humane education. In the last few years, all over the country, a visitor cannot help being astonished by the resilience and inventiveness of American higher education – ruefully so, if he happens to be an Englishman.[14]

I think also that writing as an Englishman made me insensitive to something which may, within a few years, propel the argument in another direction or which conceivably may already have started to do just that. I have been increasingly impressed by a body of intellectual opinion, forming itself, without organisation, without any kind of lead or conscious direction, under the surface of this debate. This is the new feature I referred to a little earlier. This body of opinion seems to come from intellectual persons in a variety of fields – social history, sociology, demography, political science, economics, government (in the American academic sense), psychology, medicine, and social arts such as architecture. It seems a mixed bag: but there is an inner consistency. All of them are concerned with how human beings are living or have lived – and concerned, not in terms of legend, but of fact. I am not implying that they agree with each other, but in their approach to cardinal problems – such as the human effects of the scientific revolution, which is the fighting point of this whole affair – they display, at the least, a family resemblance.

I ought, I see now, to have expected this. I haven't much excuse for not doing so. I have been in close intellectual contact with social historians most of my life: they have influenced me a good deal: their recent researches were the basis for a good many of my statements. But nevertheless I was slow to observe the development of what, in the terms of our formulae, is becoming something like a third culture. I might have been quicker if I had not been the prisoner of my English upbringing, conditioned to be suspicious of any but the established intellectual disciplines, unreservedly at home only with the 'hard' subjects. For this I am sorry.

It is probably too early to speak of a third culture already in existence. But I am now convinced that this is coming. When it comes, some of the difficulties of communication will at last be softened: for such a culture has, just to do its job, to be on speaking terms with the scientific one. Then, as I said, the focus of this argument will be shifted, in a direction which will be more profitable to us all.

There are signs that this is happening. Some social historians, as well as being on speaking terms with scientists, have felt bound to turn their attention to the literary intellectuals, or more exactly to some manifestations of the literary culture at its extreme. Concepts such as the 'organic community' or the nature of pre-industrial society or the scientific revolution are being dealt with, under the illumination of the knowledge of the last ten years. These new examinations are of great importance for our intellectual and moral health.

Since they touch on the parts of my lecture on which I have the deepest feelings, I shall revert to them once again in the next section. After that I shall leave them in the hands of those professionally qualified to speak.

One word about another passage where I showed bad judgment. In my account of the lack of communication between the two cultures, I didn't exaggerate: if anything I understated the case, as has been proved by subsequent pieces of fieldwork.[15] Yet I have regretted that I used as my test question about scientific literacy, *What do you know of the Second Law of Thermodynamics?* It is, in fact, a good question. Many physical scientists would agree that it is perhaps the most pointed question. This law is one of the greatest depth and generality: it has its own sombre beauty: like all the major scientific laws, it evokes reverence. There is, of course, no value in a non-scientist just knowing it by the rubric in an encyclopedia. It needs understanding, which can't be attained unless one has learnt some of the language of physics. That understanding ought to be part of a common twentieth-century culture – as Lord Cherwell once said, more astringently than I have done, in the House of Lords. Nevertheless I wish that I had chosen a different example. I had forgotten – like a playwright who has lost touch with his audience – that the law is called by what to most people is an unfamiliar, and therefore a funny, name. To be honest, I had forgotten how funny the un-unfamiliar is – I ought to have remembered the jocularity with which the English greeted the Russian patronymics in Chekhov, roaring their heads off each time they heard Fyodor Ilyich or Lyubov Andreievna, expressing their blissful ignorance of a formal nomenclature both more courteous and more human than their own.

So I got a laugh: but again, like an incompetent playwright, I got a laugh in the wrong place. I should now treat the matter differently, and I should put forward a branch of science which ought to be a requisite in the common culture, certainly for anyone now at school. This branch of science at present goes by the name of molecular biology. Is that funny? I think that possibly it is already well enough domesticated. Through a whole set of lucky chances, this study is ideally suited to fit into a new model of education. It is fairly self-contained. It begins with the analysis of crystal structure, itself a subject aesthetically beautiful and easily comprehended. It goes on to the application of these methods to molecules which have literally a vital part in our own existence – molecules of proteins, nucleic acids: molecules immensely large (by molecular standards) and which turn out to be of curious shapes, for nature, when interested in what we call life, appears to have a taste for the rococo. It includes the leap of genius by which Crick and Watson snatched at the structure of DNA and so taught us the essential lesson about our genetic inheritance.

Unlike thermodynamics, the subject does not involve serious conceptual difficulties. In fact, in terms of concept, it doesn't reach so deep, and it is for other reasons that it has a first claim upon us. It needs very little mathematics to understand. There are few parts of the hard sciences of which one can understand so much without mathematical training. What one needs most of all is a visual and three-dimensional imagination, and it is a study where painters and sculptors could be instantaneously at home.

It exemplifies, with extreme neatness, some of the characteristics of the whole scientific culture, its subdivisions and its community. Exponents of the 'two thousand and two cultures' school of thought will be glad to hear that only a handful of people in the world – five hundred? – would be competent to follow in detail each step of the process by which, say, Perutz and Kendrew finally disentangled the structure of the haem proteins. After all, Perutz was at haemoglobin, on and off, for twenty-five years. But any scientist with the patience to learn could get instructed in those processes, and any scientist knows it. The great majority of scientists can acquire an adequate working knowledge of what the results mean. All scientists without exception accept the results. It is a nice demonstration of the scientific culture at work.

I have said that the ideas in this branch of science are not as physically deep, or of such universal physical significance, as those in the Second Law. That is true. The Second Law is a generalisation which covers the cosmos. This new study deals only with microscopic parts of the cosmos, which may – no one knows – exist only on this earth: but since those microscopic parts happen to be connected with biological life, they are of importance to each of us.

It is very hard to write about this importance. It is better, I think, to take a self-denying ordinance and let the researches of the next ten years make it plain. But here is a statement which is not seriously controversial. This branch of science is likely to affect the way in which *men think of themselves* more profoundly than any scientific advance since Darwin's – and probably more so than Darwin's.

That seems a sufficient reason why the next generation should learn about it. The Church recognises invincible ignorance: but here the ignorance is not, or need not be, invincible. This study could be grafted into any of our educational systems, at high school or college levels, without artificiality and without strain. I dare say that, as usual, this is an idea which is already floating around the world, and that, as I write this paragraph, some American college has already laid on the first course.

V

Major scientific breakthroughs, and in particular those as closely connected to human flesh and bone as this one in molecular biology, or even more, another which we may expect in the nature of the higher nervous system, are bound to touch both our hopes and our resignations. That is: ever since men began to think introspectively about themselves, they have made guesses, and sometimes had profound intuitions, about those parts of their own nature which seemed to be predestined. It is possible that within a generation some of these guesses will have been tested against exact knowledge. No one can predict what such an intellectual revolution will mean: but I believe that one of the consequences will be to make us feel not less but more responsible towards our brother men.

It was for this reason among others that, in the original lecture, I drew a distinction between the individual condition and the social condition. In doing so, I stressed the solitariness, the ultimate tragedy, at the core of each individual life; and this has worried a good many who found the rest of the statement acceptable. It is very hard, of course, to subdue the obsessions of one's own temperament; this specific note creeps into a good deal of what I have written, as Alfred Kazin has shrewdly pointed out:[16] it is not an accident that my novel sequence is called *Strangers and Brothers*. Nevertheless, this distinction, however it is drawn, is imperative, unless we are going to sink into the facile social pessimism of our time, unless we are going to settle into our own egocentric chill.

So I will try to make the statement without much emphasis of my own. We should most of us agree, I think, that in the individual life of each of us there is much that, in the long run, one cannot do any-thing about. Death is a fact – one's own death, the deaths of those one loves. There is much that makes one suffer which is irremediable: one struggles against it all the way, but there is an irremediable residue left. These are facts: they will remain facts as long as man remains man. This is part of the individual condition: call it tragic, comic, absurd, or, like some of the best and bravest of people, shrug it off.

But it isn't all. One looks outside oneself to other lives, to which one is bound by love, affection, loyalty, obligation: each of those lives has the same irremediable components as one's own; but there are also components that one can help, or that can give one help. It is in this tiny extension of the personality, it is in this seizing on the possibilities of hope, that we become more fully human: it is a way to improve the quality of one's life: it is, for oneself, the beginning of the social condition.

Finally, one can try to understand the condition of lives, not close to one's own, which one cannot know face to face. Each of these lives – that is, the lives of one's fellow human beings – again has limits of irremediability like one's own. Each of them has needs, some of which can be met: the totality of all is the social condition.

We cannot know as much as we should about the social condition all over the world. But we can know, we do know, two most import-ant things. First we can meet the harsh facts of the flesh, on the level where all of us are, or should be, one. We know that the vast majority, perhaps two-thirds, of our fellow men are living in the immediate presence of illness and premature death; their expectation of life is half of ours, most are under-nourished, many are near to starving, many starve. Each of these lives is afflicted by suffering, different from that which is intrinsic in the individual condition. But this suffering is unnecessary and can be lifted. This is the second important thing which we know – or, if we don't know it, there is no excuse or absolution for us.

We cannot avoid the realisation that applied science has made it possible to remove unnecessary suffering from a billion individual human lives – to remove suffering of a kind, which, in our own privileged society, we have largely forgotten, suffering so elementary that it is not genteel to mention it. For example, we *know* how to heal many of the sick: to prevent children dying in infancy and mothers in childbirth: to produce enough food to alleviate hunger: to throw up a minimum of shelter: to ensure that there aren't so many births that our other efforts are in vain. All this we *know* how to do.

It does not require one additional scientific discovery, though new scientific discoveries must help us. It depends on the spread of the scientific revolution all over the world. There is no other way. For most human beings, this is the point of hope. It will certainly happen. It may take longer than the poor will peacefully accept. How long it takes, and the fashion in which it is done, will be a reflex of the quality of our lives, especially of the lives of those of us born lucky: as most in the Western world were born.[17] When it is achieved, then our consciences will be a little cleaner; and those coming after us will at least be able to think that the elemental needs of others aren't a daily reproach to any sentient person, that for the first time some genuine dignity has come upon us all.

Man doesn't live by bread alone – yes, that has been said often enough in the course of these discussions. It has been said occasionally with a lack of imagination, a provincialism, that makes the mind boggle: for it is not a remark that one of us in the Western world can casually address to most Asians, to most of our fellow human beings in the world as it now exists. But we can, we should, say it to ourselves. For we know how, once the elemental needs are satisfied, we do not find it easy to do something worthy and satisfying with our lives. Probably it will never be easy. Conceivably men in the future, if they are as lucky as we are now, will struggle with our existential discontents, or new ones of their own. They may, like some of us, try – through sex or drink or drugs – to intensify the sensational life. Or they may try to improve the quality of their lives, through an extension of their responsibilities, a deepening of the affections and the spirit, in a fashion which, though we can aim at it for ourselves and our own societies, we can only dimly perceive.

But, though our perception may be dim, it isn't dim enough to obscure one truth: that one mustn't despise the elemental needs, when one has been granted them and others have not. To do so is not to display one's superior spirituality. It is simply to be inhuman, or more exactly anti-human.

Here, in fact, was what I intended to be the centre of the whole argument. Before I wrote the lecture I thought of calling it 'The Rich and the Poor', and I rather wish that I hadn't changed my mind.

The scientific revolution is the only method by which most people can gain the primal things (years of life, freedom from hunger, survival for children) – the primal things which we take for granted and which have in reality come to us through having had our own scientific revolution not so long ago. Most people want these primal things. Most people, wherever they are being given a chance, are rushing into the scientific revolution.

To misunderstand this position is to misunderstand both the present and the future. It simmers beneath the surface of world politics. Though the form of politics may look the same, its content is being altered as the scientific revolution pours in. We have not been as quick as we should to draw the right consequences, very largely because of the division of the cultures. It has been hard for politicians and administrators to grasp the practical truth of what scientists were telling them. But now it is beginning to be accepted. It is often accepted most easily by men of affairs, whatever their political sympathies, engineers, or priests, or doctors, all those who have a strong comradely physical sympathy for other humans. If others can get the primal things – yes, that is beyond argument; that is simply good.

Curiously enough, there are many who would call themselves liberals and yet who are antipathetic to this change. Almost as though sleepwalking they drift into an attitude which, to the poor of the world, is a denial of all human hope. This attitude, which mis-interprets both the present and the future, seems to be connected with a similar misinterpretation of the past. It is on this point that representatives of the putative third culture have been speaking with trenchancy.

The argument is about the first wave of the scientific revolution, the transformation which we call the industrial revolution, and it is occupied with questions about what, in the most elementary human terms, life was like in pre-industrial as compared with industrial society. We can gain some insights, of course, from the present world, which is a vast sociological laboratory in which one can observe all kinds of society from the neolithic to the advanced industrial. We are also now accumulating substantial evidence of our own past.

When I made some remarks about the industrial revolution, I had imagined that the findings of recent research in social history were better known. Otherwise I should have documented what I said: but that seemed like documenting a platitude. Did anyone think that, in the primal terms in which I have just been discussing the poor countries of the present world, our ancestors' condition was so very different? Or that the industrial revolution had not brought us in three or four generations to a state entirely new in the harsh, un-recorded continuity of poor men's lives? I couldn't believe it. I knew, of course, the force of nostalgia, myth, and plain snobbery. In all families, at all times, there are stories of blessed existences, just before one's childhood: there were in my own. Myth – I ought to have remembered what Malinowski taught us, that people believe their myths as fact. I certainly ought to have remembered that, when anyone is asked what he would have been in a previous incarnation, he nominates – if he is modest – something like a Jacobean cleric or an eighteenth-century squire. He wouldn't have been any such thing. The overwhelming probability is that he would have been a peasant. If we want to talk about our ancestors, that is whence we came.

I was at fault, I suppose, in not trying to be more persuasive against these kinds of resistance. Anyway, there is no need for me to say much more. There are plenty of scholars professionally con-cerned with pre-industrial social history. Now we know something of the elemental facts of the lives and deaths of peasants and agricultural labourers in seventeenth- and eighteenth-century England and

France. They are not comfortable facts. J. H. Plumb, in one of his attacks on the teaching of a pretty-pretty past, has written: 'No one in his senses would choose to have been born in a previous age unless he could be certain that he would have been born into a prosperous family, that he would have enjoyed extremely good health, and that he could have accepted stoically the death of the majority of his children.'

It is worth anyone's while – in fact no one ought to escape the experience – to study the results which the French demographers have obtained in the last decade. In the seventeenth and eighteenth centuries, parish registers in France were kept with great accuracy, much more commonly so than in England – births, marriages and deaths the only tiny records, the only traces, of so many human lives. These records are now being analysed all over France.[18] They tell a story which can be duplicated in Asian (or Latin American) communities today.

In the dry but appallingly eloquent language of statistics, the historians explain to us that, in eighteenth-century French villages, the median age of marriage was higher than the median age of death. The *average* length of life was perhaps a third of ours, and appreciably less, because of the deaths in childbirth, for women than for men (*it is only quite recently, and in lucky countries, that women, on the average, have had a chance of living as long as men*). The greater part of entire communities[19] died of starvation, which appears to have been a common occurrence.

Though English records are nothing like so complete, Peter Laslett and his collaborators have discovered some late seventeenth-century registers,[20] and are actively extending their researches. The same stark conclusions stand out – except that in England there is as yet no proof of periodical famine, though it was endemic among the Scottish poor.

There is a mass of other evidence, from many kinds of provenance, all pointing in the same direction. In the light of it, no one should feel it seriously possible to talk about a pre-industrial Eden, from which our ancestors were, by the wicked machinations of applied science, brutally expelled. When and where was this Eden? Will someone who hankers after the myth tell us where he believes it was located, not in terms of wishful fancy, but in place and time, in historical and geographical fact? Then the social historians can examine the case and there can be a respectable discussion.

The present position is not respectable. One can't talk or teach false social history when the professionals are proving the falsity under one's eyes. Yet, as Plumb has publicly protested, what he calls 'this nonsense' is being taught. To anyone educated in an exact discipline it all seems very peculiar, almost as though reading itself had gone out of fashion as an activity, certainly the reading of any evidence which contradicts the stereotypes of fifty years ago. It is rather as though the teachers of physics had ignored the quantum theory and had gone on, year after year, teaching precisely those radiation laws which the quantum theory had been brought in to replace. And teaching them with that special insistence which strains the voices of priests of a dying religion.

It is important for the pre-industrial believers to confront the social historians. Then we can get a basis of fact accepted. One can teach a myth: but when the myth is seen as fact, and when the fact is disproved, the myth becomes a lie. No one can teach a lie.

I have restricted myself to primal things. It seems to me better that people should live rather than die: that they shouldn't be hungry: that they shouldn't have to watch their children die. Here, if anywhere, we are members one of another. If we are not members one of another, if we have no sympathy at this elemental level, then we have no human concern at all, and any pretence of a higher kind of sympathy is a mockery. Fortunately most of us are not so affectless as that.

Anyone who has had a physical misfortune knows that many acquaintances who would feel for him in no other circumstances, genuinely feel for him in this one. The sympathy is visceral: it is a sign that we cannot deny our common humanity.

Therefore the social condition is with us, we are part of it, we cannot deny it. Millions of individual lives, in some lucky countries like our own, have, by one gigantic convulsion of applied science over the last hundred and fifty years, been granted some share of the primal things. Billions of individual lives, over the rest of the world, will be granted or will seize the same. This is the indication of time's arrow. It is by far the greatest revolution our kind has known. We have been living through rapid change for three or four generations. Now the change is going faster. It is bound to go a great deal faster still. This is the condition in which we are both agents and spectators. Our response to it affects, and often determines, what we like and dislike in our world, what action we take, the nature of the art we value or practise, the nature of our appreciation of science. It determines also, I fancy, the way in which some straightforward proposals about education, intended to be simple and practical, have been made the jumping-off point for a debate on first and last things.

VI

We are only just beginning to live with the industrial–scientific revolution; we have taken the first positive steps to control it, to compensate for its losses as well as to absorb its gains. The modern industrial communities of, say, northern Italy or Sweden, are qualitatively different from those which first accumulated in Lancashire or New England. The whole process has not yet dived into our imaginative understanding. We who comment about it stand outside: socially in that most dangerous of positions, one tiny step more privileged than those who are taking part.

One point, however, is clear; those who are taking part have never paid one instant's attention to the lookers-on who would like them to reject industrialisation. As I said in the original lecture, this is a manifest fact in all societies all over the world. It is these witnesses whom we ought to consult, not those of us who are one step luckier, who think we know what is good for them.

The primary reason for their enthusiasm, which was set out in the last section, was so strong that men would need no others. But I believe there are others, quite deep in the individual's intuitive life, which impel most young people to elect for living in towns whenever they have a free choice, and others again which impel nearly all un-privileged people to prefer a highly organised society to one based on simple power relations.

The first class of reasons is obvious enough, and does not need explication: have you ever been young? The second is a little more subtle. Perhaps I can illustrate it by, so to speak, an example in reverse. I am reminded of D. H. Lawrence[21] reflecting on an anecdote in Dana's *Two Years Before the Mast*. The passage is a very long one, and should be read in full: it is about Dana feeling revolted when the captain of the ship has a sailor called Sam flogged. Lawrence denounces Dana for being revolted: Lawrence approves.

Master and servant – or master and man relationship is, essentially, a polarized flow, like love. It is a circuit of vitalism which flows between master and man and forms a very precious nourishment to each, and keeps both in a state of subtle, quivering, vital equilibrium. Deny it as you like, it is so. But once you *abstract* both master and man, and make them both serve an *idea*: production, wage, efficiency, and so on: so that each looks on himself as an instrument performing a certain repeated evolution, then you have changed the vital, quivering circuit of master and man into a mechanical machine unison. Just another way of life: or anti-life.

. . .

Flogging.
You have a Sam, a fat slow fellow, who has got slower and more slovenly as the weeks wear on. You have a master who has grown more irritable in his authority. Till Sam becomes simply wallowing in his slackness, makes your gorge rise. And the master is on red hot iron.
Now these two men, Captain and Sam, are there in a very unsteady equilibrium of command and obedience. A polarized flow. Definitely polarized.

. . .

'Tie up that lousy swine!' roars the enraged Captain.
And whack! Whack! down on the bare back of that sloucher Sam comes the cat.
What does it do? By Jove, it goes like ice-cold water into his spine. Down those lashes runs the current of the Captain's rage, right into the blood and into the toneless ganglia of Sam's voluntary system. Crash! Crash! runs the lightning flame, right into the cores of the living nerves.
And the living nerves respond. They start to vibrate. They brace up. The blood begins to go quicker. The nerves begin to recover their vividness. It is their tonic. The man Sam has a new clear day of intelligence, and a smarty back. The Captain has a new relief, a new ease in his authority, and a sore heart.
There is a new equilibrium, and a fresh start. The *physical* intelligence

of a Sam is restored, the turgidity is relieved from the veins of the Captain.
It is a natural form of human coition, interchange.

It is good for Sam to be flogged. It is good, on this occasion, for the
Captain to have Sam flogged. I say so.

This reflection is the exact opposite of that which would occur to
anyone who had never held, or expected to hold, the right end of the
whip – which means most of the poor of the world, all the un-
privileged, the teeming majority of our fellow men. Such a man may
not be lazy like Sam: nevertheless he doesn't like being in another's
power. He doesn't take this Rousseauish view of the virtue of the
direct expression of emotion, or 'the circuit of vitalism',[22] or 'the
blood contact of life'. *He* has suffered others' tempers, at the receiving end. *He* is not romantic at all about the beauties of the
master-and-man relation: that illusion is open only to those who
have climbed one step up and are hanging on by their fingernails.
He knows, through the long experience of the poor, what the real
condition of direct power is like – if you want it treated with ultimate
humanity and wisdom read Bruno Bettelheim's *The Informed
Heart*.

So, with singular unanimity the unprivileged have elected for
societies where they are as far away as possible from the Captain–
Sam situation – which, of course, highly articulated societies are.
Trade unions, collective dealing, the entire apparatus of modern
industry – they may be maddening to those who have never had the
experience of the poor, but they stand like barbed wire against the
immediate assertion of the individual will. And, as soon as the poor
began to escape from their helplessness, the assertion of the individual
will was the first thing they refused to take.

VII

With the scientific revolution going on around us, what has our
literature made of it? This is a topic which I mentioned in the
lecture, but about which almost everything remains to be said. Probably some sort of examination will be produced in the next few years.
For myself, I shall be glad to get this part of the controversy into

better perspective. I will make one or two comments to show some of my present thinking: to those, if I believe I can add something useful, I shall in due course return.

Let me begin some distance off the point. It happens that, of all novelists, Dostoevsky is the one I know the best. When I was twenty, I thought *The Brothers Karamazov* was by a long way the greatest novel ever written, and its author the most magnificent of novelists. Gradually my enthusiasm became more qualified: as I grew older I found Tolstoy meaning more to me. But Dostoevsky is to this day one of the novelists I most admire: besides Tolstoy there seem to me only two or three others who can live in the same light.

This confession of personal taste is not so irrelevant as it seems. Of the great novelists Dostoevsky is the one whose social attitudes are most explicitly revealed – not in his novels, where he is ambiguous, but in the *Writer's Diary* which he published once a month during the years 1876–80, when he was in his fifties and near the peak of his fame. In the *Diary*, which was produced as a single-handed effort, he gave answers to readers' problems of the heart (the advice was almost always practical and wise), but he devoted most of his space to political propaganda, to passionate and increasingly unambiguous expression of his own prescripts for action.

They are pretty horrifying, even after ninety years. He was virulently anti-semitic: he prayed for war: he was against any kind of emancipation at any time; he was a fanatical supporter of the autocracy, and an equally fanatical opponent of any improvement in the lives of the common people (on the grounds that they loved their suffering and were ennobled by it). He was in fact the supreme reactionary: other writers since have aspired to this condition, but no one has had his force of nature and his psychological complexity. It is worth noting that he wasn't speaking in a vacuum; this wasn't like Lawrence banging away with exhortations, some of them similarly regrettable.[23] Dostoevsky lived in society; his diary was influential, and acted as the voice of the ultra-conservatives, to whom he himself in secret acted as a kind of psychological adviser.

Thus I have not a social idea in common with him. If I had been his contemporary, he would have tried to get me put in gaol. And yet I know him to be a great writer, and I know that, not with detached admiration, but with a feeling much warmer. So do present day Russians know it. Their response is much the same as mine. Posterity is in the long run forgiving, if a writer is good enough.[24] No one could call Dostoevsky an agreeable character, and he did finite harm. But compare him with the generous and open-hearted Chernyshevsky, who had a sense of the future of the world flat contrary to Dostoevsky's, and whose foresight has turned out nearer to the truth. The goodwill, the social passion of Chernyshevsky have kept his memory fresh: but posterity ignores wrong or wicked judgments, and it is Dostoevsky's books which stay alive. *What is to be done?* or *The Brothers Karamazov*? – posterity, if it knows anything of the two personal histories, gives a grim, reluctant, sarcastic smile, and knows which it has to choose.

It will be the same in the future. Persons ignorant of the nature of change, antagonistic to the scientific revolution which will impose social changes such as none of us can foresee, often think and talk and hope as though all literary judgments for ever will be made from the same viewpoint as that of contemporary London or New York: as though we had reached a kind of social plateau which is the final resting-ground of literate man. That, of course, is absurd. The social matrix will change, education will change, with greater acceleration than it did between the time of the *Edinburgh Review* and the *Partisan Review*: judgments will change. But it is not necessary to go to extremes of subjectivity. Major writers are able to survive the invention of new categories; they resist the influence of ideologies, including most of all their own. As we read, our imaginations stretch wider than our beliefs. If we construct mental boxes to shut out what won't fit, then we make ourselves meaner.[25] Among near contemporaries whom I admire, I could mention Bernard Malamud, Robert Graves, William Golding: it would be a tough job to assimilate these three into any scheme or ideology, literary or non-literary, which could conceivably be associated with me. So, in a future society, different from ours, some of the great literary names of our time will still be venerated. This will be true of the major talents in the 'movement' of which Dostoevsky was a distant and eccentric precursor and which lasted, as the literature of the Western *avant-garde*, down until the very recent past.

The writers who have taken part in this movement are nowadays often called 'modernists' or 'moderns'; the terms may seem a little odd for a school which began well back in the nineteenth century and which has left scarcely any active practitioners; but literary terms are odd, and if we don't like these we can think of them as terms of art, like the adjectives in New College or *art nouveau*. Anyway, we all know what is meant: there would be fair agreement on some of the representative names – Laforgue, Henry James, Dujardin, Dorothy Richardson, T. S. Eliot, Yeats, Pound, Hulme, Joyce, Lawrence, Sologub, Andrei Bely,[26] Virginia Woolf, Wyndham Lewis, Gide, Musil, Kafka, Benn, Valéry, Faulkner, Beckett.

According to taste, and according to one's fundamental attitude to the implications of modernism, one adds names or subtracts them.[27] Thus Lukács, by far the most powerful of its antagonists, would not include Thomas Mann: while Trilling, one of its committed defenders, certainly would. And so on.

We should nearly all agree that the modernist movement includes a majority, though not all, of the high talents in Western literature over a longish period. We should further agree that the individual works of individual writers have an existence of their own; and that the greatest of the modernists' creations will, like Dostoevsky's, swim above the underswell of argument in a changing culture. But about what the movement means in social terms (that is, the social roots from which it grew and its effects upon society), its meaning in the here-and-now of our divided culture, and its influence in the future – here there is a disagreement which can't be glossed over and which may continue after most of us are dead.

There have recently appeared three interesting texts: Lionel Trilling's *The Modern Element in Modern Literature*,[28] Stephen Spender's *The Struggle of the Modern*,[29] Georg Lukács's *The Meaning of Contemporary Realism*.[30] The first striking thing is that, when they are talking of modernism and modern literature, they are talking of what is recognisably the same thing. They value it differently: their formal analysis is different: but, behind all that, the essence to which they are responding is the same.

The confrontation of Lukács and Trilling is picturesque. Each is a very clever man, and clever in somewhat the same fashion. Each brings by design to literary criticism a range of equipment from non-literary disciplines: Lukács from philosophy and economics, Trilling from Freudian psychology. They often give the common impression of being unempirical: when they try to be empirical they have a tendency to overdo it. On modernism, Lukács is temperately and courteously anti, Trilling devotedly pro. In a long and sustained analysis of modernism, Lukács sees its characteristic features as rejection of narrative objectivity: dissolution of the personality: ahistoricity: static view of the human condition (meaning by this mainly what I have called the social condition).

Trilling's views are familiar to most of us. In his recent essay there is an explicit passage:

The author of *The Magic Mountain* once said that all his work could be understood as an effort to free himself from the middle class and this, of course, will serve to describe the intention of all modern literature . . . the end is not freedom from the middle class but freedom from society itself. I venture to say that the idea of losing oneself up to the point of self-destruction, of surrendering oneself to experience without regard to self-interest or morality, escaping wholly from the societal bonds, is an 'element' somewhere in the mind of every modern person who dares to think of what Arnold in his unaffected Victorian way called the 'fullness of spiritual perfection'.

Reading these closely argued, deeply felt and often moving essays one after the other, that is, Lukács's and Trilling's, one has a curious sense of *déjà vu*. Aren't the two insights, which look so different, seeing the same phenomenon? One approves, the other disapproves, and yet there is a link. They might disagree about the social causes of modernism – but each is too subtle to think that these are simple. As Harry Levin has demonstrated,[31] the social origins of classical nineteenth-century realism are more complex than we used to think.

Lukács and Trilling are describing what has happened. The descriptions under the surface often run together. For Trilling's 'freedom from society' presupposes a static view of society. It is the romantic conception of the artist carried to its extreme. And the romantic conception of the artist only has full meaning if there is a social cushion, unaffected by change, unaffected by the scientific

revolution, to fall back on. Such an attitude, such a desire, can lead to
turning the original dichotomy on its head and taking an optimistic
view of one's individual condition and a pessimistic view of the social
one. Trilling would not do this, of course: he is too serious a man.
But it is a temptation characteristic of the worst-spirited of modernist
literature.

I find myself asking a question. It is not a rhetorical question, and
I don't know the answer. It would be a satisfaction to know it. The
question is this: how far is it possible to share the hopes of the
scientific revolution, the modest difficult hopes for other human
lives, and at the same time participate without qualification in the
kind of literature which has just been defined?

VIII

Finally, it has been said of the original lecture that it is oblivious of
politics. At first sight, this seems strange; for I have written, both in
novels and essays, more about politics, in particular 'closed' politics
(that is, the way decisions are really taken in power-groups, as
contrasted with the way they are supposed to be taken), than most
people of our time. But in fact this species of criticism is not as
strange as it seems; for those who have uttered it mean something a
good deal different from what the overt words convey. That is, they
mean by 'politics' something more limited than most of us can accept,
and something which is, in my view, profoundly dangerous. They
mean, to be brutal, by 'politics' the waging of the cold war. Their
criticism amounts to saying that I did not relate the lecture to the
cold war, as it was being waged in 1959: or, more sinister still, that I
did not accept the cold war as the prime absolute of our age, and of
all ages to come.

Of course I didn't. Not in 1959, nor for a good many years before
that. It seemed to me that nearly every indication, human, economic,
above all technological, pointed the other way. If one knew a little
about military technology, it was likely, oddly enough, not only to
make the dangers appear sharper, but also the possibility of hope:
for it was fairly clear that the discontinuities in military technology

could not possibly leave the cold war untouched for long. It was *that* kind of politics, simmering under the surface of the open formulations, with which I was concerned, and on the strength of which I made judgments which were totally unlike those of my critics. Some of mine were wrong: in the Rede Lecture I much over-estimated the speed of Chinese industrialisation. But the more significant ones, now that time has passed and we can check some of our guesses, I see no reason to change.

This leads me to the major theme of what I set out to say. Let me try again to make myself clear. It is dangerous to have two cultures which can't or don't communicate. In a time when science is deter-mining much of our destiny, that is, whether we live or die, it is dangerous in the most practical terms. Scientists can give bad advice[32] and decision-makers can't know whether it is good or bad. On the other hand, scientists in a divided culture provide a know-ledge of some potentialities which is theirs alone. All this makes the political process more complex, and in some ways more dangerous, than we should be prepared to tolerate for long, either for the purposes of avoiding disasters, or for fulfilling – what is waiting as a challenge to our conscience and goodwill – a definable social hope.

At present we are making do in our half-educated fashion, struggling to hear messages, obviously of great importance, as though listening to a foreign language in which one knows only a few words. Sometimes, and perhaps often, the logic of applied science is modifying or shaping the political process itself. This has happened over nuclear tests, where we have been lucky enough to see, what hasn't been common in our time, a triumph for human sense. The triumph might have come sooner, if the logic of applied science had been as much at educated persons' disposal as the logic of language. But still, let's not minimise our triumphs. The worst doesn't always happen, as a friend said to me in the summer of 1940. I am beginning to believe that we shall escape or circumvent the greater dangers with which science has confronted us. If I wrote the lecture again now, there would still be anxiety in it, but less dread.

Escaping the dangers of applied science is one thing. Doing the simple and manifest good which applied science has put in our power is another, more difficult, more demanding of human qualities, and in the long run far more enriching to us all. It will need energy, self-knowledge, new skills. It will need new perceptions into both closed and open politics.

In the original lecture, as now, I was isolating only one small corner of the situation: I was talking primarily to educators and those being educated, about something which we all understand and which is within our grasp. Changes in education will not, by themselves, solve our problems: but without those changes we shan't even realise what the problems are.

Changes in education are not going to produce miracles. The division of our culture is making us more obtuse than we need be: we can repair communications to some extent: but, as I have said before, we are not going to turn out men and women who understand as much of our world as Piero della Francesca did of his, or Pascal, or Goethe. With good fortune, however, we can educate a large proportion of our better minds so that they are not ignorant of imaginative experience, both in the arts and in science, nor ignorant either of the endowments of applied science, of the remediable suffering of most of their fellow humans, and of the responsibilities which, once they are seen, cannot be denied.

NOTES

1. In the United States the Lecture was published in hard covers (Cambridge University Press, 1959).
2. *Encounter*, May 1959, and subsequent issues.
3. J. Bronowski, *The Educated Man in 1984*. Closing address to the Education Section of the British Association, 1955.
4. Merle Kling, *New Republic*, 8 April 1957.
5. *New Statesman*, 6 October 1956.
6. *Sunday Times*, 10 and 17 March 1957.
7. I am referring to F. R. Leavis's *Two Cultures? The Significance of C. P. Snow* (first published, *Spectator*, 9 March 1962; republished in hard covers by Chatto & Windus in October 1962).
8. Leavis, *Two Cultures?*
9. *Spectator*, 23 March 1962, and later issues; other examples occur in the subsequent literature.
10. 'Mit der Dummheit kämpfen Götter selbst vergebens.'
11. S. T. Coleridge, *On the Constitution of Church and State* (1839), ch. v.
12. It is an interesting reflex of the British situation that the Royal Society, early

this century, deliberately excluded from its scope the social sciences and other fields of learning which, in other countries, would be regarded as part of 'science' in its universal sense.

13. cf. *The Search* (1934).
14. Good judges of the academic world, both American and English, sometimes tell me that I over-estimate American higher education.
15. cf. Kenneth Richmond's *Culture and General Knowledge* (Methuen, 1963).
16. Alfred Kazin, *Contemporaries* (Secker & Warburg, 1963), pp. 171–8.
17. That is, of course, judged by the standards of all human beings born up to the present time.
18. cf. publications of I.N.E.D. (Institut National d'Études Démographiques), Paris. See, for example, M. Fleury and L. Henry, *Des régistres paroissiaux à l'histoire de la population* (I.N.E.D., 1956); J. Meuvret, *Les crises de subsistances et la démographique de la France d'Ancien Régime. Population* (1946).
19. i.e. the peasants starved, and a small richer stratum survived. Recent research on seventeenth-century Sweden has shown that a year of semi-starvation was often followed by a year of epidemics which finished off the young, the old, and the debilitated.
20. e.g. P. Laslett and J. Harrison, 'Clayworth and Cogenhoe', in *Historical Essays 1600–1750* (A. & C. Black, 1963).
21. D. H. Lawrence, *Studies in Classic American Literature* (1924), ch. 9.
22. The pseudo-scientific jargon keeps cropping up through the entire passage.
23. *The Rainbow* (1915), ch. 12, provides one example out of many. 'Hatred sprang up in Ursula's heart. If she could she would smash the machine. Her soul's action should be the smashing of the great machine. If she could destroy the colliery, and make all the men of Wiggiston out of work, she would do it. Let them starve and grub in the earth for roots, rather than serve such a Moloch as this.'
   This is an explicit statement of Luddite convictions: note the use of 'them'. It is *those others* who are exhorted to undergo the sacrifice and pay the price. But if Dostoevsky had been recommending Luddite activities, he wouldn't have stopped at random exhortation: he would have written out a programme by which the machines could be wrecked.
24. W. H. Auden (incidentally one of the few poets for a hundred years with both a scientific education and scientific insight) put it better in 'In Memory of W. B. Yeats'.
25. In both the English and the American senses of the word.
26. There was an outburst of modernist literature (and other art) in Russia from the death of Chekhov (1904) until the Revolution and slightly after. When contemporary Russians say, as they sometimes do, that they have been through all that and don't think much of it, they are not inventing their case.
27. Dame Edith Sitwell, on being asked whether she was to be included among modernists or not, replied that whichever way was chosen she would consider it wrong.
28. *Partisan Review Anthology, 1962.* I might mention that I was perplexed by Trilling's essay about 'The Two Cultures' (*Commentary*, June 1959).

Nothing is more tedious than a writer claiming he is being misrepresented. It is usually his own fault. But I felt like saying that Trilling was attributing to me views on literature which I haven't expressed and don't hold: and attacking them by expressing views which, in the light of what he has written before and since, he doesn't appear to hold either. Martin Green has taken up the argument, more adequately, eloquently and dispassionately than I could have done: see *Essays in Criticism*, Winter 1963.

29. Stephen Spender, *The Struggle of the Modern* (Hamish Hamilton, 1962).
30. George Lukács, *The Meaning of Contemporary Realism* (Merlin Press, 1962 – originally published in German in 1957).
31. Harry Levin, *The Gates of Horn* (Oxford, 1963).
32. I examined this problem in 'Science and Government' and in the 'Appendix': see pp. 99–186.

THE CASE OF LEAVIS
AND THE SERIOUS CASE

I

In his lecture published in the *Times Literary Supplement* on 23 April 1970 ['Literarism versus Scientism: the Misconception and the Menace'], Leavis refers to 'the debate about [or between] the Two Cultures', and then says – '*There has been no debate.*'

The most recent bibliography of this topic that I have seen, compiled in an American university, lists between 1964 and 1968, in the English language alone, eighty-eight separate items.

It would have been more accurate for Leavis to say that there has been no debate between him and me. There has not: nor will there be. For one simple and overriding reason. I can't trust him to keep to the ground-rules of academic or intellectual controversy.

By 'ground-rules' here, I do not mean anything in the least complex or difficult. If I enter into discussion on any topic, intellectual, moral, practical, or whatever combination you like, it matters very little what I feel for my opponent, or what he feels for me. But I am entitled to require – or if I am not so entitled then I have to beg to be excused – that he will observe some basic and very simple rules. If he refers to words that I have said or written, he will quote them accurately. He will not attribute to me attitudes and opinions which I do not hold, and if he makes any such attributions, he will check them against the documentary evidence. He will be careful when referring to incidents in my biography, and he will be scrupulous about getting his facts right. Naturally, I have a duty to obey the same rules in return.

Nothing could be much more prosaic or straightforward; but without these ground-rules any sort of serious human exchange becomes impossible. Leavis has, however, not observed them in his references to me and others. That is why I will not enter into discussion with him.

This is a distasteful business. For years I have said nothing. I was disposed to think to myself: Oh, for God's sake, the scholars will clear it all up one day, there is not much that misses them eventually, at any rate on the plane of fact. In that spirit I should have gone on keeping silent – if it had not been for a new invention, utterly untrue, about my personal behaviour. That seemed to be more than one should properly tolerate. So, this once, I reluctantly feel it best to intervene. I will deal with the matter as briefly and factually as I can, and then proceed to more agreeable topics.

The whole episode of what Leavis calls his 'ill-famed Richmond lecture' ought to have been buried long ago. But since he has resurrected it and used it as a basis for this new and singular insinuation, I shall allow myself to make these comments.

In the lecture the simple rules to which I have just referred are broken; we find various examples. There are inaccurate quotations, wrong attributions, and incorrect biographical innuendoes. As for inaccurate quotations (cf. the text of the lecture published in book form, months after it was actually delivered) he includes approximately twenty passages which are supposed to be quoted from me. Of these, something under half are false – that is, the words he uses are not the words I wrote. Some of these misquotations are comparatively trivial: others distort and garble the meaning, so much so that if I didn't know my own work pretty well, I should be baffled about which sentences he was purporting to reproduce.

Scholars will, of course, pick up these inaccuracies in time. The texts are available, and can be compared. I mention them only because most of us, certainly I myself, tend to assume that quotations in academic discussion can be accepted as correct.

There are also a number of false attributions and false innuendoes. In his remarks about me in the Bristol lecture, there are no misquotations, since he doesn't use any quotations at all. In the space of perhaps 800 words, however, he contrives to include two false attributions, one of which I shall refer to since it has a certain bizarre humour and is of some topical interest, and one false innuendo. It is the last which is my reason for breaking silence now.

The false attribution is, as I say, mildly funny, though it might mislead those not familiar with modern Dickens studies. Leavis reports me as having the following attitude to the great creative writers of the nineteenth century and after: '. . . *they have, one gathers, what is claimed pre-eminently for Dickens: entertainment value.*'

The 'one' is presumably Leavis. The interesting question remains: who is it that is supposed to make this claim for Dickens? A claim which, obviously and fatuously, pays dismissive attention to him by stressing his 'entertainment value'.

From the context it would appear that the claim is being made, or has been made, by me. That is the opposite of the truth. I have written two articles about Dickens in my life; two and no more. One in 1956 and one this year. In both pieces I have said that Dickens, as well as being the greatest novelist in the English language, was also, through most of his career, a deliberate, serious and complex artist. There was nothing at all original or unorthodox about this opinion. It has become generally accepted. And it has been generally accepted for a good many years, during the process through which, between 1939 and 1962, Dickens's reputation has been established for what ought to be good and all.

The study of Dickens has attracted a high degree of professional scholarship, and this process, in which there seems to have been only one dissentient voice, has been charted, with exactness, from the first insights of Edmund Wilson and Orwell through the work of such scholars as Humphry House, Edgar Johnson, George Ford, Philip Collins and many younger people; aided by the (at that time) extra-academic voice of Angus Wilson, down to the publication, edited by John Gross and Gabriel Pearson, in 1962 of *Dickens and the Twentieth Century*. In this collection some of our best young academic critics swept the remains of resistance underground. After that there has been much interesting work, but the main job was done. I have just read two admirable books, by Angus Wilson and A. E. Dyson, in which they are able to take as a starting point that Dickens can, and should, be discussed with the seriousness we bring to Shakespeare.

The puzzle remains: who is making this pre-eminent claim about

Dickens's entertainment value? It can't be me. I don't use entertainment value in a pejorative sense, and the best art always possesses it, but the Dickens which I admire most (for example, *Little Dorrit* and *Great Expectations*) is not specially entertaining in the cant use of the term. Who then is it? Who is so ignorant of modern thought, who has not been able to comprehend those great later works, who is falling back on a stereotype which Edmund Wilson, Orwell and House demolished thirty years ago? Who has committed these follies for which Leavis is blaming me?

The answer may be surprising to some. It is Leavis himself.

As I have just mentioned, in the Dickens rehabilitation (or more exactly habilitation, for he was never justly appreciated until our own time) there was one dissentient voice. It occurred in Leavis's *The Great Tradition*, published in 1948. The relevant passage runs: 'But the genius [Dickens's] was that of a great entertainer and he had for the most part no profounder responsibility as a creative artist than this description suggests.' And, two sentences later: 'The adult mind doesn't as a rule find in Dickens a challenge to an unusual and sustained seriousness.'

This is the view which Leavis is now attributing to me. It has been, of course, well known to the new generation of Dickens critics, but they saw it as nonsense and swept on regardless. With the happy results that we can now read in so many admirable publications in this centenary year.

I will add, for the sake of an accurate record, that Leavis has, in recent years, shifted from his 1948 position.

I now return to the point which it would have been over-indulgent to pass over.

Leavis writes (*TLS*, *loc. cit.*):

As far as public demonstration went, as a matter of fact, I found them [the non-specialist educated], on the occasion of my ill-famed Richmond lecture, enemies: week after week following the appearance of the lecture in the *Spectator* both *its* correspondence pages and the *New Statesman*'s were charged and swollen with letters – and (I suspected) telephone communications – from the intelligentsia, denouncing me and my cruel, gratuitous and stupid assault on poor enlightened Snow, who, thus re-assured, took cover under magnanimity.

The innuendo is clear – that, in this episode, I (C.P.S.) waited to see whether I should receive any support, and that, when the support was forthcoming, I allowed it to influence, or determine, my behaviour.

The innuendo is false in general and in particular. It has been denied in unqualified terms by Mr Cyril Ray (*TLS*, 30 April 1970), the only person in a position to be a witness of truth. I confirm this denial, also without qualification.

Leavis's Richmond lecture was publicised before he gave it. From the press reports after it had been delivered, and from communications from persons present, I gathered that it was defamatory in a legal sense. In fact, I was advised by people of sober judgment to bring an action. That was a step which didn't seem to me proper. I decided at once – that is, on the morning following the lecture – not to take it, if I was the only object of attack. If, say, associates of mine had been involved, I felt that I might have to think again. At this time, I had not seen the text and wrote to Leavis asking for a copy. This he could not provide. I thought it likely, however, that anyone wishing to publish it would let me see it in advance. I should explain, for those not familiar with English law and publishing practice, that any periodical or book publisher contemplating the publication of defamatory material would, as a matter of prudence, either consult a lawyer or show it to the person attacked. In this particular case, any paper or publisher in England would have considered one of these precautions necessary.

On the Monday afternoon four days after the lecture, I received a telephone call from Mr Cyril Ray, a member of the staff of the *Spectator* and an acquaintance of mine. They had acquired rights in the lecture. Could he bring it round? His account of what followed (*TLS*, *loc. cit.*) is completely accurate. I read the lecture aloud. It contained no attack on anyone but myself. If the *Spectator* were to publish it that week, I had to give an answer on the spot. I said go ahead. They courteously offered me space to reply. I said that I had no intention of doing so either then or later.

I had no idea of any correspondence which might ensue in the columns of the *Spectator* or anywhere else. That did not enter into my decision and could not have done so. I do not remember giving it a thought. If you live to an extent in public, you have to leave some consequences of your decisions to chance.

That same week, before the publication, I received a letter of thanks from the then editor of the *Spectator*. From my side, that was all there was to it.

As I have said, I should not have referred to this episode if it had not been revived. There are two conclusions.

First, scholars investigating Leavis's writings – and detached observers of any of these discussions – will need to exert unusual vigilance in examining his statements, in particular his statements about persons and writings which he has set up in opposition to himself.

Second, he is abnormally free with words such as 'responsibility', 'morality', 'creativity' and so on. Truth telling, in the simple sense of the ground-rules to which I have been referring, is a very humble virtue: but it is essential to those more complex and lofty virtues, and they cannot exist without it (except perhaps for some of the more decadent forms of creativity).

There was an interesting letter from Mr Graham Holderness in the *TLS* of 21 May, in which he reminded us that a flexibility of moral values is necessary in our present condition of civilization. Many of us would give at least a qualified yes to that. But there are great dangers in pushing moral relativism too far. In some ways we have already abdicated responsibility for others' actions and our own, and we do not know how to put the responsibility back. That is a contemporary malaise.

Some of the roots of moral action we cannot cut away, whatever moral relativism we play with in more complex situations. Accuracy in verbal statements is better than inaccuracy. Try to pretend otherwise, and we shall find pretty soon that our lives become grittier and dirtier than we can bear.

II

Now for pleasanter things. Much of this *TLS* discussion* has been concerned with the present state of English education, and serious

* This discussion, by Lord Annan and others, went on for some months in 1970 in the *TLS*.

arguments have been put forward. Perhaps I might say a word, especially as I find myself a good deal torn about the whole matter. I don't believe for a minute that it is all easy. We know, of course, that men like Professor C. B. Cox and Mr A. E. Dyson have expressed strong views elsewhere: and we know also that they are humane, concerned and liberal men, and it is foolish for politicians or committed educational progressives to persuade themselves otherwise. I am afraid that these local disagreements – difficult to follow unless one is familiar in detail with the English educational scene – must be boring to readers who are not English. I don't know of any country where educational disputes arouse such intense and complicated emotions. But still, it is perhaps possible to extract some general reflections from our special case. After all, no society is ever satisfied with its educational arrangements. The more you live in other countries, the more you run into problems which have a bearing on our own.

The characteristic English emotional attitude to education, what we might call the English chagrin, seems to have two main causes. First, English education has for a long time been correlated with the class structure.

This is not so true of Scotland and Wales, who have escaped some of the curiosities of the English class structure, so pervasive and yet in parts so bendable. But the English have, ever since the introduction of compulsory primary education in 1870, educated a very small proportion of their children to a reasonable secondary level (though no smaller a proportion than most Western European countries). The English also set up, mainly in the nineteenth century, an unusually large sector of private education, borrowing the older name of 'public schools'; and these became the preserve of the prosperous, usually having higher academic standards than any but the very best state schools. Further, from the small proportion of children educated to a reasonable secondary level, either in state or independent schools, a very much smaller proportion reached the universities. In 1939 the number of undergraduates at English universities was less than 50,000. Of these only a negligible number came from the poorer 80 per cent of the population.

Proficient education thus became closely interwoven with the

class structure. It is an error to think that the educational arrangements, the independent fee-paying schools and the older universities,
were the cause of the class structure. That is much too simple.
Historians of English social manners have shown convincingly that
the English forms of social differentiation were already in existence
when there were effectively no schools or universities at all. That
concept of cause-and-effect ought to be dispensed with. On the other
hand, no one could possibly argue that these schools and universities
have not become a symptom of the class structure and in many ways
one of its strong supports.

Strong supports, even when the institutions themselves are
changing. People abroad, and in England itself, still believe that
Oxford and Cambridge are available chiefly to the rich. Utterly untrue. The median income of parents of Oxford and Cambridge undergraduates is remarkably low. Still, the historical feeling remains. And
the present feeling about the independent schools. And the feeling,
less precise but quite as intense, of 80 per cent of the population that
they have been shut out of all kinds of good schooling, whether it
is in grammar schools or public schools or universities or anywhere else. No one who has any intuition about this country should
underestimate the feeling of bitterness and the sense of profound in-
justice.

The second cause of the English chagrin is: out of the small proportion of students at secondary school and university, a certain
number have been educated to an exceptional level of academic
skill.

The school education has often been more specialised than that
of other countries, though recently it has been somewhat altered.
With this qualification, the able English student at eighteen has
reached a standard at least as high as anyone of his age in the world;
and the same student, graduating with a good degree from an English
university at twenty-one, has probably reached as high a standard at
that age as any contemporary.

It is this feature of our system, entirely creditable, which most
people who have profited by it don't want to lose. I should say at
once that I count myself among them. The situation would be very
much easier if this slice of English education were not, and had not

been, in a perverse and eccentric fashion so singularly good.

There are many misunderstandings from persons arguing either way, that is, from those who demand a socially more acceptable arrangement at any cost, and from those who, at any cost, would keep the specific English excellences. One or two misunderstandings can be cleared up at once.

Take one illusion of the educational optimists – that, by just and socially benevolent administration, you can soon secure the best of all possible worlds. The evidence does not suggest it (though, of course, that is no reason for not trying). The case of Oxford and Cambridge between 1890 and 1914 has some sobering lessons. The undergraduate population at the two universities put together was quite small, under 10,000. The overwhelming majority came from comfortable middle-class families or ambiences much richer than that, a very small and unrepresentative layer of turn-of-the-century England. Yet there emerged more talent of the highest class than any comparable period has been able to show since, even when the English universities were open to a far larger slice of the whole country. If between now and the year 2000, the entire English university system, with eighty times as many to educate, does half as well in terms of supreme ability, we shall all be relieved and proud.

But there is a corresponding illusion on the other side. Too many undergraduates who oughtn't to be at a university at all, academics keep saying. One cannot laugh that off. But we should remember that it would, in strict academic terms, have been much more true between 1890 and 1914. Oxford and Cambridge had in residence some of the chief glories of English intellectual history: but they also had in residence far greater numbers who would never have stood the faintest chance of getting admitted to any university nowadays. That was still the condition between the wars. Rich, intelligent and idle men often contributed something. Rich, stupid and idle men somewhat less. Rich, stupid and industrious men less still.

The average level of academic attainment has, of course, gone up, and probably the median level also. It would be astonishing, given the competition for places and the qualifications required for admission, if that were not true all over England. What hasn't gone up is an acceptance of the forms (and perhaps the necessary values) of academic life. What hasn't gone up, too, is the proportion of intellectual glory: that may very well be a feature of the entire world, and a result of the dampening effect of great masses.

There isn't a perfect solution, and possibly not a good one. I cannot be as bland as some of the committed optimists. I am sure, though, that no society in our condition could avoid spreading its education, both in its pre-university and university stages. Most of us, however humbly we were born, easily lose touch with four-fifths of our own country. It is necessary to listen to men like Sir Alec Clegg, the Chief Education Officer for the West Riding, who has lived his life among those who feel shut out. He tells us that there is no chance of human harmony in England until we pay whatever price we must (not only in money) to avoid the rancour of the educationally neglected.

That is the fundamental case for the comprehensive school. It is not an academic case. There will be some gains, as we draw in bright minds which have not up to now had the opportunity. There will certainly be some losses, mostly at the highest level of our education.

The same applies to the enlargement of university education. We are having to do it very fast. No government could go slow, against the passionate wishes of so many of its own young. Since we have to do it so fast, there will be muddle, inconvenience, waste and sometimes worse than that.

So I find myself in the following position:

(1) Strategically, the plans for educational change, both in comprehensive schools and in expansion of universities, are probably right and certainly forced.

(2) Tactically they need the most delicate and flexible handling, and the absolutism of committed educational optimists could be very dangerous. Some of the things we still do well might be destroyed within ten or twenty years, and the change would be irreversible.

(3) Even with the wisest tactical handling, there are going to be major disappointments. Education cannot become an elaborate masquerade to disguise the fact that some are more gifted than others.

Social justice is not comfortably reconciled to intellectual excellence: as a harsh possibility, it may not be reconcilable at all. Certainly the extreme of egalitarianism isn't.

These are not pretty nor consoling thoughts. Anyone is bound to have them, who has seen the ingenuity with which Soviet academics have made special enclaves for some of their brightest talent. Which leads me to a concern which has been worrying me for some time. Are we going to provide for our own brightest talent? We have a foundation to build on. But are we going, in a fit of absent-mindedness and general amiability, to forget it?

I am quite sure of one general proposition. The very bright educate one another. That has been one of the secrets of the highest-level English education: of Oxford and Cambridge 1890 to 1914, of such institutions as Manchester Grammar School. It is also the secret of Kolmogorov's and Lavrentiev's Soviet schools today. I don't care what we call such places, nor where we put them. But, unless we have them, we shall already, within a generation, have made ourselves more stupid than we need to be.

Social justice is a great value, and we shall be judged by how much of it we can achieve. But we shall also be judged by what we add to the world's mental life: and that depends on what opportunities we can make for our gifted.

Personally, I would take at least as much care of them as we take of potential athletes. Special schools, or parts of schools. If necessary, universities with higher standards than now, or parts of universities. Élitism? To him that hath shall be given? Newton, Russell, Hardy, Dirac are members of the English intellectual élite. What should we have given to the world without such as those? You can abolish an élite only by not educating anyone at all. Which, by the by, would be the most perfect form of abstract justice. How are we to treat our really bright? (There probably aren't many, however much we dig into the population. At the level I am thinking of, there may be 1 in 1,000.)

In several ways, we have in the past twenty years made some sensible improvements. The teaching of mathematics has been changed almost beyond recognition. It is now genuinely difficult for a bright student of the humanities to arrive at a university without having picked up some notion of what mathematics is: and he ought to know where to go for advice about, say, computers or statistics, which in his life-time will be taken for granted as tools of the mental life. And in reverse (remember I am confining myself to bright students) the level of artistic experience among young scientists seems to have increased. Perhaps we have been feeling our way towards a clearer concept of this distinction between scientific and non-scientific cultures. I shall try to express this briefly in a moment.

But what ought they – that is, the most academically skilful – to study in depth? Here it is foolish to lay down general rules, except maybe to say this. There are some mental exercises which become effectively impossible in later life. If you don't study hard subjects before you have graduated, you never will. And without the rigour of hard subjects, and the effect of a minority devoting themselves to them, the whole mental climate will soon become altogether too relaxing. Imagination is vital, but you breathe it in your own private air. Relevance you find for yourself if you are a human being. But intellectual rigour you don't, unless you are disciplined beyond the limits of most men. Chekhov once said: 'If I had to undertake the pursuit of art with only my imagination to rely on, I should have asked to be let off.' Chekhov was one of the truest artists who ever lived, and one with a passionate concern for his fellow-men. So I believe we should make an enclave for the preservation of hard sub-jects and the encouragement of those bright enough, and determined enough (determination is as important as native wit), to do them well. By hard subjects I mean very much what academics of a genera-tion ago would have meant. Mathematics. The physical sciences. Other sciences as they become conceptual. Classics (inflected languages, history, textual study). Difficult modern languages with major literatures. And so on. But not so on indefinitely. The criterion is, if one doesn't do such a subject between the ages of ten and twenty-one, one will not be able to make the effort again.

I don't pretend that this will be the general direction of English education. To suggest that would be crass. But for all our purposes, human and social as well as narrowly academic, we need a sprinkling of good intelligence to remind us what rigour is. It would be very

easy to become flabby. Perhaps specially easy in the flux and confusion of the next ten or twenty years.

III

In the previous section I remarked that we may be reaching a clearer
concept of the distinction between the scientific and the non-
scientific cultures. If I were giving the 'Two Cultures' lecture again,
I think I should express it rather differently. At the time I had a
major public concern: the gap between the rich and the poor
countries of the world, the dangers if it is allowed to grow. Since
then I have said a certain amount more on the subject, and I like
the prospect before us even less than I did eleven years ago.

We are walking with complacency into a situation more ominous
than any in recent history: different from previous dangers, but
quite possibly worse than any the human race has known. This is the
situation in which those whose education we are now discussing will
be living in early middle age. If they turn back to some of our present
comments, they may think that, by comparison with us, Marie
Antoinette was a remarkably deep and benevolent social thinker.

Assuming that we are going to make an effort – even though the
hope is a frail one – we have to make intelligent use of applied science.
Applied science is two-faced. It is at this moment saving India from
endemic famine, and on the other hand it gives us hydrogen bombs.
But it is the only weapon we have, unless we regard mass starvation
with indifference, sink back into parochial cosiness, and deny any
links with our fellow human beings. In which case fate will catch up
with us.

That was my original statement, and of course, I stand by it. I
also said that unless we – that is, responsible persons in rich countries
– can understand something of science, there will be no hope at all.

That led me into some account of the mutual incomprehension of
scientists and non-scientists. Descriptively the account had some
truth in it: but I now accept the criticism that, in various fashions, it
confused the issue. I probably should have separated the major
social concerns from the academic or educational ones. I might have

reached a more satisfactory formulation of the latter such as others have been putting forward. I have listened to a good many serious views, both inside the 'Two Cultures' debate (see Harold L. Burstyn, 'Tradition and Understanding', *School and Society*, November, 1969) and outside it (see J. M. Ziman, *Public Knowledge*, 1968). There have been many similar and converging suggestions defining the distinction between what Burstyn in a brilliant paper calls 'the two ways of knowing': the distinction which dimly strikes most of us, which is foggy and yet in some way real. I shall have to use a little jargon in trying to formulate this distinction. Once we have the formulation something like right then the jargon can be dispensed with. This is a sighting shot.

Two kinds of understanding. Two ways of dealing with experience. Judged by a single powerful discriminant, there really are two and only two. The phrase 'two cultures' means more than was originally intended. One of these cultures is a search, and a successful search, for agreement. That is, by limiting the content of experience which minds had to cope with, and abstracting certain parts, it was found possible to reach a level of agreement: and to build upon this, by the same process, brick by brick, incorporating what had been previously done into the growing structure. This is the culture or tradition which we call science. It only became organised and accepted as a form of mental consensus about 400 years ago (possibly the real start of science had to wait until the invention of printing): but now, so far as we can foresee, it is irreversible.

By the year 2070 there will be, within the limits in which science works, enormously more and deeper agreement about the natural world than there is now. This is the culture which cannot help showing the direction of time's arrow. It has an organic and indissoluble relation with its own past. To use a sentence of Burstyn's: 'In science, the insights of the past are digested and incorporated into the present in the same way that the genetic material of our ancestors is incorporated into the fabric of our bodies.'

This is the characteristic of science which distinguishes it in kind from the other way of knowing. No scientist, or student of science, need ever read an original work of the past. As a general rule, he does not think of doing so. Rutherford was one of the greatest of experimental physicists, but no nuclear scientist today would study his researches of fifty years ago. Their substance has all been infused into the common agreement, the textbooks, the contemporary papers, the living present.

This ability to incorporate the past gives the sharpest diagnostic tool, if one asks whether a body of knowledge is a science or not. Do present practitioners have to go back to an original work of the past? Or has it been incorporated? The English definition of science has always been stricter than that of *Wissenschaft* or *nauk*, and has in effect employed precisely that diagnostic tool.

Science is cumulative, and embodies its past. The other culture, or tradition, has and must have a different relation with its own longer and more variegated past. Take Shakespeare and Tolstoy. Anyone partaking of the 'humanist' culture (there should be a more acceptable term, but it has not yet emerged) has to read their works as they were written. They have not passed, and cannot pass, into a general agreement or a collective mind. They cannot, nor can any works of art, be incorporated into the present as scientific work is bound to be. Shakespeare and Tolstoy have to be read as the words stand on the page. And that will be true so long as man reads English or Russian.

The works endure as independent entities. Partly outside of time. Partly but not entirely: for we have to see them with a kind of double exposure, perceiving as well as we can what they meant in their own time, and (what is much easier) what they mean in ours. But, though the relation to time of humanist art is not simple, there is no direction of time's arrow. By the year 2070 we cannot say, or it would be imbecile to do so, that any man alive could understand Shakespearian experience better than Shakespeare. Whereas any decent eighteen-year-old student of physics in that year will know more physics than Newton.

There is no built-in progress in the humanist culture. There are changes, but not progress, no increase of agreement. Ask yourself, was van Eyck a worse painter than Cézanne? The answer is, he was different. Sometimes in the history of art, particularly in the visual arts, one can identify periods of what can, without absurdity, be called technical progress. But there is nothing ultimately cumulative about this passage through time: and there cannot be, in a culture which is in essence concerned with content and not with process. That is its nature. That is why it is in many ways closer to our human selves – so long as we don't forget that the abstracting, consensus-seeking mind is one of the most human things about us. In fact, the only one which, so far as we know, we don't to some extent share with the animal creation from which we sprang. It is tempting to borrow two fashionable terms and say that one of these cultures is synchronic and the other diachronic. Certainly the scientific culture is diachronic. Synchronic is partly right for the other but not quite, because of its subtle relation with its own past.

So we seem to have reached a clear divide between two cultures or traditions. One is cumulative, incorporative, collective, consensual, so designed that it must progress through time. The other is non-cumulative, non-incorporative, unable to abandon its past but also unable to embody it. This second culture has to be represented by negatives, because it is not a collectivity but is inherent in individual human beings. That means it possesses qualities which the scientific culture does not and never can: and, on the other hand, since there is a principle of mutual exclusion, it loses by its nature the diachronic progress which is science's greatest gift to the mind of man.

This method of expressing the dichotomy may be as useful as we can find, at least for the time being. It is, of course, a first approximation: but possibly it is a fairly adequate one. There exist areas of ambiguity, because some mental activities have a knack of slipping out of any conceptual net. One of the most interesting examples is history. Much of history (and of all scholarship) is cumulative and incorporative in the sense that science is. Yet, to an outsider, it often appears that modern historiography has become emphatically synchronic, not only rejecting the vulgar concept of progress, but also regarding any movement through time as a regrettable necessity. I take it that Namier's work on George III's Parliament is one of the most influential historical works of our time. One could scarcely have a major piece of historical research more synchronic than that.

It is interesting to observe that novel-writing, which often takes a course parallel to historiography, has followed a similar pattern. Just as narrative in history has become disapproved of, so to a surprising extent has narrative in the novel. It sometimes seems that Western writers no longer wish even to contemplate a future, or the passage of time.

That marks a contrast between the tone of their culture and the tone of the scientific culture, about which I commented in the original lecture. It is clear that people are drawn to one culture or the other, partly by the nature of their temperaments; further, the culture in which they live will have its own effect upon those temperaments. Men are attracted to science often because they like the concept of progress and of being engaged in a collective enterprise. Recently Dirac was saying that for him there was one supreme reward for his scientific work, the sense of having a share in the building of an *edifice*. That was said with complete unassumingness and truth, like any remark of Dirac's, which incidentally are not all that many. It was so free from ego that one had to remind oneself that Dirac's share in the edifice is probably greater than any Englishman's since Newton.

If this formulation of the two cultures is anywhere near satisfactory, then perhaps we can see whether it carries any lessons. To my mind, it may help us think sensibly about the content of education. This is not the proper time to produce any suggestions in detail. But I believe it would be possible to devise methods in ordinary academic courses to illustrate the distinction between the two kinds of knowledge. Once the distinction is grasped, then half the game has been won.

SCIENCE AND GOVERNMENT

I

ONE of the most bizarre features of any advanced industrial society in our time is that the cardinal choices have to be made by a handful of men: in secret: and, at least in legal form, by men who cannot have a firsthand knowledge of what those choices depend upon or what their results may be.

When I say 'advanced industrial society' I am thinking in the first place of the three in which I am most interested – the United States, the Soviet Union, and my own country. And when I say the 'cardinal choices', I mean those which determine in the crudest sense whether we live or die. For instance, the choice in England and the United States in 1940 and 1941, to go ahead with work on the fission bomb: the choice in 1945 to use that bomb when it was made: the choice in the United States and the Soviet Union, in the late forties, to make the fusion bomb: the choice, which led to a different result in the United States and the Soviet Union, about intercontinental missiles.

It is in the making of weapons of absolute destruction that you can see my central theme at its sharpest and most dramatic, or most melodramatic if you like. But the same reflections would apply to a whole assembly of decisions which are not designed to do harm. For example, some of the most important choices about a nation's physical health are made, or not made, by a handful of men, in secret, and, again in legal form, by men who normally are not able to comprehend the arguments in depth.

This phenomenon of the modern world is, as I say, bizarre. We have got used to it, just as we have got used to so many results of the lack of communication between scientists and nonscientists, or of the increasing difficulty of the languages of science itself. Yet I think the phenomenon is worth examining. A good deal of the future may spring from it.

In the West, we have not been very good at looking at this singularity with fresh and candid eyes. We are too apt to delude ourselves with phrases like 'the free world', or 'the freedom of science'. None of those phrases is meaningful when we are concerned with the kind of choice I am describing. Such phrases only obscure the truth. I shall come back to that point later. For the moment I will just say that all societies, whatever their political structure or legalistic formulations, are going to be faced with this same type of choice so long as we have nation-states, and that the results are going to be not only significant, but much too significant.

I know that we can draw diagrams of political responsibility which are able to make us feel that everything can be reconciled with the principles of parliamentary government. But if we do, we shall not even begin to understand what is really happening. We shall fool ourselves, as we do too often, with that particular brand of complacency, of lack of gravity, which is one of the liabilities of the West, growing upon us perhaps as we become more affluent.

The first thing, it seems to me, is to try to understand what really happens. 'We must learn to think', Don K. Price has written, 'without making use of the patterns or models taken for granted by most of the text books.'[1] It is harder than it sounds.

No one who has ever thought at all about the relations of science and government, much less anyone who has experienced part of them directly, is likely to think that positive conclusions are going to be either firm or easy to come by. Most of the concepts that administrative theorists use are at best rationalisations, not guides to further thought; as a rule they are unrealistically remote from the workaday experience.

No one that I have read has found the right answers. Very few have even asked the right questions. The best I can do is tell a story. The story is intended to contain a little of something which actually did happen. I shall not pretend that the story is not supposed to bear some relation to our present problems. I shall try to extract a few generalisations from it, or, to be more sensible, a few working rules.

II

This story is about two men and two choices. The first of the two men is Sir Henry Tizard. Let me declare my interest straight away, as they say in English board rooms. I believe, along with a number of Englishmen who are interested in recent military–scientific history, that Tizard's was the best scientific mind that in England has ever applied itself to war. I further believe, although in general I take a pretty Tolstoyan view of the influence of distinguished men upon events, that of all the people who had a share in England's surviving the air battles of July to September 1940, Tizard made a contribution at least as great as any. It has not yet been properly recognised. As he himself wrote in his diary on 8 May 1945, when he was living in what for him was high-level exile, as president of Magdalen College, Oxford, 'I wonder if the part that scientists have played will ever be faithfully and fully recorded. Probably not.'[2]

To an American audience, it is natural that I should have to introduce him from scratch: but if I was speaking of him to most English audiences, I should have to do the same. In fact I have never spoken of him before, and I am very glad that I should do so for the first time in the United States. He had much feeling for America and American science. It was owing to him, as we shall see, that, sixteen months before the United States came into the war, American scientists were told all that the English were doing and all they knew. That gesture of bold trust, forced through by him, and very like his temperament, saved both our countries quite an appreciable bit of time in the Hitler war.

I happen to know that he would have liked me to talk about him, because I once threatened him with it. He said: 'At least I can trust you to do it with the gloves off.' He meant, of course, as he said himself when writing of Rutherford, that with characters big enough one ought not to be polite. He wrote quite a lot about himself. He began an autobiography and he kept a number of fragmentary diaries. Towards the end of his life, like a good many men who have played a part in history, he wanted his own end of the record to be kept

straight. Although I knew him well, I have drawn on this documentary material as well as on other written sources. There is very little
in what follows which is my own opinion or unsupported impression.
When there is, I shall try to make it clear.

What was he like? Physically he did not alter much from middle
age, when I first met him, until he died in 1959. He was English of
the English. His whole appearance, build, and manner were something one does not often see outside England, or even outside the
English professional class from which he sprang. He was not pretty.
There were times when he looked like a highly intelligent and
sensitive frog. His hair, what was left of it, was reddish. His face was
unusually wide across the jaw line. But his expression was trans-
figured by his eyes, which were transparent light blue, sparkling with
dash and interest. He was middle-sized, and like nearly all successful
men of affairs, he was in a muscular sense strong. But that tough
physique, that alert, confident, commanding manner, that warm rasp
of a voice, hid certain disharmonies. He was not all of a piece.

He came into a room, and he had an authority, a pugnacity, that
made men attend to him. He had a lively satirical tongue, of a kind
that seemed a little stylised to my generation. 'Andrade [who was
looking after wartime inventions] is like an inverted Micawber,
waiting for something to turn down.' Of the personal antagonism
with which I shall soon be dealing: 'The hatchet is buried for the
present: but the handle is conveniently near the surface.' And so on.
There were heaps of Tizardisms – but they were to an extent misleading.

True, he knew he was a gifted man; he knew his own capacity
pretty well; but the confidence which made men follow him was not
the deep-rooted, relaxed confidence of those who have their creative
achievement safely behind them – the relaxed creative confidence,
for example, of his idol Rutherford. Tizard did not always find himself easy to live with. The bold face he put on did not completely
mask the strains of his inner life.

In the same way, his tough powerful physique was not as impregnable as it looked. All his life he seems to have been vulnerable
to infections, suddenly knocked out by mysterious high temperatures.
He was lucky in his family, and had sons of very high ability: but he

had a great need for affection, not only in his family, but among his friends. Friendship mattered more to him than it would have done if he had been the self-sufficient man he looked. Fortunately for him, he had the energy and warmth to make friends of all ages. I sometimes thought he was at his happiest in the Athenaeum – he had the curious distinction of being able to make the Athenaeum cosy – among people who not only admired him, but were fond of him.

He was born in 1885. His father was a naval officer – a naval officer of strong scientific leanings, who became assistant hydrographer to the Navy and a Fellow of the Royal Society, but first and foremost a naval officer. That had a direct importance to Tizard, both in his attitudes and in what he was able to achieve. All his life he had the simple, unquestioning, absolute patriotism of a regular officer: and he had a complete intuitive understanding of what soldiers and sailors were like. Except for a physical chance, in fact, he would have been one himself. He would – as a matter of course in such a family – have entered the Navy, if it had not been discovered, just before the examination, that he had a blind patch in one eye. Tizard says, 'I must have taken this verdict philosophically at the time, for I don't remember being disappointed or relieved: but it was a bad blow for my father. . . . He went to a friend in the Admiralty and said, "What would you do with a boy who cannot get into the Navy ?" '[3]

These traditional loyalties were very deep in Tizard. In scientific and technical things his mind was radical: but emotionally he remained until he died bound to that upright, intelligent, dutiful, conservative line. His family were always short of money. Running true to form of the conservative English service families, they both had a certain contempt for money and were constantly worried about it. That stayed so with Tizard. He was worried about money till his death. He never made any, and when he retired from the public service no proper provision was made for him, owing to the changes and chances of his career. His one bitter complaint, in his old age, was that he did not know how he was going to live.

Instead of entering the Navy, he went through an orthodox professional English education – Westminster and Oxford. He was dazzlingly clever at anything he put his hand to. Later on he thought he might have made a goodish academic mathematician, and wished he had tried. Actually, he specialised in chemistry, which was at the time the only adequate scientific school in Oxford. Oxford is now, of course, highly developed in scientific subjects, and it is a bit startling to be reminded that the young Tizard in 1908, bursting with both academic honours and promise, anxious to make a start in research, could find no one in Oxford to work under. Like other bright young Englishmen and Americans of that period, he decided that Germany was the place to find the masters of research. He went off to Berlin to work under Nernst.

As it turned out, he did not bring off anything of scientific interest during his year there. But he brought off something else. For it was in Nernst's laboratory that he first met the other main character in this story. There is a difficulty about this other character because of the English habit of changing names and styles. Thirty odd years later, as the right-hand man and grey eminence of Winston Churchill, he became known as Lord Cherwell. But nearly all the way through his friendship and enmity with Tizard he was called F. A. Lindemann. That is the name by which Tizard in his papers always refers to him. For clarity's sake I shall stick to the same convention.

III

These two young men met in Berlin in the autumn of 1908. We do not know the exact circumstances. It would be nice to know, for even if we eliminate what was to happen, they were two of the most remarkable young men alive, and there cannot have been many such meetings. Lindemann was, by any standards, a very odd and a very gifted man, a genuine heavyweight of personality. I did not know him as well as I did Tizard, but I talked to him a good many times. As he thought I was relatively sensible about the job I was doing, he gave me some tough support. He even made a speech about me in the House of Lords.[4] More important than that, as far as I was concerned, his was the sort of character that makes a novelist's fingers itch. So, although in the two issues I am going to use for analytical purposes I have no doubt that he was wrong and Tizard right, I have a soft spot for him and a complex of respect. I do not think that I should be so interested in the Tizard–Lindemann struggles if I did not have that kind of feeling for both men.

I said that Tizard was English of the English. Lindemann was quite un-English. If one met him for the first time in middle age, I have always thought that one would have taken him for a central European businessman – pallid, heavy-featured, correctly dressed, one who had been a notable tennis-player in his youth and was now putting on weight. He spoke German as well as he did English, and there was a faint Teutonic undertone to his English, to his inaudible, constricted mumble. No one seems to know to this day what his father's nationality was.[5] He may have been a German or an Alsatian. It is possible, though I doubt it, that he was Jewish. No doubt this rather silly mystery will be cleared up in the official biography which Lord Birkenhead is now writing. But it is certain that Lindemann's father was distinctly rich, and Lindemann himself, unlike Tizard, had the attitude to money of a rich man, not of a member of the professional classes.

There was a similar sharp difference in the nature of their patriotism. As I have said, Tizard's was the patriotism of a naval officer, which came to him as naturally and unselfconsciously as breathing. Lindemann, who was not an Englishman but became one, had the fanatical patriotism of someone who adopts a country which is nevertheless not, in the deepest sense, his own. No one cared more about England than Lindemann, in his own way: but it was a way that, with its flavour of the patriotism of the converted exile, struck men like Tizard as uncomfortable and strained.

A great deal else of Lindemann's personality struck them also as uncomfortable and strained. About him there hung an air of indefinable malaise – so that, if one was drawn to him at all, one wanted to alleviate it. He was formidable, he was savage, he had a suspicious malevolent sadistic turn of what he would have called humour, though it was not really that. But he did not seem, when it came to the most fundamental things, to understand his own life, and despite his intelligence and will, he did not seem good at grappling with it. He enjoyed none of the sensual pleasures. He never drank. He was an extreme and cranky vegetarian, who lived largely on the whites of eggs, Port Salut cheese, and olive oil. So far as is known, he had no sexual relations. And yet he was a man of intense emotions.

Tizard, whose emotions were also deep and difficult to control, had an outgoing nature, which, luckily for him, found him wife and family and friends. Lindemann's passions were repressed and turned in upon himself. You could hear the difference in their kind of joke. Tizard, as I mentioned, had a tongue which was harsh, which could be rough with pretentious persons, but which was in the long run good-natured. Lindemann's had the bitter edge of repression.

I remember being in Oxford one morning when the Honours List had been published. I think this must have been during the war. I was talking to Lindemann. I happened to remark that the English honours system must cause far more pain than pleasure: that every January and June the pleasure to those who got awards was nothing like so great as the pain of those who did not. Miraculously Lindemann's sombre, heavy face lit up. His brown eyes were usually sad, but now they were glowing. With a gleeful sneer he said: 'Of course it is. It wouldn't be any use getting an award if one didn't think of all the people who were miserable because they hadn't managed it.'

In that kind of venom, in almost everything he did, he was much more intense than most men. His passions were a bit bigger than life-size; they often took on the inflated monomania of the passions in Balzac's novels. He was altogether a bit bigger than life-size. As I have already said, he was a character who made a novelist's fingers itch. And yet, thinking of him and Tizard, I am not sure which would interest me more as a novelist. When I was younger, Lindemann certainly. Now that I have found my interest gradually change from what we call 'abnormal' to 'normal' personalities – I am using these words, of course, as a shorthand jargon – I think it might be Tizard. He was externally a far less odd man than Lindemann. In the structure of his personality he was probably more complex.

IV

One would like to know what they talked about, in Berlin that winter of 1908. Science, of course. Both had an unshakeable faith that science was the supreme intellectual manifestation of the mind of man, a faith they never lost. Tizard had strong interests in literature, but Lindemann none, nor in any other art. Maybe they talked about politics. Both were conservative, but Tizard had the receptive tolerant conservatism of the Establishment, while Lindemann was eccentrically, and often extremely, reactionary. I do not think they talked of love or young women, as men of that age might be expected to.

There was a romantic story, dear to some in Whitehall who met them in the days of their power and unpatch-up-able quarrels, that they had once been inseparable. I believe, from the quotation from Tizard's autobiography which follows and from other evidence, that that is overdoing it. It is true that Tizard was writing long after the event: but he was also deliberately composing his autobiography with the Lindemann feud as its chief dramatic conflict, and he was too much of a natural storyteller to have underplayed their original friendship, if honesty had not compelled him to do so.

F. A. Lindemann and I became close but not intimate friends. [This is the first reference to Lindemann in the autobiography.] There was always something about him which prevented intimacy. He was one of the cleverest men I have known. He had been to school in Germany, and talked German very well – as well as he talked English – and was fluent in French. He was a very good experimenter. He also played games well. He wanted me to share rooms with him [in Berlin] but I refused. I think my chief reasons for doing so at the time were that he was much better off than I was and I could hardly compete with his standard of living, and also that we should be speaking English all the time, for he would take no trouble to teach me German. It was lucky that I refused because we had a minor row later on. I had discovered a gymnasium in Berlin which was run by an ex-lightweight champion boxer of England, so I used to go there for exercise. I persuaded Lindemann to join and box with me.

Now one of his greatest defects was that he hated anyone of his own age to excel him in anything. He was a clumsy and inexperienced boxer, and when he found that I, who was much shorter and lighter than he was, was much quicker with my hands and on my feet, he lost his temper completely, so much so that I refused to box with him again. I don't think he ever forgave me for that. Still, we remained close friends for over twenty-five years, but after 1936 he became a bitter enemy.[6]

After that year in Berlin, Lindemann stayed in Germany, where he had his entire education, high school, undergraduate, and post-graduate. Tizard returned to England and became a scientific don at Oxford. As he wrote himself,[7] in view of his subsequent career it was strange that he did not remember taking the slightest interest in the application of science to war before 1914. At that time, all his ambitions were in pure science, and they were broken only by the beginning of the war and by a friendship, a hero-worshipping friendship, with Rutherford. That sounds a paradox, since Ruther-ford was the supreme creative expression of pure science, but it makes good psychological sense, and I will deal with it in a moment.

In the 1914–18 war both Tizard and Lindemann, in their early thirties, played picturesque parts. Both happened to be not only brave, but abnormally brave, in the starkest physical sense. Both happened to find their way into the primitive aircraft experimenta-tion of the time. They volunteered for it, because they were not allowed to fight behind machine guns. Tizard was offered flying training, but only in weather *too rough* for the normal flying cadets. 'Done,' he said. Lindemann, for experimental purposes, deliberately put his aircraft into a spinning nosedive. It was against the statistical probabilities that either remained alive, let alone both.

After the war their lives interweaved again. Tizard went back to teach chemistry at Oxford. He put in a word with the electors to the chair of experimental philosophy on behalf of Lindemann,[8] who was duly elected, much to the astonishment of the English physicists, since Lindemann had never been inside an English university. Lindemann became godfather to one of Tizard's children. For two or three years it seemed that they might lead a scientific renaissance in Oxford, the first since the seventeenth century.

But then something began to happen to them both – quite clearly to Tizard, more foggily to Lindemann, who had far less introspective insight. What happened was simple. They knew they were never going, by high standards, to make a success of pure science. Tizard was explicit about it, both in conversation, 'I knew I should never be any *real* good', and in his autobiography, 'I now convinced myself that I would never be outstanding as a pure scientist. Younger men were coming on of greater ability in that respect.'[9] By this he meant that he could not fight at the same weight as Rutherford and his friends. Rutherford, who had become a major influence in his life, had set him a standard to judge scientific achievement by. Tizard did not expect to be a Rutherford. They occurred once in three hundred years. But he was a proud man, he had a sense of his own powers, and he wanted at least to be as good as the next rung down. He felt he was not, and that settled it.

In all this I am reminded of Alfred Kazin's comment about Englishmen weighing themselves and each other up as though they were so much horseflesh. All I can say is, it happened. With Lindemann, it took more time, and it was not so incisive. But he was an even prouder man than Tizard, and internally more convinced that he had a great intellect. He could not tolerate not being able to compete on the one hand with Rutherford and the new generation of Rutherford's pupils, Chadwick, Cockcroft, Kapitza, Blackett, or, on the side of mathematical physics, with Bohr, Heisenberg, Dirac, and a dozen others. It just wasn't good enough. So they each, one consciously and the other gropingly, took their separate ways out.

It is interesting to wonder whether they were right. If they had had more creative confidence, which they both seriously lacked, would they have left a real scientific memorial behind them? After all, they were out of comparison more intelligent than many scientists who have made major discoveries. In his last years Tizard certainly – here I cannot speak for Lindemann – would have given up all his other achievements if he could have had even a quarter of a Rutherfordian *œuvre* to his credit. With more luck, with less pride, could he, could either of them, have done it? As I think that, I hear, from twenty years ago, the clear voice of G. H. Hardy: 'For anything worth doing [by which Hardy meant creative work, which he took for granted was the only thing worth doing] intelligence is a very minor gift.'

Probably, one is forced to believe, their intelligence would not have compensated, and they were right when they contracted out. Tizard had a very broad scientific comprehension. He was the kind of scientist, of which Willard Gibbs was a supreme example, who builds great systems: but Tizard had not the special insight which would have let him see which system, in his own time, was there to be built. Lindemann was the opposite. Apart from his zest in destructive criticism, he was a gadgety scientist, inventive, on the lookout for ingenious tricks. To make use of that gadgety talent, one has to have the obsessive force that can keep one thinking over one device for year after year. Aston could do that, so could C. T. R. Wilson, so could Thomas Merton.[10] But Lindemann soon got tired. That was why he remained an amateur among professionals: which, by the way, was how the leaders of physics, such as Rutherford, always regarded him.

V

So, though they both became fellows of the Royal Society at an early age – earlier than they could have hoped to become in the conditions of today – Tizard and Lindemann slipped out of pure science. And their ways of slipping out brought about the two great collisions. Tizard became a high-level scientific administrator. That was less than forty years ago, but England had only just begun to spend money on applied science. It was during the 1914–18 war that the Department of Scientific and Industrial Research was started. Tizard, who had made a great reputation in applied science during the war,[11] succeeded to the job of permanent secretary, that is, the chief official responsible to a minister. Such chief officials in England have greater power, and more influence in determining policy, than their opposite numbers in the United States. In England they are right at the heart of the power-structure, and in a good many ways are more steadily and continuously important than their political bosses. Tizard fitted into that world from the start. He was not exactly an administrator's administrator, but he was liked and trusted by the high officials. They were in origin and in general attitude, if we forget his streak of scientific radicalism, very much like himself. He liked Whitehall. He liked the Athenaeum. He liked his colleagues, men like himself devoted, upright, and tough, though nothing like so outspoken as he was. When he moved off to become rector of the Imperial College, London, in 1929, he did not leave this inner English official world.

During those same years, Lindemann was making his way in

quite a different English world – the world of high society and
conservative politics, which at the time, when 'Society' had a
practical function that is now obsolescent or dead, still overlapped.
It may seem odd that it was so easy for someone without any social
connections, who was not even English by birth, who was about as
little like a typical specimen of the English upper classes as one can
comfortably imagine, to penetrate right into the inner sanctums. But
it is really very simple. It is only a puzzle if one approaches English
society with Proustian illusions. Lindemann was rich: he was also
determined. For generations English society has been wide open to,
defenceless against, rich and determined men. The more so if they
happen to be intelligent. So within a matter of months rather than
years Lindemann was eating his singular vegetarian meals at a good
many of the great English houses. He became known among smart
people, with somewhat unfortunate infantilism, as 'the Prof'. He
was very soon an intimate of Lord Birkenhead (F. E. Smith), and
through Birkenhead he met Winston Churchill and began, apparently
almost at first sight, a friendship which determined the rest of his
life.

This friendship was utterly loyal on both sides, and continued so
until Lindemann's death. A good deal of Lindemann's social progress
was snobbish, an escape from inner defeats. But his devotion to
Churchill was the purest thing in his life. It was quite unaffected, or
perhaps more strengthened than weakened, by Churchill's ten
years out of office (1929–39) when it looked as though he were one
of a hundred great men *manqués*, one of those with a brilliant future
behind them. Churchill's loyalty to Lindemann was also absolute.
Later on, Lindemann, as Churchill knew well enough, became a
cause of friction with Churchill's other intimates, something of a
political liability. Churchill didn't budge an inch.

Why this friendship? a good many people have asked. They
appeared a pretty incompatible pair. Churchill does not seem at first
glance the obvious soulmate for a fanatical ascetic, a teetotal non-
smoking vegetarian. But the question, like a similar question about
Roosevelt and Harry Hopkins, is without meaning unless one knew
both men, not just well, but as well as they knew each other. Why
any friendship, as far as that goes?[12]

VI

In 1934 both Tizard and Lindemann were nearly fifty. Of the two, Tizard had been by a long way the more successful, though even he, judged by the standard he set himself, had not lived up to his promise. He was a trusted man of affairs, he had been knighted, he was head of a university institution, but in his own eyes he had not done much.

As for Lindemann, he had done much less. The professional physicists did not take him seriously as a scientist, and dismissed him as a cranky society pet. Scientifically his name was worth little. He was the intimate friend of a politician whose name was scarcely worth as much.

Then, quite suddenly, Tizard was given the chance for which he was made. England was strategically in a desperately vulnerable position, for reasons – the tiny size of the country, the density of the population – which apply more harshly today. In 1934 Baldwin was the main figure in the government, and it was only two years since he had said lugubriously: 'The bomber will always get through.'

In public, rebellious politicians like Churchill were attacking the whole of the government's defence policy. In secret, the government scientists, the military staffs, the high officials, were beating round for some sort of defence. There was nothing accidental about this. It was predictable that England, more vulnerable to air attack than any major country, would spend more effort trying to keep bombers off. But there was something accidental and unpredictable in Tizard being given his head.

The Air Ministry, under the influence of their scientific adviser, H. E. Wimperis, himself prodded by a bright young government scientist called A. P. Rowe,[13] set up a Committee for the Scientific Study of Air Defence. Its terms of reference were as flat as usual: 'To consider how far advances in scientific and technical knowledge can be used to strengthen the present methods of defence against hostile aircraft.' The committee was nothing very important to start with.

No one took much notice when its membership was announced. There may have been slight curiosity about the appointment, which was entirely due to Wimperis,[14] of Tizard as chairman. The appointment would not and could not have happened, though, if Tizard had not been so well connected in official life.

Well, that committee was called the Tizard Committee almost from its first meeting. It is slightly touching that in his diary Tizard, who could not use that title, never seems to have been quite certain what its official title really was.

From the first meeting on 28 January 1935 he gripped the problems. This was the job for which he was born. Quite soon, by the summer of that year, small ripples of confidence oozed under the secret doors and penetrated Whitehall, almost the only ripples of confidence that touched the official world during those years. Tizard insisted on a very small committee which he chose himself. Wimperis had to be there, Rowe was brought in as secretary, but at the beginning there were only two members of independent standing, A. V. Hill and P. M. S. Blackett. Both of these were eminent scientists, of a quite different order of accomplishment from Tizard or Lindemann. Hill was one of the most distinguished physiologists in the world and had won a Nobel prize in 1922. Blackett, who was only thirty-seven at this time, was one of Rutherford's most brilliant pupils, and later himself won a Nobel prize.[15]

I doubt if their scientific stature was Tizard's first reason for choosing them. He was an exceptionally good picker of men. Like all good pickers, he was not distracted by much; he was thinking of what the men could do. It did not matter to him that Hill was a very unorthodox conservative, hotly out of sympathy with the Baldwin–Chamberlain policy, the policy of Tizard's own Whitehall friends. It did not matter to him – as it would certainly have done to more cowardly men – that Blackett was a radical, the most distinguished figure among all the radical young scientists, who were bitterly antifascist and who distrusted every move that our own government made. I can say that without hedging, because I was one of them myself.

Tizard did not care. He knew that Hill and Blackett were men who were equipped not only with technical insight, but with strong characters and capacity for decision. That was what he wanted. There was not much time to play with. And I have, though I can produce no evidence for it, a strong feeling that he wanted just one other thing. He wanted the members of his committee to have a natural sympathy for and identification with military men. Hill had been successful in the Army in the First World War, and had edited a classical work on anti-aircraft gunnery. Blackett, before he turned to physics, had been a professional naval officer.

That was a factor in their success, I am convinced. Because the first task was not only a scientific choice, which they made quickly, but also an effort of indoctrination in the services (and a mutual give and take between serving officers and scientists) without which the choice was useless. The choice itself faced them like an 'either/or'. *Either* what was later called by its American name of radar, but in these aboriginal days was known as R.D.F., was the device to back: *or* there was nothing to back.

The committee made up its mind about that before the device really existed. Watson Watt, who was the pioneer of radar in England, working in the Radio Research Laboratory of the D.S.I.R., had done some preliminary experiments. This device might, not certainly but possibly, work in real war in three or four years. Nothing else possibly could. Tizard, Hill, Blackett had faith in their own reasoning. Without fuss, and without backward glances, the choice was made. That was only a resolution on paper, and they had to make it actual.

The administrative mechanism by which this was done is itself interesting. In form the Air Minister, Lord Swinton,[16] arranged for a new high-level committee which was to act as a subcommittee of the Committee of Imperial Defence. Over this new body he himself presided, and on to it was brought the government's chief military critic, Winston Churchill. In fact, however, one has got to imagine a great deal of that apparently casual to-ing and fro-ing by which high English business gets done. As soon as the Tizard Committee thought there was something in radar, one can take it that Tizard would lunch with Hankey[17] at the Athenaeum; Hankey, the secretary of the Cabinet, would find it convenient to have a cup of tea with Swinton and Baldwin. If the inner circles had not trusted Tizard as one of their own, there might have been a waste of months or years. In fact, everything went through with the smoothness, the lack of friction, and the effortless speed which can only happen in England when those inner circles are behind one. Within a very short time the Tizard Committee were asking for millions of pounds, and getting it without a blink of an eye. Two successive secretaries of the Cabinet, Hankey and Bridges,[18] did much more than their official duty in pushing the project through.

The second active job was, in particular, to persuade the serving officers of the Air Staff that radar was their one hope and, in general, to make scientists and military people understand each other. Here again this might have been impossible. In fact, with the exception of those concerned with bombing policy, the senior officers were ready to be convinced as soon as Tizard started to talk.[19] They often thought of putting him in uniform: but that would have defeated his whole virtue as an interpreter between the two sides. 'I utterly refuse to wear a busby,' he used to say. Fairly soon he had not only got radar stations in principle accepted and hoped for, but also succeeded, with the help of Blackett's exceptional drive and insight, in beginning to teach one lesson each to the scientists and the military, lessons that Tizard and Blackett went on teaching for twenty years.

The lesson to the military was that you cannot run wars on gusts of emotion. You have to think scientifically about your own operations. This was the start of operational research,[20] the development of which was Blackett's major personal feat in the 1939–45 war.[21] The lesson to the scientists was that the prerequisite of sound military advice is that the giver must convince himself that, if he were responsible for action, he would himself act so. It is a difficult lesson to learn. If it were learnt, the number of theoretical treatises on the future of war would be drastically reduced.

The committee met for the first time, as I said, in January 1935. By the end of 1935 its important decisions were in effect taken. By the end of 1936 most of those decisions were translated into action. It was one of the most effective small committees in history. But before it clinched its choices, there was a most picturesque row.

The committee had been set up, as we saw, from inside the Air Ministry. One of the reasons was, no doubt, to forestall criticism from outside, which came most loudly and effectively from Churchill. In 1934 he had publicly challenged the government's underestimate of the size of Hitler's air force. His figures, which had been produced by Lindemann, were much nearer the truth than the government's. Thus, simultaneously, there were going on the secret deliberations and discussions of the Tizard Committee, and an acrimonious military argument in full light in the House of Commons and the press, with Churchill the anti-government spokesman.

It is one of the classical cases of 'closed' politics co-existing with 'open' politics. Passing from one to the other, an observer would not have known that he was dealing with the same set of facts. By the middle of 1935 Baldwin, who had just in form as well as fact become Prime Minister, wanted to reduce the temperature of the 'open' military argument. He used the orthodox manœuvre of asking Churchill in. Not into the Cabinet: the personal rifts were too deep for that, but on to the new Swinton Committee, the *political* committee to which I have just referred, which was to keep a supervisory eye on air defence.

The history is very tangled at this point. No minutes have ever been published, but if I know Hankey and his colleagues at all – and I had the good luck to work under them a short time later – I have not much doubt that on the one hand they felt confident that they could give the Tizard Committee its head (Tizard sat himself on the political committee and made his requests for money to it), and that on the other hand it could not do harm, and might do good, if Churchill were given exact information of what was actually being done, rather than inexact.

Roughly that was what happened, but there were other consequences. Churchill entered the political committee, retaining the right to criticise in public and insisting that Lindemann, as his personal scientific adviser, be given a place on the Tizard Committee. Both these conditions were reasonable enough: but then the private war began.

Almost from the moment that Lindemann took his seat in the committee room, the meetings did not know half an hour's harmony or work undisturbed. I must say, as one with a taste for certain aspects of human behaviour, I should have dearly liked to be there. The faces themselves would have been a nice picture. Lindemann, Hill, and Blackett were all very tall men of distinguished physical presence – Blackett sculptured and handsome, Hill ruddy and English, Lindemann pallid, heavy, central European. Blackett and Hill would be dressed casually, like academics. Tizard and Lindemann, who were both conventional in such things, would be wearing black coats and striped trousers, and both would come to the meetings in bowler hats. At the table Blackett and Hill, neither of them specially patient men nor overfond of listening to nonsense, sat with incredulity through diatribes by Lindemann, scornful, contemptuous, barely audible, directed against any decision that Tizard had made, was making, or ever would make. Tizard sat it out for some time. He could be irritable, but he had great resources of temperament, and he knew that this was too serious a time to let the irritability flash. He also knew, from the first speech that Lindemann made in committee, that the friendship of years was smashed.

There must have been hidden resentments and rancours, which we are now never likely to know and which had been latent long before this. No doubt Lindemann, who was a passionate man, with the canalised passion of the repressed, felt that he ought to have been doing Tizard's job. No doubt he felt, because no one ever had more absolute belief in his own conclusions, that he would have done Tizard's job much better, and that his specifics for air defence were the right ones, and the only right ones. No doubt he felt, with his fanatical patriotism, that Tizard and his accomplices, these Blacketts, these Hills, were a menace to the country and ought to be swept away.

It may have been – there are some who were close to these events who have told me so – that all his judgments at these meetings were due to his hatred of Tizard, which had burst out as uncontrollably as love. That is, whatever Tizard wanted and supported, Lindemann would have felt unshakeably was certain to be wrong and would have opposed. The other view is that Lindemann's scientific, as well as his emotional, temperament came in: it was not only hatred for Tizard, it was also his habit of getting self-blindingly attached to his own gadgety ideas that led him on. Whatever the motive was, he kept making his case to the committee in his own characteristic tone of grinding certainty. It was an unjustifiable case.

The issue in principle was very simple. Radar was not yet proved to work: but Tizard and the others, as I have said, were certain that it was the only hope. None of them was committed to any special gadget. That was not the cast of their minds. There was only a limited amount of time, of people, of resources. Therefore the first priority must be given to radar – not only to making the equipment, but to making arrangements, well in advance even of the first tests, for its operational use. (It was in fact in the operational use of radar, rather than in the equipment, that England got a slight tactical lead.)

Lindemann would not have any of this. Radar was not proved. He demanded that it should be put lower on the priority list and research on other devices given as high a priority. He had two pet devices of his own. One was the use of infra-red detection. This seemed wildly impracticable then, to any of the others and to anyone who heard the idea. It seems even more wildly impracticable now. The other putative device was the dropping, in front of hostile air-craft, of parachute bombs and parachute mines. Mines in various forms had a singular fascination for Lindemann. You will find Rube Goldberg-like inspirations about them – aerial mines, fluvial mines, and so on – all over the Churchillian minutes from 1939–42.[22] They keep coming in as a final irritation to a hard-pressed man in Tizard's records of his conversations with Churchill. All these mine inspirations originated from Lindemann. None of them was ever any practical good at all.

For twelve months Lindemann ground on with his feud on the committee. He was tireless. He was ready at each meeting to begin again from the beginning. He was quite unsoftened, quite impregnable to doubt. Only a very unusual man, and one of abnormal emotional resistance and energy, could sit with men so able and not be affected in the slightest regard.

They themselves were not affected so far as choice was concerned. Tizard went ahead with the radar decisions and they let Lindemann register his disagreement. But gradually they got worn down. Neither Blackett nor Hill was phlegmatic enough to endure this monomaniac tension for ever. In July 1936,[23] when the committee were preparing a report, Lindemann abused Tizard in his usual form, over the invariable issue of too much priority for radar, but in terms so savage that the secretaries had to be sent out of the room.[24]

At that point Blackett and Hill had had enough of it. They resigned and did not try to give an emollient excuse for doing so. Whether this was done after discussion with Tizard is not clear. No discussion was really necessary. They all believed that this friction was doing too much harm. They were all experienced enough to know that, with Churchill still out of office, they could make their own terms.

Within a short time the committee was reappointed. Tizard was still chairman, Blackett and Hill were still members. Lindemann, however, was not. He was replaced by E. V. Appleton, the greatest living English expert on the propagation of radio waves. Radar itself was an application of Appleton's fundamental work. The announcement of his name meant, in the taciturn eloquence of official statements, a clear victory for radar and for Tizard. The radar stations and the radar organisation were ready, not perfect but working, in time for the Battle of Britain. This had a major, and perhaps a decisive, effect.

This cautionary story of the first Lindemann–Tizard collision seems to me to contain a number of lessons, some of them not obvious. But there is one, at the same time so obvious and so ironic that I shall mention it now. It is simply that the results of closed politics can run precisely contrary to the results of open politics. That is an occupational feature of the way in which closed politics works and the way in which secret choices are made. Probably not more than a hundred people had any information whatever about Tizard's first radar decision; not more than twenty people took any effective part in it, and at the point of choice not more than five or six.

While that was going on, so also was violent open politics, the open politics of the thirties, the most ferocious and deeply felt open politics of my lifetime. Nearly everyone I knew of my own age who was politically committed, that is, who had decided that fascism had at all costs to be stopped, wanted Churchill brought into the government. Partly for his own gifts, partly as a symbol of a country which was not going to let the Nazis win by default. We signed collective letters about Churchill; we used what influence we had, which in those years was not much. We wanted a government which would resist, the kind of government we finally got in 1940. That was the position, I think, of Blackett and most of my liberal friends. It was certainly my own. Looking back, I think we were right, and if put back in those years again I should do what I did then.

The ifs of history are not very profitable – but if Churchill had been brought back to office, if open politics had gone the way my friends and I clamoured and implored that it should? We should, without any question, have been morally better prepared for war when it came. We should have been better prepared in the amount of war material. But, studying the story I have just told, I find it hard to resist the possibility that, in some essential technical respects, we might have been worse prepared. If Churchill had come into office, Lindemann would have come with him, as happened later. It is then very hard to imagine Lindemann not getting charge of the Tizard Committee. As I have said, I take a pretty Tolstoyan view of history in the large. In a broad sense I cannot easily accept that these small personal accidents could affect major destinies. And yet . . . with Lindemann instead of Tizard, it seems at least possible that different technical choices would have been made.

These retrospective fears are not profitable. But I do not know of a clearer case where open and closed politics appear to tell such different stories and point to such different fates.

VII

The first round in the Tizard–Lindemann duel thus went to Tizard. When war came, he had got his air defence system working. He himself became scientific adviser to the Air Ministry, and his diary between September 1939 and May 1940 is quick, hurried, and lively, written at night after visits to airfields, on the job that he did better than anyone in any country, getting scientific methods into the heads of the young officers, infusing them with his own enthusiasm and his own sense of scientific fact.

Things were going pretty well scientifically that winter, but he had another preoccupation. He had arranged for A. V. Hill to be sent on a mission to Washington, and both of them had become convinced that there were overwhelming arguments for telling the American scientists the whole of our radar and other military scientific secrets. Nearly all the English scientists agreed – Cockcroft, Oliphant, Blackett all pressed the matter. Nearly everyone else disagreed.[25] The written record is simultaneously comic and dreary, with just the kind of comic dreariness one always meets when people get seized by the euphoria of secrecy. Various nodding heads said that United States security could in no circumstances be trusted. Various others, including some who should have known better, thought the United States had nothing to offer.

Tizard became distinctly irascible, but otherwise was getting a good deal of his own way. Churchill had become First Lord of the Admiralty as soon as war broke out, and Lindemann was in Whitehall as his personal adviser. But for the moment there was an uneasy balance of power; Lindemann could not touch the air arrangements. From the papers it looks as though Tizard was as happy and as occupied in those months as at any time in his public life.

Then came 10 May, the German attack on France, Churchill in power. Tizard knew the military dangers as well as anyone alive. He also probably knew that his own days of authority would not last long. If so, his diary entries for that day and 11 May are among the masterpieces of English phlegm.

Friday, May 10. Left Oxford 9 a.m. for Farnborough by air. Saw de Burgh and discussed with him experimental work on A. I. In particular some work on frequency modulation. R. A. E. have made progress in aerial design to eliminate some of the effects of ground reflection, and Mitchell is optimistic: too much so, I think. No clear evidence that method of frequency modulation is better than the pulse method.

Saturday, May 11. From Hill Head to Tangmere. Discussed flying trials of A. I. Was told that ordinary C. H. interception was so bad that there was little hope of getting good A. I. interception by night until day interception was improved. I told them that I thought it better to concentrate on day interception with the help of A. I. rather than do night interceptions now.[26]

The German armies cut through France. Churchill and Lindemann were in 10 Downing Street, getting ready to take control of the
war, including the scientific war. Tizard's diary goes on just like
those two extracts, full of his actions, advice, memoranda. Of course,
there is a great inertia behind anyone living the active life. It is a
characteristic of a man of action, and Tizard was very much a man of
action, that he goes on with his activity until he is stopped.

He was soon stopped. He was stopped in a somewhat peculiar
fashion. On 4 June he was summoned to see Lindemann at 10
Downing Street. Maddeningly, there is no record of the conversation; I doubt if anything very direct was said on either side. The
diary simply reports: 'June 4. Thence to see Lindemann at 10
Downing Street. Apparently he had been told by the P. M. to "drive
ahead" with anything new that may be of use this summer, and there
is enough overlapping of responsibility to hinder almost anything
useful being done.'[27]

Tizard must have known that he was out. But the particular way
in which he was shown to be out may have come as a surprise. On
7 June he attended a meeting of his own Ministry, of which he was
still the official scientific adviser – with his own Minister in the
chair. The air marshals and permanent officials were there. So was
Lindemann. And it was Lindemann who laid down what the
scientific programme should be. Tizard wrote that night: 'Doubtful
whether S. of S. really expected me. I tried to keep them straight
about use of A. I. and G. L. for searchlights – but do not know if I
succeeded. I left before the meeting was over as it did not appear that
good could be done by staying.'[28]

In the next few days Tizard went on with his work and at times
saw his friends. A good many of them seem to have thought that a
man who had already been proved right so often could not be got rid
of so contemptuously.

Friday, June 21. Meeting at 10 Downing Street to consider enemy
methods of navigation. P. M. in chair – present Lindemann, S. of S.,
C. A. S., C. in C's Bomber and Fighter Command, Watson Watt, R. V.
Jones and myself. Various decisions reached but would have been reached
without those commotions in ordinary way. Afternoon meeting presided

over by S. of S. to discuss progress on new developments. As unsatisfactory as previous meeting. Afterwards went to Athenaeum and wrote letter definitely resigning. Showed it to C. A. S. who agreed it was inevitable and asked me to suggest a post of authority for myself. Said this was better left for two or three weeks.[29]

The Chief of Air Staff, Sir Cyril Newell, was, like most of the military people, a devoted supporter of Tizard's. But when they talked of a post of authority, even Tizard, usually clear-sighted, was deluding himself. He was to perform one more first-rate service that year: he was to take part in the classical scientific–military quarrel in 1942; but, in the sense he had known it, there was to be no more authority for him in that war.

In a few weeks they had thought up something for him to do. Someone, possibly to tempt or mollify him, had revived his old idea of scientific exchange with the United States.

July 30. A meeting with Fairey in the hall of M. A. P. He said, 'I am going to be a member of your staff.' I said, 'What staff?' He replied that Beaverbrook had just told him that I was to lead a mission to America and that he, Fairey, was to be a member. As Beaverbrook could not see me, Rowlands, the Permanent Secretary of M. A. P., took me to his room and explained that the P. M. wanted me to lead a mission to America for the exchange of technical information. . . . I was given a provisional list of 'secrets' I could impart, and of information I was to ask for. I said I certainly would not go unless I was given a free hand. . . . It looked to me at first sight as rather a neat method of getting a troublesome person out of the way for a time![30]

That was, of course, at least part of the truth. If Tizard had been playing politics he would not have gone. In times of crisis, as all kinds of men have found out, from Trotsky downwards, the first mistake is to absent oneself. But Tizard had always believed in what such a mission could do.

August 1. Called on Prime Minister at 5.45. Had to wait some time as the Archbishop was with him, which, as the private secretary explained, had quite thrown out the timetable. The P. M. quite emphatic that the mission was important and that he particularly wanted me to lead it. I asked if he would give me a free hand and would rely on my discretion. He said 'of course' – and would I write down exactly what I wanted. So I said I would go, and went into the lobby and wrote out a paper which I left with his secretary. Then I rang up Rowlands and told him that I had accepted and that the P. M. was going to give me full discretion. He said that was quite different from what the P. M. had previously said![31]

Flying the Atlantic in August 1940 meant that a man put his affairs in order. Before he left Tizard arranged that, in case of accidents, his war-time diaries should go to the Royal Society. Those are the diaries from which I have been quoting. He had a proper pride in what he had achieved, and a proper rancour for the way he had been treated. He did not doubt that, if and when competent persons studied the evidence – the diaries and notebooks are full of scientific arguments from 1935 to 1939, which it would not be suitable to quote here – he would get his due.

But no accidents happened, and the mission, on which John Cockcroft was his second in command, was one of the successes of both their lives. American scientists, both at the time and since, have spoken, with extreme generosity, of the effect that visit made. It is true that, mainly because the English had been forced to think in order to survive at all, in most military scientific fields they were ahead. This was pre-eminently true of radar. Although English, American, and German scientists had all begun developing radar at about the same time – which incidentally tells one something of the nature of 'secret' discoveries – by 1940 the English had carried it further.

Tizard and Cockcroft carried with them a black leather suitcase which Miss Geary, Tizard's secretary, was forced to keep under her bed. She did not know it contained nearly all the important new English war devices – and, of a different order of importance from the rest, the new cavity magnetron. Mr James Phinney Baxter, writing the story of the American scientific war, has called the black box 'the most valuable cargo ever brought to our shores' and 'the single most important item in reverse lease-lend'. The magnetron, which was invented by Randall and Boot in Oliphant's laboratory at Birmingham, was probably the most valuable single device in the Hitler war.[32] The sight of it set American scientists working all out

sixteen months before the United States was in the war at all. As
Blackett has said:

This imaginative act of trust, which Tizard and A. V. Hill first envisaged
and finally forced through Whitehall, had immensely beneficial effects on
the scientific aspects of the allied war effort. Cockcroft reminds us that
the mission was magnificently organised by Tizard, and that he had the
inspiration to bring a mixed team of serving officers and scientists. For the
first time our American friends heard civilian scientists discussing
authoritatively the instruments of war, and then heard the Service people
following on with practical experience.[33]

When he returned from the mission, Tizard found that he was still
out. There was no real job for him. He worked, as a kind of free-lance
scientific adviser, in the Ministry of Aircraft Production. Then the
R.A.F., which had throughout been loyal to him, put him on the
Air Council. But neither of those posts made anything like a full call
on his powers. In fact, no post could, while Lindemann was making
all the major scientific decisions on the English side of the war.

I saw something of Tizard at the time. He was a very high-spirited
man, too high-spirited to be bitter. He was also remarkably free
from self-pity. He got a lot of fun out of the solemn paraphernalia of
English official life. The dinners at City Companies, the various
Boards of Governors of which he was a member – to most of us all
that would not have been much consolation, but it was to him. Still,
he was only fifty-six, he was at the height of his abilities, he was
chafing at the leash. I think he welcomed the final row with Lindemann, not only because he was certain he was right, but also because
it gave him something to do.

VIII

The row occurred in 1942, and it occurred over strategic bombing.
We have got to remember that it was very hard for the Western
countries to make any significant military effort in Europe that year.
The great battles were taking place on the Russian land. So it was
natural, and good military sense, that the Western leaders were
receptive to any idea for action. It is also true – and this was not such

good military sense – that the English and Americans had, for years past, believed in strategic bombing as no other countries had. Countries which had thought deeply about war, like Germany and Russia, had no faith in strategic bombing and had not invested much productive capacity or many élite troops in it. The English had, years before the war began. The strategy had not been thought out. It was just an unrationalised article of faith that strategic bombing was likely to be our most decisive method of making war. I think it is fair to say that Lindemann had always believed in this faith with characteristic intensity.

Early in 1942 he was determined to put it into action. By this time he was Lord Cherwell and a member of the Cabinet, and he produced a cabinet paper on the strategic bombing of Germany. Some cabinet papers are restricted to members of the Cabinet only, and Lindemann occasionally used this technique for circulating a scientific proposal; since he was the only scientist in the Cabinet, discussion was reduced to a minimum. But the paper on bombing went out to the top government scientists.

It described, in quantitative terms, the effect on Germany of a British bombing offensive in the next eighteen months (approximately March 1942–September 1943). The paper laid down a strategic policy. The bombing must be directed essentially against German working-class houses. Middle-class houses have too much space round them, and so are bound to waste bombs; factories and 'military objectives' had long since been forgotten, except in official bulletins, since they were much too difficult to find and hit. The paper claimed that – given a total concentration of effort on the production and use of bombing aircraft – it would be possible, in all the larger towns of Germany (that is, those with more than 50,000 inhabitants), to destroy 50 per cent of all houses.

Let me break off for a minute. It is possible, I suppose, that some time in the future people living in a more benevolent age than ours may turn over the official records and notice that men like us, men well educated by the standards of the day, men fairly kindly by the standards of the day, and often possessed of strong human feelings, made the kind of calculation I have just been describing. Such calculations, on a much larger scale, are going on at this moment in the most advanced societies we know. What will people of the future think of us? Will they say, as Roger Williams said of some of the Massachusetts Indians, that we were wolves with the minds of men? Will they think that we resigned our humanity? They will have the right.

At the time I heard some talk of the famous cabinet paper. I have to say this about my own attitude and that of the people I knew best. We had never had the conventional English faith in strategic bombing, partly on military and partly on human grounds. But now it came to the point it was not Lindemann's ruthlessness that worried us most,[34] it was his calculations.

The paper went to Tizard. He studied the arithmetic. He came to the conclusion, quite impregnably, that Lindemann's estimate of the number of houses that could possibly be destroyed was five times too high.

The paper went to Blackett. Independently he studied the arithmetic. He came to the conclusion, also quite impregnably, that Lindemann's estimate was six times too high.

Everyone agreed that, if the amount of possible destruction was as low as that calculated by Tizard and Blackett, the bombing offensive was not worth concentrating on. We should have to find a different strategy, both for production and for the use of élite troops. It fell to Tizard to argue this case, to put forward the view that the bombing strategy would not work.

I do not think that, in secret politics, I have ever seen a minority view so unpopular. Bombing had become a matter of faith. I sometimes used to wonder whether my administrative colleagues, who were clever and detached and normally the least likely group of men to be swept away by any faith, would have acquiesced in this one, as on the whole they did, if they had had even an elementary knowledge of numerical thinking. In private we made the bitter jokes of a losing side. 'There are the Fermi–Dirac statistics,' we said. 'The Einstein–Bose statistics. And the new Cherwell nonquantitative statistics.' And we told stories of a man who added up two and two and made four. 'He is not to be trusted,' the Air Ministry then said. 'He has been talking to Tizard and Blackett.'

The Air Ministry fell in behind the Lindemann paper. The

minority view was not only defeated, but squashed. The atmosphere was more paranoid than is usual in English official life; it had the faint but just perceptible smell of a witch hunt. Tizard was actually called a defeatist. Strategic bombing, according to the Lindemann policy, was put into action with every effort the country could make.

The ultimate result is well known. Tizard had calculated that Lindemann's estimate was five times too high. Blackett had put it at six times too high. The bombing survey after the war revealed that it had been ten times too high.

After the war Tizard only once said 'I told you so.' He gave just one lecture on the theory and practice of aerial bombing. 'No one thinks now that it would have been possible to defeat Germany by bombing alone. The actual effort in manpower and resources that was expended on bombing Germany was greater than the value in manpower of the damage caused.'

During the war, however, after he had lost that second conflict with Lindemann, he went through a painful time. It was not easy, for a man as tough and brave as men are made, and a good deal prouder than most of us, to be called a defeatist. It was even less easy to be shut out of scientific deliberations, or to be invited to them on condition that he did not volunteer an opinion unless asked. It is astonishing in retrospect that he should have been offered such humiliations. I do not think that there has been a comparable example in England this century.

However, the Establishment* in England has a knack of looking after its own. At the end of 1942 he was elected to the presidency of Magdalen College, Oxford. This is a very honourable position, which most official Englishmen would accept with gratitude. So did Tizard. There are no continuous diary entries at this period, although now he had plenty of time. For once his vitality seems to have flagged.

I think there is little doubt that, sitting in the Lodgings at Magdalen during the last thirty months of war, he often thought of Whitehall with feelings both of outrage and regret. Here he was, in one of the most splendid of honorific jobs, but his powers were rust-

* I use a cliché which is neither very accurate nor very useful. I mean a group of people, largely independent of politics, with links in official life and some assumptions in common.

ing – powers that were uniquely fitted for this war. He knew, more accurately than most men, what he was capable of. He believed, both in his dignified exile in Oxford and to the end of his life, that if he had been granted a fair share of the scientific direction between 1940 and 1943, the war might have ended a bit earlier and with less cost. As one goes over the evidence it is hard not to agree with him.

After the war, he and Lindemann were never reconciled. In Whitehall they performed a Box and Cox act which had a note of sarcastic comedy. In 1945, with the political defeat of Churchill, Lindemann went back to his professorial chair at Oxford. Tizard was promptly invited by the Labour Government to become chairman of the Advisory Council on Scientific Policy, and also of the Defence Research Policy Committee, that is, to become the government's chief scientific adviser, very much in the mode in which Killian and Kistiakowsky have been employed in the United States. In 1951 Churchill and Lindemann returned to power. Tizard rapidly resigned.

It caused a good deal of comment that Tizard was never put in the House of Lords, but that did not trouble him. The only thing he was known to grumble about was his pension, which, as I previously mentioned, was derisory. In his very last years, when he and Lindemann were both getting old, he had to take some directorships to make money for himself and provide for his wife. Lindemann died in 1957. Tizard outlived him by two years.

IX

There ends my cautionary story. Now I want to suggest just which cautions we can reasonably extract from it. First we have got to allow for those features of English government and administration which are peculiar to us. There are some features which do not travel, which are inexplicable and boring to Americans and Russians involved in their own problems of science and government. These features are, as American publishers used to say in pained tones of English novels, too British. The chief of them, I think, is the small size, the tightness, the extreme homogeneity, of the English official world. I. I. Rabi once told me that, on his first visit to England in wartime, I believe in 1942, he found Churchill actually handling the prototype of a new radar set in No. 10 Downing Street. Rabi wondered, why did the English insist on running the war as though it were a very small family business?

It is perfectly true that the English unconsciously adopt all sorts of devices for making their population, genuinely small by world standards, seem a good deal smaller than it really is: just as the United States, it seems to me, does exactly the reverse.

But, though that is true, I do not think it affects the major lessons of my story. There is a great deal in closed politics which is essentially the same in any country and in any system. If we are going to begin to understand what goes on, and so do better, I am sure it is wise to take for granted that other countries are much the same as ourselves, not vastly different. To a friendly observer, it often seems that Americans endanger themselves most when they get most possessed by a sense of their own uniqueness. In all the problems I am now discussing, government science, closed politics, secret choices, there is no such uniqueness.

In these matters, by the sheer nature of the operations, all countries have to follow very similar laws. No country's governmental science is any 'freer' than any other's, nor are its secret scientific choices. I beg you to listen to this.* It is said by someone who knows you a bit, who loves you a lot, and who is passionately anxious to see your generous creative forces set loose in the world. You have no special advantages in this domain of science and decision. Listening to American and Soviet scientists, trying to study the way in which you both do your government science, I am struck, not by the differences, but by the similarities. If there is any difference, it is perhaps that, because of the special privileges and autonomy of the Soviet Academy, Russian scientists take a slightly loftier attitude: and also, though this may be a superficial impression, I fancy their major choices involve more scientific minds, are slightly more broadly based, than with you or us.

So I believe we are in the same boat and that all countries can learn from each other's concrete experience. We all know the ideal

* This lecture was, I should perhaps reiterate, addressed to an American audience.

solutions. First, you can abolish some, though probably not all, secret choices as soon as you abolish nation-states. Second, the special aura of difficulty and mystery about these choices will at least be minimised as soon as all politicians and administrators have some trace of scientific education, or at any rate are not scientifically illiterate. Neither of these ideal solutions is in sight. We may therefore not be entirely wasting our time if we try to analyse some phenomena of scientific choice in 'closed' politics.

I have used the phrase 'closed politics' before. I mean any kind of politics in which there is no appeal to a larger assembly – larger assembly in the sense of a group of opinion, or an electorate, or on an even bigger scale what we call loosely 'social forces'. For instance, some of the struggles in an English Cabinet partake of the nature of closed politics: but this is not pure closed politics, since the Prime Minister or any member can if pressed move from personal to mass opinion. On the other hand, almost all the secret scientific choices are something like pure closed politics.

In my type-specimen, during the whole of his conflicts with Lindemann, Tizard had no larger body of support to call on. If he had been able to submit the bombing controversy[35] to the Fellows of the Royal Society, or the general population of professional scientists, Lindemann would not have lasted a week. But of course Tizard could do no such thing: and that is true of most conflicts in government science and of all secret choices.

So we find ourselves looking at the classical situations of closed politics. The most obvious fact which hits you in the eye is that personalities and personal relations carry a weight of responsibility which is out of proportion greater than any they carry in open politics. Despite appearances, we are much nearer than in ordinary government to personal power and personal choice. A crude result is that, at this moment, all countries are not unlikely to be at the mercy of scientific salesmen.

In the Tizard–Lindemann story, we saw three of the characteristic forms of closed politics. These three forms are not often completely separable, and usually fuse into each other, but they are perhaps worth defining. The first is committee politics. There is, of course, a complex morphology of committee politics, and everyone who has ever lived in any society, in a tennis club, a factory dramatic group, a college faculty, has witnessed some of its expressions. The archetype of all these is that kind of committee where each member speaks with his individual voice, depends upon his personality alone for his influence, and in the long run votes with an equal vote.

The Tizard Committee itself was a good example. The members did not represent anyone but themselves. Their only way of affecting conclusions was by their own mana and their own arguments. If it came to a disagreement, then the ultimate decision, which any official committee leans over backwards to avoid, was by means of 'counting heads'. That was what happened, though the circumstances were dramatic, when Lindemann was opposing Tizard over the priority for radar. Everyone round the table knew that it was three to one against Lindemann.[36] In this archetype of a committee, with personalities of approximately equal toughness, with no external recourse except a Churchill out of power and so possessing only nuisance value, that meant his case was lost.

I have just said that any official committee, certainly any English official committee, is reluctant about taking an open vote. I believe that such a vote has only with extreme infrequency been taken in the English Cabinet: but of course the substance of a vote, the way opinion has divided, is obvious enough. If you want open votes, so as to see the committee operation in its full beauty, you need to go to societies which do not damp down the friction of personalities – such as the smaller colleges of my own Cambridge, which cheerfully proceed to open votes on all sorts of controversies, including personal appointments. I suppose the most famous open vote of this century happened when, in October 1917, smuggled for safety into the house of a political enemy, Lenin moved his resolution to the Central Committee of the Bolshevik party 'That . . . [very long parenthesis defining the conditions] . . . the Bolsheviks do now seize power.' The voting was ten to two in favour, with Kameniev and Zinoviev voting against.

There is nothing, by the way, in committee politics which is specially connected with American or English parliamentary institutions. The Venetian oligarchy were great masters of committee work and carried out most of their government by its means. The

Council of Ten (which usually sat as a body of seventeen) and the Heads of the Ten (who were an inner committee of three) made most of the executive decisions. I doubt if there is much that any of us could have taught them about committee politics. In a book of mine some years ago I wrote about a meeting of high officials:

These men were fairer, and most of them a great deal abler, than the average: but you heard the same ripples below the words, as when any group of men chose anyone for any job. Put your ear to those meetings and you heard the intricate, labyrinthine and unassuageable rapacity, even in the best of men, of the love of power. If you have heard it once – say, in electing the chairman of a tiny dramatic society, it does not matter where – you have heard it in colleges, in bishoprics, in ministries, in cabinets: men do not alter because the issues they decide are bigger scale.[37]

I should still stand by each word of that.

The second form of closed politics I think I had better call 'hierarchical politics' – the politics of a chain of command, of the services, of a bureaucracy, of a large industry. On the surface these politics seem very simple. Just get hold of the man at the top, and the order will go down the line. So long as you have collected the boss, you have got nothing else to worry about. That is what people believe – particularly people who are both cynical and unworldly, which is one of my least favourite combinations – who are not used to hierarchies. Nothing could be more naïve.

Chain-of-command organisations do not work a bit like that. English organisations, our Civil Service, our armed Services, are moderately well disciplined, by existing standards. Certainly our serving officers do not show the same enthusiasm for publicising their point of view, especially when they cut across higher authority, as some American officers appear to show. But, in reality, though not on the surface, both our countries work much the same way.

To get anything done in any highly articulated organisation, you have got to carry people at all sorts of levels. It is their decisions, their acquiescence or enthusiasm (above all, the absence of their passive resistance), which are going to decide whether a strategy goes through in time. Everyone competent to judge agrees that this was how Tizard guided and shoved the radar strategy. He had the political and administrative bosses behind him from the start (Churchill and Lindemann being then ineffective). He had also the Air Staff and the Chiefs of Commands. But he spent much effort on persuading and exhorting the junior officers who would have to control the radar chains when they were ready.

In the same way, he was persuading and exhorting the scientists who were designing the hardware, and the administrators who had to get it made. Like all men who understand institutions, Tizard was always asking himself the questions 'Where to go to? For which job?' Often, for a real decision as opposed to a legalistic one, the chap who is going to matter is a long way down the line. Administrators like Hankey and Bridges were masters of this kind of institutional understanding, and they were able to prod and stroke, caress and jab, the relevant parts of the English organism, so that somehow or other, in a way that made organisational diagrams look very primitive, the radar chain got made.

I remember myself, very early in the war, being sent for by a high functionary, much to the bafflement and, I am afraid, to the irritation, of my official superiors. I was a junior official, having gone in as a temporary a few months before: but I had taken on myself the job of producing large numbers of radar scientists. As usual, everyone had forgotten the sheer human needs, in terms of numbers of trained minds, of a new device. I got my summons and went off to the Treasury. My interlocutor was so many steps above me in the hierarchy that no regular communication was possible. That did not matter. Later on, we became friends. The interview, however, took about five minutes. Was this scheme going all right? Should we get enough men? At the right time? The answer to those questions was yes. Did I need any help? No, not just then. That was all. That is the way hierarchical politics sometimes has to work. Granted a serious objective, granted a long-term and unspoken respect for certain rules, it often works very well.

This is a form of politics which has not yet received the attention it needs, if one is going to have any feel, not for how an elaborate organisation is supposed to operate, but for how it does in fact.[38] It cuts across all kinds of romantic stereotypes of official power. The top bosses of great corporations like General Motors, or General

Electric, or their English equivalents, could not act even if they wanted to, could not act by the intrinsic nature of their organisation, like the proprietors of a small film company. Blissful expressions of power, such as hire and fire, get more remote from reality the more elaborate your organisation is, and the nearer you are to the top of it. I suspect that hierarchical politics are probably more interesting and complex in the United States than in any country in the world, certainly more interesting than in any country in the West.

The third form of politics in the Tizard–Lindemann story is the simplest. I shall call it 'court politics'. By court politics I mean attempts to exert power through a man who possesses a concentration of power. The Lindemann–Churchill relation is the purest example possible of court politics.

In 1940, as I described it, Lindemann asked Tizard to call on him at 10 Downing Street. At that time Tizard was the most senior scientific adviser in government employment. Lindemann had no official position whatever; he was the confidential friend of Churchill. Before the end of their conversation Tizard knew that his authority was over. Within three weeks he had resigned.

For another eighteen months, until the end of 1941, Lindemann still held no official position whatever: but he had more direct power than any scientist in history. Roosevelt had a court too, and there must have been a lot of court politics throughout his administrations; but, so far as I know, no scientist ever got near to being intimate with him, and Vannevar Bush and his colleagues were operating at the ordinary official distances and through the ordinary official techniques. Hitler had a court, but he, to an extent quite unparalleled, kept the power to himself. Incidentally, no scientist seems to have got anywhere near him, though he was interested in weapons. His total lack of scientific comprehension was fortunate for the world.

Churchill and Lindemann, however, really did work together, on all scientific decisions and on a good many others, as one mind. In his early days as grey eminence to the Prime Minister, Lindemann made it obvious, by holding his interviews in 10 Downing Street or by threatening Churchill's intervention. Very soon this was not necessary. Bold men protested to Churchill about Lindemann's

influence,[39] and were shown out of the room. Before long everyone
in official England knew that the friendship was unbreakable, and
that Lindemann held real power. Before long also men had accustomed themselves to that degree of power and jumped up behind
it; for an overwhelming majority of men find a fascination in seeing
power confidently used, and are hypnotised by it. Not entirely
through self-seeking, though that enters too.

The fact that the bombing policy was forced through with so little
opposition is a typical example of the hypnosis of power. A good
many men read the Tizard and Blackett papers. A certain proportion
felt, men being men, that, if a scientific statesman like Tizard could be
ignominiously swept aside, lesser persons had better keep quiet. It
is very easy, in an atmosphere of crisis, in the midst of secret
decisions, for men to surrender both their reason and their will. I
can still hear someone, a man normally tough and intelligent, saying
to me one black night: 'The P.M. and Prof. have decided – and who
are we to say them nay?'

Judged by the simple criterion of getting what he wanted, Lindemann was the most successful court politician of the age. One has to
go back a long way, at least as far as Père Joseph, to find a grey
eminence half as effective. Incidentally, there exists a romantic
stereotype of the courtier – as someone supple, devoid of principle,
thinking of nothing except keeping his place at court. Now Lindemann was, in functional terms, a supreme courtier; and yet no one
could be more unlike that stereotype. Life is not as simple as that,
nor as corrupt in quite that way. Throughout his partnership with
Churchill, Lindemann remained his own man. A remarkable
number of the ideas came from him. It was a two-sided friendship.
There was admiration on Lindemann's side, of course, but so there
was on Churchill's. It was a friendship of singular quality – certainly
the most selfless and admirable thing in Lindemann's life, and in
Churchill's, much richer in personal relations, it nevertheless ranked
high. It is ironical that such a friendship, which had much nobility
and in private showed both men at their human best, should in
public have led them into bad judgments.

In all closed politics the three forms I have isolated – committee
politics, hierarchical politics, court politics – interweave, interact,

and shift from one to the other.[40] That is independent of the objectives, which may be good or bad; it is simply the way men have to operate, in order to get anything done at all. I do not mean that as satire. Satire is cheek.[41] It is the revenge of those who cannot really comprehend the world or cope with it. No, I mean my description of politics to be taken as neutral statements. So far as I have been able to observe anything, this is how the world ticks – not only our world, but also the future world one can imagine, juster and more sensible than ours. It seems to me important that men of good will should make an effort to understand how the world ticks; it is the only way to make it tick better.

X

After looking at the Tizard–Lindemann story, and reflecting a bit on the kinds of politics, can we find any guide to action? Is there any way, in this great underground domain of science and government, in which we can arrange to make choices a little more reasonably?

Let me say at once that I have no easy answers at all. If there were any easy answers, they would have been found by now. The whole problem is an intractable one, one of the most intractable that organised society has thrown up. It is partly the expression, in political and administrative terms, of the split between two cultures that I have said something about elsewhere.[42]

But, though the answers have not presented themselves, I think we have advanced far enough to know certain things to avoid. We know some of the sources of bad judgments and bad choices. I think most of us would agree that it is dangerous to have a solitary scientific overlord. It is specially dangerous to have him sitting in power, with no scientist near him, surrounded by politicians who think of him, as some of Churchill's colleagues thought of Lindemann, as the all-wise, all-knowing Prof. We have seen too much of that, and we should not like it to happen again.

And yet, as I say that, I wonder if I am becoming too cautious, too much in love with an old country's predilection for checks and balances. Lindemann made some bad choices, but he also drove some things through as a nonscientist could not have done. Imagine that, in that same position of solitary scientific power, Tizard had been installed: or that Vannevar Bush had been as close to Roosevelt as Lindemann was to Churchill. In either of those cases the positive good would have been startling. Still, I do not think it is overcautious to remember that that has never happened. The chances of getting a Tizard or a Bush as scientific overlord are pretty remote. On the whole, I am still inclined to believe that the obvious dangers outweigh the vestigial possibility of good.

That is fairly clear. We ought not to give any single scientist the powers of choice that Lindemann had. It is even clearer, in my mind at least, that there is a kind of scientist to whom we ought not to give any power of choice at all. We have seen some examples of how judgments were distorted, enough to specify some of the people to fight shy of. Various kinds of fear distort scientific judgments, just as they do other judgments: but, most of all, the self-deceiving factor seems to be a set of euphorias. The euphoria of gadgets; the euphoria of secrecy. They are usually, but not invariably, combined. They are the origin of 90 per cent of ill-judged scientific choices. Any scientist who is prone to these euphorias ought to be kept out of government decisions or choice-making, at almost any cost. It doesn't matter how good he is at his stuff. It doesn't matter if the gadgets[43] are efficacious, like the atomic bomb, or silly, like Lindemann's parachute mines for dropping on airscrews.[44] It doesn't matter how confident he is; in fact, if he is confident because of the euphoria of gadgets, he is doubly dangerous.

The point is, anyone who is drunk with gadgets is a menace. Any choice he makes – particularly if it involves comparison with other countries – is much more likely to be wrong than right. The higher he climbs, the more he is going to mislead his own country.

The nearer he is to the physical presence of his own gadget, the worse his judgment is going to be. It is easy enough to understand. The gadget is *there*. It is one's own. One knows, no one can possibly know as well, all the bright ideas it contains, all the snags overcome. I have felt something like it at second hand, over gadgets I have seen developed. Seeing the first English jet flying in 1942, I could not believe this was not unique. It was like denying one's own identity to credit there was anything else like that in existence. As a matter of fact, of course, there were in existence quite a lot like that. The Germans had already got a jet flying even more impressively. In cold blood the probabilities dawn again, just as they dawned upon anyone connected with radar, who found the same gadgets being developed in the same loving secrecy in England, in the United States, in Germany and elsewhere.

The overriding truth is a bleak one, if one is living in the physical presence of gadgets and spends one's creative force developing them: that societies at about the same level of technology will produce similar inventions. In military technology in particular, where the level of the United States and the U.S.S.R. is very much the same and where the investment of scientists and money is also similar, it would be astonishing if either society kept for long anything like a serious, much less a decisive, technical lead.

It is overwhelming odds that one country will get its nose in front in one field for a short time, the other somewhere else. This situation, fluctuating in detail but steady in the gross, is likely to continue without limit. It is quite unrealistic, and very dangerous, to imagine that the West as a whole can expect a permanent and decisive lead in military technology over the East as a whole. That expectation is a typical piece of gadgeteers' thinking. It has done the West more harm than any other kind of thinking. History and science do not work that way.

If one is not existing in the immediate presence of gadgets, it is a little less impossible to keep a kind of rudimentary common sense. The news of the first atomic pile reached a few of us in England in 1943. In the somewhat inelegant language of the day, we knew the atomic bomb was on. We heard people, intoxicated by the discovery, predicting that it would give the United States unheard-of power for so long as one could foresee. We did not believe it. We had no special prescience, but we were outside the area of euphoria. We speculated on how long it would take a country with the scientific and technical capacity of Russia to catch up, once the discovery was known. We guessed about six years. We were wrong. One always overestimates these periods. It took them four.

It is one of the firmest convictions of most of the best administrators I have known that scientists, by and large, could not do their job. There are many reasons for this conviction, including various human frailties, and I shall return to it at the end. But there is one good one. Many administrators have had to listen to the advice of scientist-gadgeteers. To Bridges and his colleagues, to a good many of the high civil servants who played a part in the Tizard–Lindemann story, it must have appeared scarcely human that men should be so lacking in broad and detached judgment.[45] Most administrators would go on to feel that there is something of the gadgeteer hiding in every scientist.

I have to admit that there is something in it. I should phrase it rather differently. The gadgeteer's temperament is an extreme example of a common scientific temperament. A great many scientists have a trace of the obsessional. Many kinds of creative science, perhaps most, could not do without it. To be any good, in his youth at least, a scientist has to think of one thing, deeply and obsessively, for a long time. An administrator has to think of a great many things, widely, in their interconnections, for a short time. There is a sharp difference in the intellectual and moral temperaments. I believe, and I shall lay some stress on this later, that persons of scientific education can make excellent administrators and provide an element without which we shall be groping: but I agree that scientists in their creative periods do not easily get interested in administrative problems and are not likely to be much good at them.

The euphoria of secrecy goes to the head very much like the euphoria of gadgets. I have known men, prudent in other respects, who became drunk with it. It induces an unbalancing sense of power. It is not of consequence whether one is hugging to oneself a secret about one's own side or about the other. It is not uncommon to run across men, superficially commonplace and unextravagant, who are letting their judgment run wild because they are hoarding a secret about the other side – quite forgetting that someone on the other side, almost indistinguishable from themselves, is hoarding a precisely similar secret about them. It takes a very strong head to keep secrets for years, and not go slightly mad. It isn't wise to be advised by anyone slightly mad.

XI

I could go on accumulating negatives and empirical prescriptions. We know something about what not to do and whom not to pick. We can collect quite a few working tips from the Tizard–Lindemann story. For instance, the prime importance, in any crisis of action, of being positive what you want to do and of being able to explain it. It is not so relevant whether you are right or wrong. That is a second-order effect. But it is cardinal that you should be positive. In the radar struggle Tizard and his committee were positive that theirs was the only hope, and Lindemann had only quibbles and fragmentary ideas to set against it. Over bombing, Lindemann was positive that he had the recipe to win the war. Tizard was sure he was wrong, but had nothing so simple and unified to put in its place. Even at the highest level of decision, men do not really relish the complexity of brute reality, and they will hare after a simple concept whenever one shows its head.

We also saw that a committee like the Tizard Committee is, in the right conditions, as sharp a tool for doing business as government can find. What are the conditions? As a sighting shot I should say:

1. The objective must be clear and not too grandiloquently vast. A scientific committee set to advise on the welfare of all mankind is not likely to get very far. The objective of the Tizard Committee – to defend England in a foreseeable short-term future against air attack – is about as much as anyone can hope actually to cope with.

2. The committee has got to be 'placed' within the government structure. It is usually not difficult to do this, if one has people who know the government machine (or organism, since machine is a bad word) by touch. Different government machines need a different touch, and as a rule a foreigner, however well he knew the country, would dither about where the optimum place should be. To fit the local English structure, the Tizard Committee could not have been better placed, partly by good management, partly by good luck. It was not so high as to get out of touch with the working administrators and the serving officers, or to arouse too much envy (very important

in a compact country). But it had its own links with ministers and top civil servants. In the United States, if I have not got it wrong, there is not the same problem of fitting into a highly organised and very powerful civil service. On the other hand, the committee has to survive in a welter of constitutional and contractual complications, much more elaborate than any the English know. As for the Soviet Union, I have an impression that the correct placing would bring in a good many questions of academic status.

3. To be any real good, the committee has to possess (or take, as the Tizard Committee took) powers of action. It needs, at the least, the power of inspection and follow-up. If it does not have those, it will be too far from the reality it is trying to decide about, and too far from the people who are supposed to carry out the decisions. Advisory committees, if they are confined to pure advice and never get near the point of action, fade away into a kind of accidie.

As a matter of historical fact, these conditions for an effective committee have quite often been achieved. In any particular case, it ought to be reasonably easy to achieve them again. It is – and this is bad luck for us all – specially easy to do this for military objectives. Military objectives are nearly always more precise than benevolent ones: which is why military technology has been easier for ingenious men to think about.

Again unfortunately, the constraints of secrecy, though they disturb the comparative judgment, do not disturb the scientific process. In more liberal days, in the days of Rutherford's Cambridge, Bohr's Copenhagen, Born's Göttingen, scientists tended to assume, as an optimistic act of faith, as something which ought to be true because it made life sweeter, that science could only flourish in the free air.

I wish it were so. I think everyone who has ever witnessed secret science and secret choices wishes it were so. But nearly all the evidence is dead against it. Science needs discussion, yes: it needs the criticism of other scientists: but that can be made to exist, and of course has been made to exist, in the most secret projects. Scientists have worked, apparently happily, and certainly effectively, in conditions which would have been thought the negation of science by the great free-minded practitioners. But the secret, the closed, the climate which to earlier scientists would have been morally intolerable, soon becomes easy to tolerate. I even doubt whether, if one could compare the rate of advance in one of the secret sciences[46] with one of those which is still open to the world, there would be any significant difference. It is a pity.

There is a difference, though, in the rate at which the sciences open to the world get into action. Since those sciences are by definition the ones which cannot be pointed at a military objective, they get into action slower. The exceptions, though perhaps only partial exceptions, are the cluster of sciences which can be applied to medicine. In medicine the objectives are often as clear-cut as in military science.[47] In fact, there is a certain grim family resemblance. This gives edge and sharpness to the deployment of medical research. For it is not the nature of the objective that makes for speedy action, whether it is destructive or on the side of life. All that matters is that there should be an objective at all.

I am speaking very much as an outsider here, and even if I were not, it is difficult to be sure what one means when one speaks of the efficiency of research and development. But, if that phrase means anything, I should have thought the efficiency of medical research in both the United States and England is a good deal higher than of military research. The choices, often because they are not so much all-or-nothing, have been more sensibly made. This is true, although the administrative techniques in the two countries are not the same. Our Medical Research Council, working with funds Americans would think derisory, is an unusual example, very much admired among people who are studying the arts of government, of a government organ which is acting not so much as a controlling force, but as an impresario.

So in military science, and on a lesser scale in medical science, government manages to get some results. But an awful lot of life doesn't consist either of trying to accelerate people's deaths or alternatively to delay them. In the application of science to this vast mid-range of human life, the problems are vaguer, the impetus is less, the pressures of government do not weigh so heavy. A good many benevolent initiatives get lost, although government in the United States, and with slightly less conviction in England, might think that (*a*) this was not their business, (*b*) the initiatives will work their way out elsewhere in the society. It is arguable that that is so, but I am by no means convinced. And governments are not convinced either, because they have set out some sort of springboard where these initiatives can get started. In the United States, unless I am wrong, this springboard ought to be provided by the National Research Council. In England, by the Advisory Council on Scientific Policy. In the Soviet Union, by the Academy of Sciences itself, which is a much smaller body than the U.S. National Academy of Sciences or than the Royal Society of London. The Soviet Academy of Sciences is made up of something like 250 full Academicians, and about 150 corresponding members. It contains historians, economists, various kinds of literary scholars, and even creative writers. About 70 per cent are scientists in the restricted Western sense. It is difficult to guess how completely they succeed as a source of scientific initiative. As for us, I do not think anyone would claim that our organs are well designed for the job.

Does that matter? Is there a job? Hasn't the West in particular got so much applied science in so many quarters that it doesn't need any encouragement?

Does anyone in his senses need more material possessions than the ordinary comfortably off professional American? Or indeed as many? I have some sympathy with anyone who asks me that. And yet, with the ultimate attitude behind it, I haven't so much sympathy after all.

Why not leave well alone? You have said yourself that not many scientists make good administrators. Why worry about science and government? Why not keep the scientists in their place, as we used to, and just call them out to give advice to wiser men?

Isn't the first, the only serious problem of our time, to save the peace? Why does it matter what we do with the scientists? Isn't it the statesman's job to save the peace? What does it matter about scientists?

I am familiar with those questions. They are asked by intelligent men. There is a lot of truth in some of them. And yet they are no good. Or rather, they spring from roots from which spring also many of our dangers and our losses of hope. One of those dangers is that we are beginning to shrug off our sense of the future.

This is true all over the West. True even in the United States, though to a lesser extent than in the old societies of Western Europe. We are becoming existential societies – and we are living in the same world with future-directed societies. This existential flavour is obvious in our art. In fact, we are becoming unable to accept any other kind of art. It is there to be seen in quarters much nearer the working mechanism of our society, in the deepest of our administrative arrangements, in the way we make the secret choices that I spoke of at the beginning, in the nature of the secret choices themselves. We seem to be flexible, but we haven't any model of the future before us. In the significant sense, we can't change. And to change is what we have to do.

That is why I want scientists active in all the levels of government. By 'scientists' here I mean people trained in the natural sciences, not only engineers, though I want them too. I make a special requirement for the scientists proper, because, partly by training, partly by self-selection, they include a number of speculative and socially imaginative minds, while engineers – more uniform in attitude than one would expect a professional class to be – tend to be technically bold and advanced but at the same time to accept totally any society into which they may have happened to be born. The scientists proper are nothing like so homogeneous in attitude, and some of them will provide a quality which it seems to me we need above everything else.

I do not merely mean here that, if we had scientists of any kind diffused through government, the number of people helping to influence secret choices is bound to increase. That is true. In my view, and it is one of the points from which I started, it would be a real gain. It is a clear advantage to the Soviet Union that they have, right at the top of the political and administrative trees, a fairly high proportion of men with scientific or technical training. The proportion of these men in the top executive organs, or among high-ranking diplomats, seems to be somewhere between 35 and 45 per cent, which is far higher than in the United States or England. In the fields where they have made better technical choices than either of us, and there are plenty, this collective influence has no doubt been a help. But, though that is a real gain, it is secondary to what I have most in mind. I believe scientists have something to give which our kind of existential society is desperately short of: so short of, that it fails to recognise of what it is starved. That is foresight.

I am not saying, of course, that all scientists have foresight and no one else has. Foresight is a fairly rare quality. Mr Secretary Stimson showed some of it, more than other political figures at the time, in his memorandum to President Truman, dated 25 April 1945, about the consequences of the atomic bomb.[48] But compare the kind of prescience in this memorandum with that of Franck and the Chicago scientists in their famous letter ten weeks later.

Stimson had to rely on his political sense. Franck and his colleagues had training and something which we can loosely call knowledge behind them. It was not quite knowledge. It was much more an expectation of knowledge to come. It was something that a scientist, if he has this kind of sensitivity latent in him, picks up during his scientific experience.

I believe it is something we grossly undervalue: rather like paleolithic men, before arithmetic had been invented, jeering at someone who had a knack of counting on his fingers. I suppose most scientists possess nothing of this foresight. But, if they have any trace of the capability, then their experience, more than any experience at present open to us, gives them the chance to bring it out. For science, by its very nature, exists in history. Any scientist realises that his subject is moving in time – that he knows incomparably more today than better, cleverer, and deeper men did twenty years ago. He knows that his pupils, in twenty years, will know incomparably more than he does. Scientists have it within them to know what a future-directed society feels like, for science itself, in its human aspect, is just that.

That is my deepest reason for wanting scientists in government. I have tried a shot at an explanation why in their youth they are often not good at the arts of administration. As one thinks back to the operations of the Tizard Committee, it is worth remembering that their decisions were carried out by professional administrators. If these had been replaced by scientists, the scientists would almost certainly have done worse.

But that is only half of it. I spent twenty years of my life in close contact with the English professional administrators. I have the greatest respect for them – as much respect, I think, as for any professional group I know. They are extremely intelligent, honourable, tough, tolerant, and generous. Within the human limits, they are free from some of the less pleasing group characteristics. But they have a deficiency.

Remember, administrators are by temperament active men. Their tendency, which is strengthened by the nature of their job, is to live in the short term, to become masters of the short-term solution. Often, as I have seen them conducting their business with an absence of fuss, a concealed force, a refreshing dash of intellectual sophistication, a phrase from one of the old Icelandic sagas kept nagging at my mind. It was: 'Snorri was the wisest man in Iceland who had not the gift of foresight.'[49]

Foresight in this quotation meant something supernatural, but nevertheless the phrase stayed with me. The wisest man who had not the gift of foresight. The more I have seen of Western societies, the more it nags at me. It nags at me in the United States, just as in Western Europe. We are immensely competent; we know our own pattern of operations like the palm of our hands. It is not enough. That is why I want some scientists mixed up in our affairs. It would be bitter if, when this storm of history is over, the best epitaph that anyone could write of us was only that: 'The wisest men who had not the gift of foresight.'

NOTES

1. Don K. Price, *Government and Science* (New York University Press, 1954), p. 30. Much the most interesting and experienced book on the subject that I have read. Nothing written on government and science in England remotely compares with it.
2. Tizard Papers, diary, 8 May 1945.
3. Tizard Papers, autobiography, MS., f. 17.
4. House of Lords *Hansard* (1957), weekly no. 323, pp. 482–96. He was referring to an article of mine in the *New Statesman* (6 September 1956) called 'New Minds for the New World'. As I was still in Government employment at the time, my friends in Whitehall preferred me not to sign this article; but the authorship was an open secret.
5. R. F. Harrod, *The Prof* (Macmillan, 1959), pp. 15, 107. Sir Roy Harrod's book is a biographical memoir of Lindemann. Harrod knew his subject intimately, but would not claim to understand Lindemann's scientific life.
6. Tizard Papers, autobiography, MS., f. 52.

7. Ibid., f. 66.
8. Ibid., f. 122.
9. Ibid., f. 124.
10. F. W. Aston spent years of his life developing the mass spectrograph, and Wilson years of his on the cloud chamber: both were Nobel prize winners. Sir Thomas Merton is a distinguished spectroscopist and, incidentally, a distinguished art connoisseur and collector.
11. He had become second-in-command to Bertram Hopkinson, who was in effect head of aircraft research. Hopkinson, the most eminent academic engineer of his generation, was killed piloting his own aircraft in 1918: he, more than anyone, taught Tizard what military science meant.
12. One can, of course, make psychological guesses. It would be fairly easy to make plausible guesses about both Roosevelt-Hopkins and Churchill-Lindemann.
13. Rowe played an important part, easy to underestimate because the whole of it was secret, in the scientific war, 1935–45. He is best known as the superintendent of the Telecommunication Research Establishment, the most brilliant and successful of the English wartime research establishments.
14. It is worth noticing that Wimperis, who was a peace-loving, sweet-natured man, ill-at-ease among violent disputes, both got the committee going and selected Tizard.
15. In 1948.
16. Lord Swinton's part in these preparations, like Rowe's, though for different reasons, has been constantly underestimated.
17. At this time Sir Maurice, later Lord, Hankey. One of the great invisible influences in English affairs, particularly military affairs, for a generation.
18. Later head of the Civil Service and Lord Bridges.
19. cf. P. M. S. Blackett, 'Tizard and the Science of War', *Nature* 185 (1960), pp. 647–53.
20. 'Operations research' in the United States. But the English started it, and I much prefer the English name. In the 1914–18 war, A. V. Hill's scientists were testing anti-aircraft gunnery and were carrying out what we should later have called operational research.
21. P. M. S. Blackett, 'Operational Research', *Brassey's Annual* (1953), pp. 88–106.
22. cf. W. S. Churchill, *The Second World War* (Cassell, 1948), vol. 1, pp. 399–401, 593–4.
23. Not 1937 as stated in Churchill, *Second World War*, vol. 1, p. 120. There are other inaccuracies in the chapter ('Problems of Sea and Air, 1935–1939', pp. 115–28).
24. This is Blackett's account. Rowe is inclined to think, without being certain, that this critical quarrel took place before a meeting. It may easily have happened that, since a row was expected, the secretaries were told not to come in at the beginning.
25. Except Hankey. That most discreet of men, who never let slip a secret in his life, thought this was the time to do so.
26. Tizard Papers, diary, 10, 11 May 1940. R.A.E. is the Royal Aircraft Establishment; A.I. is air interception; C.H. is the first-stage chain interception; G.L. is the training of searchlights in combination with anti-aircraft guns.

27. Tizard Papers, diary, 4 June 1940.
28. Ibid., 7 June 1940. S. of S. is Secretary of State.
29. Ibid., 21 June 1940. C.A.S. is Chief of Air Staff.
30. Ibid., 30 July 1940. M.A.P. is Ministry of Aircraft Production.
31. Ibid., 1 August 1940.
32. The magnetron is a device for producing beams of high-frequency radio waves. All the advances in radar after 1940 depended upon it.
33. Blackett, 'Tizard and the Science of War', *Nature* 185.
34. Harrod, *The Prof*, pp. 74-5, had clearly not been told the nature of the argument, either in this matter or (pp. 176-8) in the prewar quarrel.
35. The controversy would have had to be submitted with a large amount of factual background, such as the way in which aircraft are actually operated in practice. It was precisely in the misuse of this factual background that Lindemann's calculations went wrong.
36. That is, of the independent scientific members. Wimperis and Rowe were also on Tizard's side.
37. *The New Men* (Macmillan, 1954), pp. 278-9.
38. An interesting field of investigation would be the British Broadcasting Corporation, which, despite the Kafka-like impression it makes on outsiders, must provide some textbook examples of hierarchical politics.
39. There is a story that a small deputation of Fellows of the Royal Society called on Churchill and said that they distrusted Lindemann's scientific judgment. It would have made a pleasing scene; but I have, with regret, satisfied myself that the story is not true.
40. Some examples of these political processes enter into my novels, cf. *The Masters, The New Men, Homecomings, The Affair*.
41. I owe this remark, which seems to me truer the more I think of it, to Pamela Hansford Johnson.
42. *The Two Cultures and the Scientific Revolution* (Cambridge University Press, 1959). This was the Rede Lecture for 1959. See pp. 13-46.
43. I am using 'gadget' to mean any practical device, from an egg-beater to a hydrogen bomb. The kind of mind which is fascinated by the one is likely to be fascinated by the other.
44. Rowe, who saw more of the English scientific choices between 1935 and 1945 than any single man, is inclined to think that, of all the scientists he met, Lindemann had the worst judgment. Judgment, that is, of science applied to war. (Letter to C.P.S., 3 August 1960.)
45. They did not feel this, of course, about Tizard himself.
46. That is, those parts of science which are directly applicable to war.
47. It is, of course, also true that the feeling of society is deeply involved in military and medical science, and lays great stress upon them. If a similar stress were laid on the problems of transport, we might get scientific solutions quite quickly.
48. cf. Elting E. Morison's biography of Stimson, *Turmoil and Tradition* (Houghton Mifflin, 1960), pp. 613-43.
49. *Saga of Burnt Njal*, ch. 113. 'Foresight' in modern translations sometimes appears as 'prescience'.

APPENDIX TO
'SCIENCE AND GOVERNMENT'

I

THE Godkin Lectures on 'Science and Government' were delivered in December 1960 and published in April 1961. They make quite a short book, not more than 20,000 words or so. There have been a great many more words, however, in the shape of discussions, reviews, articles, and private communications – probably more than in the original piece. Then in October 1961 the four-volume history of the strategic bombing offensive, *The Strategic Air Offensive against Germany 1939–1945* (H.M. Stationery Office), by the late Sir Charles Webster and Dr Noble Frankland, appeared at last. These volumes are an essential source for anyone interested in the themes I myself was writing about. They are, of course, much more than that. In their turn they received a remarkable amount of comment and controversy, far more, which was natural and right, than my little book had done. Finally, in November 1961, Lord Birkenhead published his official biography of Lord Cherwell (F. A. Lindemann) called *The Prof. in Two Worlds*. More arguments started: sometimes the same arguments repeated, sometimes new ones, now the amount of material open to inspection had become greater.

We can now study a good many more documents than I was able to when I first prepared my lectures. It may be some years before we are given any new documents of importance. There are still two official caches which, when broken open, will clear up some of the areas of doubt. I will mention these potential sources later, but it is unlikely that they will do more than sharpen the knowledge we already possess.

Other official sources are at present being explored (for example, the history of the British side of atomic energy). Some of these may give more spectacular results. So may domains of the scientific war, particularly those connected with the army, which so far as I know are still being left in obscurity. It is always possible that we shall have memoirs or autobiographies from some of the major scientists of the war, as, if he had lived longer, we should have had Tizard's.

For the present, however, we must make do with what we have. It ought to be enough to bring us, on most issues, to sensible conclusions. Some of the arguments will remain, and some of the mysteries. But these will not look so numerous, once the dust has settled. With every new batch of documents so far, acrimonious words have been exchanged. I don't intend to add to these. I shall permit myself one subdued grumble on my own account: but that apart – and it does not matter much anyway – I have no doubt what is the most useful thing I can do. I have asked myself a simple question. There is now a lot of information which was not published when I gave the Godkin Lectures. If I had had this information, how would it have affected what I wrote?

II

I must not raise false expectations. If I were doing it again, I should say, in essence, the same things. I should alter it a little in emphasis, a little in tone, I should make rather more qualifications, but in the end I should come, with an even greater sense of urgency, to the same conclusions. The main lessons I wanted to draw seem to me, after almost twelve months' preoccupation with scientific–military history, above all with the history of the strategic bombing offensive, to matter more vitally than they ever did; and I am using the word 'vitally' in its original and naked sense. I regret only that I did not make those lessons clearer. By a failure of literary tact, I allowed the anecdote or parable of Tizard–Lindemann to distract too much attention from the lesson it was supposed to teach. If I were doing it again, I should try to get the lesson and the parable into better proportion. But I should still use the parable. It is the best example in our time of what I was trying to explain, and of what we ought to know. In the light of what I have learned, I should introduce some amendments and speculations: but, again in the light of what I have learned, the anecdote seems to me not weaker, but stronger – sadder, harsher, but more illuminating.

The original lectures can, for convenience, be divided into five parts: (*a*) the statement of the problem, that is, the problem of decision-making in 'closed' politics, in particular, decision-making in scientific affairs; (*b*) the character, scientific qualities, and achievements of Tizard; (*c*) the character, scientific qualities, and achievements of Lindemann; (*d*) the Tizard–Lindemann conflicts; (*e*) the lessons, negative and positive, and the problem of scientific judgment, in particular scientific judgment as applied to military operations. I will now try to have another look at each of these in turn.

III

Decision-making in Closed Politics

I wish that on pages 131–7 I had said much more and said it more sharply. The longer I think about the way decisions have been taken, are being taken, and will continue to be taken, the more frightened I get. I have been accused, by friendly critics, of liking closed politics too much. In one sense there is something in what they say. I have devoted a lot of attention and interest to closed politics: I understand them pretty well: and at times in my life I have been at home there. It is a fairly short step from being at home with something to liking it more than one should. There is a genuine corruption of familiarity.

All that is true. Yet, the more I learn about these methods of taking decisions, the more the dangers appal me. Not only the practical dangers, but the moral dangers too. I do not believe that any person, moderately detached and moderately sentient, can read the sombre pages of *The Strategic Air Offensive* without a feeling of something like vertigo – that *this* is the way we have to make cardinal choices. The Chief of Air Staff on 15 February 1942 writes a minute:

Ref the new bombing directive: I suppose it is clear that the aiming points are to be the built-up areas, *not*, for instance, the dockyards or aircraft factories where these are mentioned in Appendix A.

This must be made quite clear if it is not already understood.[1]

As a piece of information, what percentage of Americans and English realised that this was their countries' intention? It is a very interesting example of collective moral responsibility. In the long future, perhaps the history of our times, and our methods of making war, will be written by some Asian Gibbon: if so, *The Strategic Air Offensive* will provide him with a good many of his most sardonic laughs.

How else can we make this type of decision, though, so long as we have nation-states? It would be nice to think that the United States and the Soviet Union might suddenly renounce all scientific–military decisions taken in secret; it would be nice to think so, but not very sensible. Take, for example, the decisions on nuclear testing. It is clear that the scientific–military part of the argument will not be conducted in public, either in the United States or anywhere else. And it is that part of the argument which, among the pressures and in the typical conditions of closed politics, is certain to prevail.

As for open politics, in any parliamentary democracy, just as much as in a communist society, it would be easy for any government, once the secret decision is taken, to get it not only accepted but applauded. That would be true, whatever the nature of the decision. A government has only to state any of the following propositions:

1. Nuclear testing is essential for the country's military strength;

2. Nuclear testing will make a perceptible addition to the country's military strength, enough to outweigh other considerations;

3. Nuclear testing will make a perceptible addition to the country's military strength, but not enough to outweigh other considerations;

4. Nuclear testing will make a negligible addition to the country's military strength.

None of these propositions can possibly be examined, even by scientifically trained citizens, unless they have access, which by definition they can't have, to the secret arguments; while for most citizens, including the highly intelligent, the propositions could not be examined, even if the secret arguments were thrown open. Because, while secrecy is a major obstacle, the difficulty of communicating scientific arguments is nearly as absolute. Throughout the whole of these discussions of the past year, about strategic bombing, priority for radar, Tizard and Lindemann, I have been more than ever impressed by this gap in communication. Some of the most intelligent people in the world cannot really comprehend the nature – and the fallibility – of scientific judgment. So that, over the hard core of the argument on nuclear testing, just as over the major scientific arguments of the 1939–45 war, politicians, responsible in form for the final decision, have in the long run to trust their scientists. Of course, it is not always easy to know which scientists to trust.

This is still our condition. There are some palliatives, but for the present, by which I mean the next ten or twenty years, there is no root-and-branch solution. In the long run we are forced to depend, much more than is healthy for a society, on scientific judgment. That is, the scientific judgment of a comparatively small number of men. By 'scientific judgment' here I mean *scientific judgment as applied to practical affairs, and especially to military affairs.* I don't mean scientific judgment *tout court*, which is one of the greatest gifts a pure scientist can possess, the gift which tells him the problems worth doing and the problems which will 'go'. Rutherford had this gift to a superlative degree. So did Fermi. So did most, though not quite all, of the major scientific figures of this century. It is sometimes, but not invariably, combined with scientific judgment in the more mundane sense. It is this second kind of scientific judgment which governs our major decisions. It is, often without our knowing it, the heart of our problem. In the rest of this appendix, when I use the phrase, I shall, unless I specify otherwise, be intending it in this sense, scientific judgment as applied to practical (often military) affairs.

Scientific judgment has a good many of the properties of ordinary human judgment, judgment as we talk about it in everyday speech. It is a kind of informed and experienced guessing. It is not a 'logical' process, or at least only in part. It is not necessarily connected with the highest creative talent in science, or with the most sparkling scientific or intellectual brilliance. It can be, but it need not be. It is not a romantic gift. It consists very largely in having a feel for limits, of sensing what brute nature will or will not do, of having a nose for what is 'on'.

Again, as with ordinary human judgment, no one possesses this gift completely or all the time. That is, everyone is fallible: but some are a good deal more fallible than others.

There is one difference from ordinary human judgment. It is not easy, in either case, to predict in advance whether a man possesses the quality. With scientific judgment, however, it is usually possible to test the result after the event.

Since everyone is fallible, no one's scientific judgment ought to be relied on uniquely and by itself. That is one simple lesson to which I shall return. But it is also imperative to identify men of good scientific judgment and get them near the decisions. We now know enough at least to be suspicious of bad scientific judgment, and to some extent of the kinds of personal–scientific temperament which are most likely to possess it. This is negative guidance, but it is better than nothing. Just realising the dangers is in itself a good deal better than nothing.

IV

Tizard

The picture of Tizard that I gave and which others[2] had given before me has not been seriously challenged. Even those who disagree with me on other points[3] have gone out of their way to pay the highest tributes to Tizard and his achievements. Both in print and in private letters there has been a rush of praise. Praise which has that special tone and quality which only happens when people are genuinely relieved to give it. There has been a solitary criticism, but a surprising one. Lord Birkenhead in his official biography of Lord Cherwell, *The Prof. in Two Worlds*, has suggested[4] that Tizard was resistant to new ideas, unless they were his own. This is the opposite of the truth. It has been contradicted by those[5] who have occupied the highest places in English governmental science and who saw Tizard in action over a period of twenty years.

In fact, Tizard did not have much opinion of his own ideas. He was not an inventive scientist at all, in that sense. His supreme gift lay in judging the ideas of others, of knowing which to back and which not to back, and, above all, of being able to introduce the workable ones into military operations. Scientific ideas are no good in war unless they can be made into hardware with which soldiers can be taught to fight. It was this insight, both intellectual and intuitive, into actual military operations, that made Tizard so valuable in the science of war.

There is, fortunately, no doubt about his value. It is on the record, and cannot be argued with. To him, as much as to any single man, we owed the fact that there was an adequate fighter defence in 1940 – only just adequate, but still it dragged us through. Of this fighter system, radar was only one part, though an essential one. Tizard's was the strongest scientific mind behind the whole system. He was at one throughout with the serving officers. This mutual trust enabled him and his committee to introduce the operational use of radar just in time.

The introduction of radar into Fighter Command between 1937 and 1940 is a textbook example of the successful application of science to war. It ought to be studied in staff colleges: and it ought to be studied by anyone who still thinks that scientific war is an affair of bright ideas. Radar was invented – that is, wireless waves were shown to be echoed from aircraft – almost simultaneously by government scientists in the United States, Great Britain, and Germany, entirely unknown to each other. As a matter of history, two Americans in the Navy Department got in first. But the British had two advantages. First, the British inventor, Watson Watt, believed passionately and imaginatively in what he was doing. Second, Tizard right from the start realised that this was the only scientific defence worth looking at, and had the power and the military insight to teach the Air Force so. *Tizard actually persuaded the Air Force to base their defensive planning on the assumption that radar would work long before the stations existed as practical systems.* This was an act of astonishing intellectual courage. Not only Tizard deserves the highest credit for it, but also the officers of Fighter Command.

By 1940 German radar was technically somewhat more sophisticated than the British: but the combination of Tizard and the officers of Fighter Command had ensured that the British knew better how to use it as a weapon of war.

That was Tizard's greatest service to the country. He did another, almost equally important, of a not dissimilar kind. Watson Watt reports[6] that as early as February 1936 he (Watson Watt) was pressing for the development of short-wave radar. It was obvious that, if one could produce a powerful source of centimetric waves, the efficacy of radar would increase – almost out of belief, by the standards of 1936. But the invention of such a source became one of the most difficult problems of the entire scientific war. Tizard, so Cockcroft has told us,[7] got the Cavendish scientists thinking about it by 1938. At some date early in the war[8] Lindemann was setting his own team on to the problem. Over this development there was no disagreement, and Lindemann, when he had full power, threw it behind centimetric techniques.

Almost everyone, however, was concentrating on a device called the klystron, which, though useful, was not the final answer. Without anyone really knowing, an approach to the final answer had been set in motion earlier. Tizard had not only talked to the Cavendish, but to Oliphant's laboratory at Birmingham. In August 1939 a number of Oliphant's staff paid a visit of several weeks to the chain station at Ventnor. In an interview with the Australian periodical *Meanjin Quarterly* Sir Mark Oliphant has stated:

I must say that I agree completely with Blackett's appraisement of the 'history' of the Lindemann–Tizard controversies. I was a colleague of Blackett's in Cambridge from 1927 to 1933 and he has been a close friend since then. I knew Tizard well, from about 1932 until his death, and was fortunate to become his friend. Lindemann and I became closely associated from about 1937, although I knew him much earlier. However, although our relationship was always friendly, I cannot claim to have become close enough to him personally to call him other than a professional colleague.

When war broke out I had been associated, as a nuclear scientist, with the appraisal of the possibilities of using nuclear fission to produce a powerful military weapon, and some work was going on in my laboratory. However, through the vision of Tizard and Blackett, many of us who were physicists had been introduced to the concept of radar and had spent some weeks at the newly created chain of radar stations along the eastern and southern coasts of Britain. I was then Professor of Physics in Birmingham, and in view of the national situation I agreed to drop the work on atomic energy and to devote the efforts of my team to the further development of radar. We undertook, in particular, to try to develop generators and detectors of radio waves of far greater frequency than was then available.

J. T. Randall's account in the paper compiled at the request of S.R.E. Department, Admiralty, 1943, *Development of the Multi-Resonator Magnetron in the University of Birmingham*, gives much more detail.

The Birmingham scientists took over the centimetric problem. Even here nearly everyone was trying to make improvements to the klystron. Randall and Boot, in Randall's own words,[9] were standing on the side lines. Suddenly the idea broke through. Within a time that still seems magically short, Randall and Boot had a cavity magnetron working. The idea of the magnetron and its design were on paper in November 1939, and it operated in its crude form (with sealing-wax joints and so on) before the end of February 1940.

It was a device – if one is going to use such words – of genius. James Phinney Baxter was writing of the cavity magnetron when, in describing the Tizard–Cockcroft mission to the United States in 1940, he said it was the most valuable cargo ever brought to American shores.[10] Of all the scientific inventions in the Hitler war, the cavity magnetron was the most valuable.

Tizard's contribution to the scientific war is, as I have said, on the record. It is not ambiguous, and we can leave it there.

Now I should like to introduce two reflections about it, on my own account. The first has arisen by implication in some of the discussions. The second has come to me as I have thought over the whole story.

In my original lectures, I said that Tizard's was the best scientific mind that in England had ever applied itself to war. I knew precisely what I meant: but the phrase may have conveyed something slightly different from what I intended. I should now use instead of 'best' the same adjective that I have just applied to the magnetron. I should write that Tizard's was the 'most valuable scientific mind that in England had ever applied itself to war'.

I did not mean, though I now see that I could be taken to mean, that he was the best scientist, *as a scientist*, who happened to have had a share in military decisions. That would be quite untrue. Tizard, who was very modest about his scientific attainments, would have said trenchantly that it was untrue. Take the English physicists who were active in the 1939–45 war, Blackett, Chadwick, Cockcroft, Appleton, Thomson: all Nobel Prize winners and scientists of the highest class. Tizard knew that he did not fight at the same scientific weight. He knew also that he did not fight at the same scientific weight as Oliphant, Bullard, Dee, Bernal, and a good many others. I am fairly sure, though I don't remember discussing it with him, that he would have thought Lindemann, as a pure scientist, markedly better than himself.

It is true that, just at the end of the war, Tizard's name was seriously mentioned as the next President of the Royal Society, the highest official honour that English science can give. But he took it to be right that ultimately the election went to Robert Robinson, one of the most distinguished organic chemists in the world.

Tizard was not, and probably could never have been, one of the great pure scientists. On the other hand, you would have to go a long way to find his equal for scientific judgment applied to practical affairs. That was his gift. It was because of it that he was able to make his major contribution.

The second point which I have considered is a quality of Tizard's own nature. The description I gave of him is, I think, all right as far as it goes. But I couldn't dig very deep within the limits of this kind of essay, and Tizard's was one of those characters which got more complex, more intricate in structure, the further one got into it. That was why, on page 106, I mentioned that he might draw the attention of the mature novelist. The contrast between the controlled and disciplined behaviour of the high scientist-administrator and the inner nature which he had to control and discipline would be a fascinating job. But Tizard, it now seems to me, paid a price for this self-discipline, heavier than most of us realise. I suspect that, quite apart from the inner strains, he sometimes paid a price in action.

He had adapted himself to play the game according to the rules, the rules of the English governing and administrative classes. Like a good many deep and turbulent natures who adapt themselves so, he did it a shade too thoroughly. For most of his official life, this did not affect him; but when, as in the strategic bombing controversy, he found himself in a situation not played according to the rules, he was at a loss.

The result was, he surrendered a little easily. A less disciplined character might have made more of a row, kicked over the apple-cart, risked a public scandal – there were ways of doing this, difficult and painful but still possible, even in wartime. The younger scientists could not have done it with effect, but Tizard might.

For him, however, it was psychologically inconceivable. He had made a refuge for himself – and to an extent from himself. The refuge was precious to him. It was the good opinion, the company, fellowship, and support of the scientists of the Royal Society, the serving officers, the administrators, the Athenaeum. In the long run, he couldn't break away. Any action that they would condemn, even though they sympathised with him, he couldn't manage. Anything they couldn't do, he couldn't do either.

V

Lindemann

I am going to begin with my one modest grumble. Quite a number of critics – most of them not familiar with these events and not committed to either side in any of these controversies – have scolded me, good-temperedly and charitably, for setting the issue in terms too black and white. They conclude – and in many cases this has been intended as an excuse for me – that the imagination of a novelist had been too strong. I had succumbed to the hypnosis of my own technique, they said with good nature: I had written this anecdote as though it had occurred in one of my own novels. This has been said by people who know and understand my novels very well.[11]

When they said it, though, they must have forgotten what my novels are really like. Take this situation. A is a man almost universally popular with his professional colleagues; B is, on the contrary, very widely distrusted and disliked. They are put in the middle of major decisions. A turns out to be almost invariably right; B is, on the contrary, singularly and often perversely wrong. I ask mildly: does that sound like a situation from any piece of fiction that I have written or am ever likely to write? In fiction, of course, I should have played every kind of finesse. By the time I had finished you wouldn't have known which was liked and which was disliked: you certainly wouldn't have known which was right and which was wrong.

Lord Birkenhead[12] complains that I have gone in for melodrama. Well. Have another look at A and B. Once they were bosom friends. They were associated in great hazards in the 1914–18 war. Afterwards they advanced each other's careers, were allies at the university, were linked by family life. Suddenly, without A's knowing it, B's feeling changes. He begins to talk of A as 'that wretched little man'. They are brought together as members of a committee, in a task on which the safety of the country may depend. B abuses A, in front of the committee, in terms of uncontrolled violence. Other members force B off the committee. A has a period of great influence. Again a twist of fortune: B is given the authority. The time is the summer of 1940, the country is in danger, A sends a message through a common friend: can't they patch up the quarrel and work together? B returns the answer: 'Now that I am in a position of power, a lot of my old friends have come sniffing round.'

Melodrama? Certainly. But whose melodrama? The story comes direct from Lord Birkenhead's official biography.

I could never have invented anything like that. But life is sometimes more grotesque than art. It is not sensible to talk about a novelist's temptations, when those are temptations no decent novelist would ever feel, much less succumb to.

That is my only personal grumble. Having uttered it, I have no other complaints to make. Let us try to get back to the plane of reason. We ought to remember from the start that, except for the authors of *The Strategic Air Offensive*, none of the persons who have taken part in these discussions are, in any sense, trained historians. So far as I know, only one eminent professional historian has inspected the most recent evidence, Professor J. H. Plumb. He has pointed out[13] the inadequacies in method in Lord Birkenhead's handling of his material, and the questions a professional historian would ask. I am sure that similar criticisms apply to me. No doubt the historians will come along in time. Meanwhile, the best we can do is to go ahead in our own amateur fashion, and see if we cannot get a bit nearer to the truth.

Lindemann's personality is likely to puzzle historians, when they look into these events. We now know a good deal about his *behaviour*, not only in his official, but in his private life. For instance, he quarrelled with his sister because she married a man he disapproved of, and didn't speak to her for forty years.[14] He cut his younger brother just as completely out of his life.[15] After boyhood, he was on bad terms with his mother.[16] In all these intimate relations, he showed a life pattern which might have come out of a psychiatrist's case book. I am very chary of shorthand explanations, but I do not think it is fanciful to pick out the same life pattern in his behaviour to Tizard.

Yet, though there was so much in his behaviour that no one in his senses could defend, those who liked him best insist – and this I respect – that there was a kind of essential Lindemann, different in kind from much that he did or said. As I wrote on page 104 of 'Science and Government', he was a heavyweight of personality. He proved himself vindictive in action, outside the ordinary human run. At the same time, he inspired passionately protective feelings in many,[17] as though he were a man longing for happiness, not knowing what was wrong with him, crying inarticulately for help. He struck his friends with the pathos of an intensely passionate man, lacking in self-knowledge, constantly struggling with a major repression or conflict which he could neither dislodge nor resolve.

Detached observers, reading these various accounts of him, will form their own judgment, according to their interpretations of personality and their human values. In his summing up, Lord Birkenhead[18] speaks of 'the fundamental simplicity of his nature'. Paradoxically, to me that sounds right. His behaviour was bizarre, but the structure of his nature, unlike Tizard's, may not have been complicated at all.

My essential concern, in telling this parable or anecdote, was to draw a practical lesson. From that point of view, it doesn't matter that people will form different opinions of what Lindemann was really like. Of course, it is fascinating to speculate about his character if one in interested in the human variety. It is fascinating, but it is not the point.

I should be happy if anyone who wanted to follow my practical argument read the two biographical studies of Lindemann,[19] made his own picture of the man, and read it into my story. For myself, I can accept much of the psychological portraiture of both these books. (Harrod in particular had a depth of insight any novelist would be proud of.) It is not Lindemann's character which is vital to this story.

In the same way, we need not spend much time on his accomplishments as a pure scientist. These are, in any case, less mysterious than human character, and more susceptible to objective evaluation. Scientists are judged, not by what their friends say about them, nor their enemies either, but by what they have done. Lindemann's publications are in print in the scientific journals. Anyone who wants to do so can inspect them, and any physicist can form an opinion of how important his achievement was. The language of science is international. The opinions formed by, say, Japanese or Swedish physicists would be near enough the same. I will return in a moment to what they would be likely to be.

Meanwhile I should like to mention two contributions of Lindemann's which no one has ever disputed or would wish to dispute. Neither of them was in the narrow sense scientific, but the second had big scientific consequences, I did not mention these contributions in the Godkin Lectures, except for one passing reference, on page 116. I have since regretted this. Neither was strictly relevant to my narrative, but leaving them out made the account more grudging in spirit than it should have been.

The first was Lindemann's recognition of the danger of Hitler right from 1933. This recognition was, of course, common enough in radical intellectual circles; but it was fairly rare among Tories, and to have it proclaimed, with a characteristic intensity, by Lindemann, a man far out on the right, did great good.

The second contribution followed from the first. Lindemann, believing that Hitler meant what he said about the Jews, went round Germany rescuing some of the best Jewish scientists. It didn't matter that Lindemann himself professed a rather silly anti-Semitism.[20] He brought some of the best scientific minds in Europe – Francis Simon, Kurti, the Londons, Mendelssohn, Kuhn – to Oxford. Lindemann had already done something by 1933 to improve the reputation of the Clarendon Laboratory, but it was still pretty low. The introduction of Simon and his colleagues meant that within twenty years the Clarendon was a laboratory among the top three or four in England, and perhaps in some respects the best. This must be put to Lindemann's permanent credit.

Others have made great physics laboratories. In almost every case they have been men who themselves were scientists in the full radiance of their own creative work. This was true of Rutherford at the Cavendish, Born and Franck at Göttingen, Bohr at Copenhagen, Ernest Lawrence at Berkeley. I can think of only two exceptions. Between 1922 and 1938 Rome suddenly became one of the great physical centres of the world, and produced masters like Fermi, Segré, Rasetti, Amaldi. But we have been told that the origin of this efflorescence was none of them, but a father-figure called Corbino, senator, banker, impresario, man of affairs, who had, in the intervals of making a fortune, presided over the laboratory, found the money, collected the talent. He brought together a great laboratory until Fascism destroyed it. Lindemann's achievement with the Clarendon was not dissimilar in kind.

As for his own original achievement in pure science, that – if it were not for the fact that he was, by common consent, both an exceptionally clever man and a controversial figure – does not leave room for genuine disagreement. Studying his publications, out of range of the aura of his personality, our putative Swedish and Japanese referees would report that:

(a) Between 1910 and 1914 he produced nearly twenty papers. There are signs of overmuch diversion of effort, but some of these papers are original and deep.

(b) After 1919 he produced a number of notes and letters on many subjects, but little substantial work; although he was working at a period when physics, both theoretical and experimental, was wide open to discovery as it may not be again for generations, he did not find a profitable field. None of this would surprise the referees very much. There are many physicists and mathematicians who make a good start and then find their creative impulse dry up very early. Some of them undergo bitter personal suffering on this account.

But Lindemann's *œuvre* as a pure scientist does not bear much on the problems of his public career, any more than his personality does. If he had had the personality of a Schweitzer and the scientific *œuvre* of a Rutherford or a Bohr, the problems would still remain. The discussion, at its core, is not concerned either with personality or with creative work. It is concerned with scientific judgment.

VI

It was in the struggles with Tizard that Lindemann's scientific judgment was called most violently into question – though there were similar controversies where Tizard was not concerned, which, as the histories are written, we shall hear more about in the next ten years. One or two of these I shall mention in passing. For the present, it is enough to see what more we can learn about the struggles with Tizard.

The Personal Story

There is not much to add; and what there is (compare the last paragraph of Section v) does not really affect the central problem. Possibly no one will ever know when and why the personal antagonism blew up. It does not seem quite so surprising, now that we have learned of Lindemann's unilateral breaches inside his family. It certainly seemed surprising to Tizard, however. There have been attempts to represent it as a straight struggle for power: but that is an oversimplification. On Lindemann's side the hatred went on till death. There was nothing like the same emotional involvement on the part of Tizard. To say he felt specially benevolent to Lindemann would be sentimental, but, in his last years, he spoke of Lindemann and the whole story with a kind of sardonic and lively detachment. He went out of his way to reiterate[21] that Lindemann was one of the cleverest men he had ever met.

The Tizard Committee and Radar

A lot of people have become baffled and lost by what has seemed a conflict of evidence. Sir Robert Watson Watt[22] has gone on record that Lindemann encouraged his radar work and gave him active support in 1936, during the period when Lindemann was sitting on the Tizard Committee. Professor R. V. Jones says[23] that he remembers discussing with him in 1935 the possibilities of radar. Both these are men of complete integrity.

On the other hand, there were five people who were witnesses of all that happened on the Tizard Committee throughout its life – Tizard himself, Wimperis, Blackett, Hill, and Rowe. Of these five, Tizard and Wimperis are dead. Before he died, Tizard gave an account of Lindemann's behaviour on the Committee which was essentially identical with mine. Tizard gave this account, not in ordinary conversation, though he did that too, but in reply to questions by an official historian.[24] Wimperis in conversation gave the same account. So did Blackett in print, a year before my lecture was delivered, and again in confirmation of what I had said.[25] Rowe, who was secretary of the Committee throughout, has publicly confirmed my account.[26] Hill did so privately while it was in manuscript,[27] and had himself, though this has generally not been realised, published the only first-hand description of the proceedings actually written at the time.[28]

The integrity of all these men, just as with Watson Watt and Jones, is complete.

It might seem that the collision is head-on. Who is wrong? Whose memory is defective? Where is the contradiction?

The answer is undramatic and something of an anticlimax. No one is wrong. No one's memory is defective. There is no contradiction.

The confusion has arisen very largely because most people are not familiar with the nature of scientific–military arguments. The technical dispute on the Tizard Committee, like eight out of ten scientific–military arguments, was about priorities. Priorities mean what they say. They are arrangements in order of importance. Given infinite resources, in scientific war, one would often like to try almost everything – as the Americans did in making the fission bomb. But usually that is not possible, even in America. One has to establish priorities, to see that the best chance is not missed, even if it means sacrificing lesser chances.

Stripped of its violent personal emotion, the issue before the Committee was a judgment of priorities. The technical disagreement was about that, and nothing else. It is now almost certain that before the Committee ever met Tizard had decided that radar had to be given something like absolute priority. Sir Philip Joubert[29] remembers him late in 1934 dismissing the possibilities of air defence one after the other – 'Infra-red. No *real* good', and so on, then telling the officers that he was pretty sure they had got the answer: and, even as early as that, beginning to talk in terms of military use. He never budged from this position. He wanted as near absolute priority for radar as he could get, not only in technical development but, at least as imperatively, in terms of indoctrinating the services. It is very rare, of course, to be able to get any absolute priority in the literal sense for any scientific–military scheme. Tizard and the Committee were prepared to expend a little effort on (that is, give a low but finite priority to) other schemes such as infra-red detection, though it seemed highly improbable it could be any use in time for a war in 1939 or 1940. But they were not ready to make many compromises about priority, and in fact never did so.

As soon as Lindemann took his place on the Committee, he wanted to alter Tizard's order of priorities. He was actively interested in Watson Watt's work, but he was not prepared to give radar the near-absolute priority that the Committee had already settled on. The Committee's preoccupation – its all-important preoccupation – with the operational use of radar meant nothing to him. He had his own order of priorities. This order appears to have varied from time to time. He had a number of his own specifics – wire-carrying shells, aerial mines carried by parachutes, bombs carried by wires, as well as infra-red detection – which he was determined to press on to the Committee. His favourite devices seem to have been bombs dangled by wires in front of enemy aircraft and the parachute-carried aerial mines. Sometimes he argued that the parachute mine deserved higher priority than radar. At no time was he prepared to accept it as being less than equally important or as carrying less than equal priority.

Lindemann's general idea of appropriate priorities – about which the evidence of all present is unanimous – we can, fortunately, confirm by the aid of two documents written at the time. We shall only know the precise details when the minutes of the Committee are made public. It seems a pity that these minutes, which were kept by Rowe, are not already available. They would say the last word on an interesting piece of scientific–military history. However, we have two documents written in 1936. The first was composed in verse by A. V. Hill, shortly before the Committee was coming to its final arguments. It is published in his book *The Ethical Dilemma of Science*, 1959, with the following prefatory note:

The following poem, in the style of the Earl of Derby's translation of the Iliad (1864), purports to represent the Minutes of a meeting of a Committee of the Air Ministry in 1936, together with a summons to the next one. These meetings were *secret*, and even today, twenty-three years later, considerations of propriety, if not of security, require that pseudonyms should be used: this may explain how a Norse deity and a Geheimrat somehow got mixed up with a lot of Greek characters on a Trojan Committee.*

> Attending there on ancient Sigma sat
> The Elders of the City: Omega
> And Theta and von Alpha-plus and Phi.
> All these were gathered at Adastral House,
> By age exempt from war, but in discourse
> Abundant as the cricket that on high
> From topmost bough of forest tree sends forth
> His music: so they sent their Minutes forth,
> And all men wondered, even Odin wept
> With tears of joy that Ilium was safe.
>
> Von Alpha-plus arose and thus began,
> 'O ancient Sigma eminent in war
> And in the council wise: thy present words
> No Trojan can gainsay, and yet the end
> Thou hast not reached, the object of debate.

* Characters in the poem in order of appearance:

Sigma	Tizard
Omega	Wimperis
Theta	Blackett
von Alpha-plus	Lindemann
Phi	A. V. Hill
Odin	Sir Winston Churchill
Lambda-Mu	Roxbee Cox ⎫ who attended some meetings of the
Hermes	Joubert ⎭ Committee
Rho	A. P. Rowe
Hopskipjump	Lord Caldecote (at this time Sir Thomas Inskip)

This city cannot be immune from war
Until a hail of parachuting mines
Descend unceasing at its eastern gate.
So shall the long-haired Greeks remain at home
Nor lay their infernal eggs upon our streets.'

Thus angrily, and round his body flung
His cloak, and on his head a billycock,
Then passing cocked a snook at Lambda-Mu,
Last called his shiny Rolls of eighty steeds
And soon without the tent of Odin stood.
Him, from his godlike sleep, he sought to rouse
Loud shouting: soon his voice his senses reached:
Forth in his slumber-suit bearlike he came
And spoke to deep designing Alpha-plus,
    'What cause so urgent leads you through the camp,
    In the dark night to wander thus alone?'

To whom von Alpha-plus of deep design replied,
'O Odin, godlike son of destiny, awake:
For ancient Sigma's professorial crew,
With Hermes of the glancing wings and Rho
Who keeps the minutes but who wastes the hours,
Will not be happy till the long-haired Greeks
Upon this city lay their infernal eggs.
They have no mind to fill the sky with mines
Attached to parachutes: and precious days they waste
In vain experiment with R.D.F.
If, godlike son of destiny, we two
In place of Hopskipjump and Sigma were
Thy sky would rain with parachuting mines
Unceasing, and the land be safe.' So spake
Von Alpha-plus of deep and bold design.
Him answering, Odin, son of destiny, replied,
'Many indeed, and fierce, the bombs I've dropped,
But never 2-oz. mines attached by wires
To parachutes, by day and night alike,
In billions at our eastern gate. The like
Has never been before. We two will take
The tidings to the Minister of State.

With Odin Lord Almighty of land and sky and sea
And Alpha-plus to help him, how happy all will be!'

So ancient Sigma and his stag-eyed crew,
Theta with bright ideas, Phi with none,
Rho with the Minutes, weary Omega,
Sat long and silent in the deepening gloom,
While Lambda-Mu went out and hanged himself,
Snook-cocked by Alpha-plus of deep design.
At last with downcast visage Sigma spoke:
'The game is up. Without von Alpha-plus,
Of wily counsel and of deep design,
Who speaks with politicians and the Press,
And soon may be M.P. for Oxenbridge,
All hope is gone and many-murdering Death
Will hunt his victims in our streets.' To which
Theta of bright ideas, Phi of none,
Rho of the Minutes, weary Omega,
Had nothing printable to add. But set
A day to meet Geheimrat Alpha-plus
And pray for mercy from his mighty friends,
From Odin, godlike son of destiny,
And from himself, the man of deep design.
Then ancient Sigma and his stag-eyed crew
Will make submission to von Alpha-plus
(Except for Lambda-Mu who hanged himself).
Your presence is requested at 11:
The number of the room is 008.

The second document – and this is the most satisfactory kind of evidence – was written by Lindemann himself. In a letter to Churchill dated 27 February 1936 he said:

The only part of the Committee's work which has so far been successful has been the development of methods of detection and location. The reason for this seems to be that it has been put in the hands of a man who suggested the method and believed in it and that he could and did push ahead with whatever experiment he thought necessary.

I suggest however that the only way of making progress with the equally important development of aerial mines and the related question of shell-burst which remain effective for some reasonable period, is to put them in the hands of some enthusiastic believer who is not compelled to come back to the Committee every time he wants to make a fresh experiment.

It was the 'equally important development of aerial mines' with which he had worn the Committee down. Anyone who could suggest giving this device equal priority with radar seemed to them so lacking in scientific judgment as to be a danger. Scientists are used to harsh argument, but they were not prepared to argue indefinitely about aerial mines and wire-carried bombs. These ideas made no technical sense. Time was being wasted, and wasted in an atmosphere of extreme hostility. The only sane course was to get back to the highest priority for radar and for the operational use of radar.

There has been some speculation as to what – on the level of reason and purpose – Lindemann was really after. One view, which Rowe is inclined to hold,[30] is that he was determined to wreck the Committee at any cost, using any scientific idea regardless of its merit, so that in the long run he could get the power himself. This, of course, would be irresponsible behaviour by any standards, since this Committee was the only body in the country working out a scientific defence, and war was very near.

The second view is simply that in advancing these fantasy projects, in haranguing the Committee about them, he really believed what he said. This is entirely consistent with some of his behaviour later in his career. It is also consistent with the fact that, after he had had been forced off the Committee, he was still pressing the wire-carrying shell and the aerial-mine parachute on to various Government departments.[31]

If I were writing my account of the Tizard Committee again, I should include some of what I have just said, but otherwise alter nothing. I should underline the question of priorities, though in fact in my original account I chose my words with care (see page 118 of 'Science and Government' where the issue of priorities is precisely stated). I should include the two documents I have just quoted. They make the whole dispute clear.

There is one omission I should now make. I should leave out the last three paragraphs of Section VI, pages 119–20. I should not have permitted myself to go in for such a speculation. I should now finish the story of the Tizard Committee by saying something plain and prosaic. It is clear that any body, setting up a scientific air defence in Great Britain in 1935, had to do three things: (1) it had to give high priority to radar; (2) it had to make an act of faith, and persuade the serving officers of the use of radar before the apparatus was so much as in existence: it had to go on concentrating on the operational use of radar; (3) it had to let university physicists into the secret, so as to get them thinking about centimetric radar. No other policy would have given us much chance of surviving. Fortunately for us, this was the policy of Tizard and his Committee.

Strategic Bombing

Over the 1942 controversy on the effects of strategic bombing, the facts are more eloquent than any lucubrations about them. These facts, which are now known in detail, are almost exactly as I stated them. Lindemann's scientific judgment was wrong. He overestimated the effects of bombing by at least ten times. Tizard's judgment was much more nearly accurate. Blackett's was better still. The only documents of importance which remain to be examined are Blackett's memoranda, still hidden in the Admiralty files. Since Blackett, partly for interdepartmental reasons, took the argument considerably further than Tizard did, his papers are needed to complete the story. We have, however, his published recollections of these events.

The facts are so eloquent that, if I had had the Lindemann and Tizard papers before me, I should just have printed them without comment. Let me quote the official history (the footnotes are part of the quotation):

It was at this moment of the crisis of strategic bombing that Lord Cherwell intervened. On 30th March 1942, he addressed a minute to the Prime Minister in which he said:

'The following seems a simple method of estimating what we could do by bombing Germany:

'Careful analysis of the effects of raids on Birmingham, Hull and elsewhere have shown that, on the average, 1 ton of bombs dropped on a built-up area demolishes 20–40 dwellings and turns 100–200 people out of house and home.

'We know from our experience that we can count on nearly 14 operational sorties per bomber produced. The average lift of the bombers we are going to produce over the next 15 months will be about 3 tons. It follows that each of these bombers will in its life-time drop about 40 tons of bombs. If these are dropped on built-up areas they will make 4,000–8,000 people homeless.

'In 1938 over 22 million Germans lived in 58 towns of over 100,000 inhabitants, which, with modern equipment should be easy to find and hit. Our forecast output of heavy bombers (including Wellingtons) between now and the middle of 1943 is about 10,000. If even half the total load of 10,000 bombers were dropped on the built-up areas of these 58 German towns the great majority of their inhabitants (about one-third of the German population) would be turned out of house and home.

'Investigation seems to show that having one's house demolished is most damaging to morale. People seem to mind it more than having their friends or even relatives killed. At Hull signs of strain were evident, though only one-tenth of the houses were demolished. On the above figures we should be able to do ten times as much harm to each of the 58 principal German towns. There seems little doubt that this would break the spirit of the people.

'Our calculation assumes, of course, that we really get one-half of our bombs into built-up areas. On the other hand, no account is taken of the large promised American production (6,000 heavy bombers in the period in question). Nor has regard been paid to the inevitable damage to factories, communications etc. in these towns and the damage by fire, probably accentuated by breakdown of public services.'*

. . . The Cherwell minute, therefore, involved certain matters of high policy such as the production programme for heavy bombers and the concentration of the bombing offensive upon certain strategic objectives. It also involved calculations of probability such as the average life of an operational bomber in 1942 and 1943 and the effect of a certain weight of bombs upon a given number of German towns. Clearly the results which Lord Cherwell foresaw in consequence of his probability calculations would not be achieved unless policy decisions were taken in the sense which his minute suggested as necessary. On the other hand, these policy decisions could not be justified by the probability calculations themselves

* Min. Cherwell to Churchill, 30 March 1942. Circulated by the Prime Minister to Defence Committee on 9 April 1942. The whole text of the minute is transcribed above.

because the calculations seemed probable only to those who, in any case, believed in the policy. To those who did not, they seemed to be wholly improbable and, in this connection, one scientist could easily be answered, or at least questioned, by another. Sir Henry Tizard, for example, observed that 'the risk entailed by this policy is so great that it is necessary to be convinced not merely that it has a chance of success but that the probability of success is very great'.*

To Sir Henry Tizard it seemed that Lord Cherwell's calculations contained certain important fallacies. He pointed out that the Ministry of Aircraft Production programme provided for the construction of 3,585 Wellingtons and 5,219 heavy bombers between the beginning of April 1942 and the end of June 1943. 689 of the Wellingtons were earmarked for Coastal Command. Thus, the bomber programme provided for 8,115 aircraft. Experience had taught Sir Henry Tizard 'that we cannot rely on more than 85% of the target programme' and he therefore estimated that Bomber Command would receive 7,000 and not 10,000 aircraft in the period reviewed by Lord Cherwell.

Even if this difficulty could be overcome, Sir Henry Tizard immediately saw another in the assumption that each of these aircraft would on the average complete fourteen operational sorties. This would mean that they would all be destroyed and that 'we should be left at the end of the period with a front line strength no greater than it is at present, which is surely quite unthinkable'. The two difficulties led Sir Henry Tizard to the conclusion that Bomber Command would be able to drop on Germany only half the tonnage which had been estimated by Lord Cherwell.

The next point which struck Sir Henry Tizard as 'much too optimistic' was the assumption that the '58 towns of over 100,000 inhabitants' would be easy to find and hit. He thought that Lord Cherwell had underestimated the difficulties which would confront the bomber crews operating at night in the face of heavy opposition. *Gee*, he pointed out, had a limited range and would have a limited life. New radar aids were not expected by Sir Henry Tizard to come into service until April 1943.† He therefore, thought it unsafe to assume that more than twenty-five per cent of the bombs lifted would find their targets. Thus, he calculated that in the period reviewed by Lord Cherwell and on the assumption that all heavy bombers were concentrated exclusively on the task,‡ not more than

* Memo. by Tizard, 20 April 1942.
† In which expectation he was not far wrong.
‡ Which concentration, Sir Henry Tizard thought, would be neither wise nor possible.

50,000 tons of bombs would fall on the built-up areas. If this was spread over the fifty-eight towns the effect might, on the average, be three or four times as great as that produced by the Germans in Hull and Birmingham. This, Sir Henry Tizard thought, 'would certainly be most damaging but would not', he said, 'be decisive unless in the intervening period Germany was either defeated in the field by Russia, or at least prevented from any substantial further advance, e.g. to the Russian or Iranian Oilfields'.

Thus, although Sir Henry Tizard had by no means fully realised the extraordinary resilience and determination with which the Germans were to meet both the bombing of their towns and the defeat of their armies in Russia, he had sounded a note of warning against the assumptions upon which the Cherwell minute was based and so against the policy into which Bomber Command was drifting. The concluding paragraph of his memorandum is worth quoting in full:

'I conclude therefore,' he wrote:
'(a) That a policy of bombing German towns wholesale in order to destroy dwellings cannot have a decisive effect by the middle of 1943, even if all heavy bombers and the great majority of Wellingtons produced are used primarily for this purpose.
'(b) That such a policy can only have a decisive effect if carried out on a much bigger scale than is envisaged in [the Cherwell minute].'*

. . . Nevertheless, as the Prime Minister also remarked, 'there must be a design and theme for bringing the war to a victorious end in a reasonable period. All the more is this necessary when under modern conditions no large-scale offensive operation can be launched without the preparation of elaborate technical apparatus.' Lord Cherwell's minute, despite its largely and inevitably fallacious 'forecasts',† had done no more and no less than to acknowledge a 'design and theme' for the air offensive, and Lord Cherwell exerted a much greater influence upon the Prime Minister than did Sir Henry Tizard.

The Air Staff, as has been shown, had already devised this theme

* Memo. by Tizard, 20 April 1942. Sir Henry Tizard sent his note to Sir Archibald Sinclair and Lord Cherwell.

† There were, of course, many fallacies, some less inevitable than others, besides those remarked upon by Sir Henry Tizard. For example, Lord Cherwell had assumed that if one ton of bombs dropped on a built-up area made between a hundred and two hundred people homeless, then forty tons would make four thousand to eight thousand people homeless. This, however, did not necessarily follow.

towards the end of 1941 and Lord Cherwell had added little that was new. All the same, because of the position which he occupied and the time at which he submitted his minute, Lord Cherwell's intervention was of great importance. It did much to insure the concept of strategic bombing in its hour of crisis.[32]

To which marmoreal account I should have wished to add only one comment. The use of the word 'inevitably' seems semantically a little odd. Of course, as I have said before, all scientific judgments are informed guesses. But some informed guesses turn out nearer the truth than others.

The argument about scientific judgment is clear enough. But there was also, closely connected with it, an argument about strategic judgment. Certainly Blackett, and, I think, Tizard (though in his case I have to rely on my memories of conversations at the time, which is not good evidence), had major strategic objections to the bombing policy as a whole. They also, and this is incontrovertibly well documented, had a precise strategic objection to the bombing policy of 1942–3. They, like the Naval Staff, believed that long-range aircraft should be used for anti-submarine purposes, largely, though not entirely, in the Battle of the Atlantic. If this battle was lost, the war was lost. On the other hand, a victory over the submarines in 1942 would transform the shape of the war. To Tizard and Blackett such a victory seemed technically possible, for a relatively small investment of bombers and of radar apparatus which – according to the Air Staff–Lindemann bombing doctrine – should be hoarded for mass bombing. The official history of the naval war says:

The basic issue which had to be settled by the Cabinet was, therefore, whether, taking account of the prevailing shortage of aircraft, a balance could be struck between the accepted Allied policy of bombing Germany and Italy as heavily as possible and the urgent need to improve the protection of our convoys. One fundamental requirement was to estimate just how effective the bombing of Germany had already been, and also how effective it was likely to become. Lord Cherwell forecast that in 1943 bombing of built-up districts would deprive about one-third of the population of Germany of their homes, and that this might be decisive . . .

In the early summer the Admiralty's anxiety deepened. U-boat sinkings remained very high, in the Mediterranean 'the situation was pre-carious', the Far East 'was in a state of disintegration', and our ability to hold the Indian Ocean 'was in balance'. 'Ships alone', they said, were 'unable to maintain command at sea . . . a permanent and increased share in the control of sea communications had to be borne by [the] air forces.' The requirements were once again analysed, and a deficiency of 800 air-craft was arrived at. But the Air Ministry still felt that 'to dissipate the Royal Air Force's strength' in order to reinforce Coastal Command would be a strategic error. They held that, as the bombing of Germany gained momentum, the threat to our sea communications was bound to diminish. By reducing the weight of our bombing we might merely postpone the day when the rising curve of Allied merchant ship construction would overtake our losses. To this argument the Admiralty's reply was that, quite apart from the great value of the ships lost, every one of their cargoes was of immense importance to the nation's war effort; that there was a real danger of our war production and transport slowing down, or even coming to a stop, through failure to bring in the essential imports of food and raw materials; that losses on the present scale could not continue without the morale of the Merchant Navy suffering; and finally that unless stronger air escorts were provided the enemy's rising U-boat strength would over-whelm the defenders of our convoys.[33]

Blackett takes up the story at this point:

From my talks with Lindemann at this time [the summer of 1942] I became aware of that trait of character which Snow so well emphasizes: this was his almost fanatical belief in some particular operation or gadget to the almost total exclusion of wider considerations. Bombing to him then seemed the one and only useful operation of the war. He said to me (unfortunately I have no record of this conversation, but he probably said the same to others) that he considered any diversion of aircraft production and supply to the antisubmarine campaign, to army co-operation or even to fighter defence – in fact, to anything but bombing – as being a disastrous mistake. Lindemann even suggested that the building up of strong land forces for the projected invasion of France was wrong. Never have I encountered such fanatical belief in the efficacy of bombing.

The high priority given thereafter to everything pertaining to the bombing offensive made it very difficult to get adequate air support for the vital Battle of the Atlantic. If this had got worse there would have been no more bombing offensive for lack of fuel and bombs, and no invasion of France in 1944. I remember that during the winter of 1942 and 1943 the

Admiralty had to enlist President Roosevelt's personal influence to ensure that a squadron of that admirable antisubmarine aircraft, the B-24, was allocated to Coastal Command (where they were brilliantly successful) and not, as the Air Staff wanted, sent to bomb Berlin, for which they were not very suitable. However, at the Casablanca Conference in January, 1943, a combined American and British bombing offensive was formally adopted as a major part of the British war strategy.

No part of the war effort has been so well documented as this campaign, which had as its official objective 'the destruction and dislocation of the German military, industrial and economic system and the undermining of the morale of the German people to the point where their capacity for armed resistance is fatally weakened'. Immediately after the war the U. S. Strategic Bombing Survey was sent to Germany to find out what had been achieved. A very strong team (which included two men who are now advisers to President Kennedy, J. K. Galbraith and Paul Nitze) produced a brilliant report, which was published in September, 1945. Without any doubt the area-bombing offensive was an expensive failure. About 500,000 German men, women and children were killed, but in the whole bombing offensive 160,000 U. S. and British airmen, the best young men of both countries, were lost. German war production went on rising steadily until it reached its peak in August, 1944. At this time the Allies were already in Paris and the Russian armies were well into Poland. German civilian morale did not crack.

Perhaps it is not surprising that the report of the Strategic Bombing Survey seems to have had a rather small circulation; it is to be found in few libraries and does not appear to have been directly available, even to some historians of the war.

If the Allied air effort had been used more intelligently, if more aircraft had been supplied for the Battle of the Atlantic and to support the land fighting in Africa and later in France, if the bombing of Germany had been carried out with the attrition of the enemy defences in mind rather than the razing of cities to the ground, I believe the war could have been won half a year or even a year earlier. The only major campaign in modern history in which the traditional military doctrine of waging war against the enemy's armed forces was abandoned for a planned attack on its civilian life was a disastrous flop. I confess to a haunting sense of personal failure, and I am sure that Tizard felt the same way. If we had only been more persuasive and had forced people to believe our simple arithmetic, if we had fought officialdom more cleverly and lobbied ministers more vigorously, might we not have changed this decision?[34]

I have nothing to add, except the sombre words of the naval historian:

For what it is worth this writer's view is that in the early spring of 1943 we had a very narrow escape from defeat in the Atlantic; and that, had we suffered such a defeat, history would have judged that the main cause had been the lack of two more squadrons of very long range aircraft for convoy escort duties.[35]

Window

There was a third and final wartime argument between Lindemann and Tizard. I did not know enough about it to mention it in my original lectures. The subject was not of the order of importance of the other two. The official history of the bombing offensive, however, deals with the controversy in terms severely critical of Lindemann.

The full story (which the official history does not give) shows Lindemann deserving of credit at an early stage, although at the decisive time his scientific judgment of military operations was once more at fault.

As early as 1937, it had been suggested that defensive radar systems could be interfered with by the very simple device of dropping from aircraft strips of paper coated with metal. Lindemann had received this idea from R. V. Jones[36] and in 1942 gave another of his friends, Derek Jackson, the power to make operational tests.[37] So that he was responsible for the inception of a really valuable device. It is at this point that the official history introduces the topic.

Experiments had shown that the dropping of metallised strips of paper in quantity produced a reaction on radar screens operating on certain frequencies and prevented accurate measurements being made on them. These metallised strips, which subsequently came to be known as *Window*, had the great advantage of being cheap, easy and quick to produce, and it seemed that their immediate introduction would confer upon Bomber Command an important advantage in the air battle which was now joined. For these reasons the Air Staff suggested in April 1942 that the use of *Window* should be authorised at once and the Chiefs of Staff had little difficulty in agreeing to the request. . . .

It was at this stage, however, that Lord Cherwell intervened with the pertinent suggestion that *Window* might also disrupt night-fighter radar interception and after a meeting which he held with Sir Archibald Sinclair and Sir Arthur Harris early in May 1942, it was decided to defer the introduction of *Window* until these possibilities had been investigated.

Thus, at a time when the Bomber Command offensive was rapidly gaining momentum in the face of heavy and increasing casualties and at a time when the German air offensive was diminishing to negligible proportions, a cardinal weapon, favouring the bombers and hindering the defences, was cast aside for more than another whole year. It was not until the night of 24th July 1943 that Bomber Command was able to use *Window* for the first time and the sensational success which it then achieved in the famous Battle of Hamburg is, indeed, a grave verdict on the many decisions to defer its earlier introduction.[38]

And the story is continued in the second volume of the official history:

Thus, one of the principal reasons for withholding *Window*, namely the danger of revealing it to the enemy, was seriously undermined from the outset and seemed to have been completely destroyed by the end of October 1942 when an Air Scientific Intelligence report indicated that it was 'certain' that the Germans fully understood the *Window* principle.

This consideration of the secret being out seemed, in the view of Sir Henry Tizard, to complete the argument for the immediate introduction of *Window*, but there were others who persevered with a different view. . . . This attitude and the absence of Sir Henry Tizard at a meeting at the Air Ministry on November 4, 1942 left the floor to those who were preoccupied with the dangers and not the advantages of *Window*, the introduction of which was consequently again postponed.

By the end of March 1943 when the Battle of the Ruhr had begun, the case against *Window* was, however, palpably crumbling. The obvious fact that the German bomber force was an almost negligible factor and that the German fighter force was one of increasingly decisive importance was at last beginning to exert some influence upon the discussions. Indeed, it now appeared that of the losses inflicted by enemy action upon Bomber Command no less than seventy per cent were due to German night fighters. About half these losses to night fighters were, it was estimated, attributable to radar-controlled fighters which might be substantially put out of action by *Window*. Of the remaining thirty per cent of the casualties which were attributed to flak, it was thought that two-thirds were due to radar-controlled guns which similarly might be dislocated by *Window*. Thus, it seemed probable to the Air Staff that the introduction of *Window* would save from destruction no less than thirty-five per cent of the aircraft which were then being shot down by enemy action. This would amount to 1.7 per cent of the total Bomber Command sorties being despatched.

There were, of course, astonishing defects in this optimistic argument, which, for example, assumed that the dislocation of radar would result in the G.C.I.s and A.I.-equipped night fighters and the radar-controlled anti-aircraft guns achieving absolutely no results at all. Nevertheless, the argument for introducing *Window* did seem to be overwhelming especially in view of the great weakness of the bomber force remaining to Germany with which to retaliate. . . .

Even this was not the end of an already sad story. The Chiefs of Staff now decided that *Window* should be further delayed until after the projected invasion of Sicily had been carried out. By the middle of June 1943, however, even Lord Cherwell was beginning to recognise 'on the whole that the time is rapidly approaching when we should allow it (*Window*) to be used'. Even so, he advised the Prime Minister that the introduction of *Window* should not be allowed to endanger allied plans in the Mediterranean. Meanwhile, in the strategic air offensive, British bomber losses between 1st April and 14th July 1943 amounted to 858 aircraft. German bomber losses in the same period were, it seemed, twenty-seven aircraft. It appeared to Sir Charles Portal that if *Window* had been used in these months, Bomber Command might have saved 230 bombers and crews and the Germans might have saved sixteen.[39]

VII

In the war Lindemann had, so Lord Birkenhead says, 'power greater than that exercised by any scientist in history'.[40] That is dead true. It is precisely for that reason that his record of judgment has to be examined, if we are to extract lessons which are necessary to us all. There are two primary lessons. I don't want to labour the first. Flogging dead horses is no fun for anyone. But I also don't want to leave any vestige of ambiguity. This first lesson is not to do with how nice a man Lindemann was, nor with how good a scientist he was. It is to do, inescapably, with his scientific judgment in the sense I defined it on page 155, that is, his scientific judgment applied to practical affairs, in particular to military operations. This kind of scientific judgment is not a thing which has to be left to subjective evaluation for ever. To a meaningful extent, it can be tested. What a man recommended or predicted can be measured against what actually happened. His suggestions and decisions are on paper, and as a rule we can see what came of them. Technological history, even in the confusion of war, is more precise and ruthless than any other kind of history. By these standards, Lindemann's scientific judgment was unusually bad.

The phrase 'unusually bad' is not a loose one. It doesn't mean that we are thinking of an ideal certainty of judgment which human beings never attain. It means that, compared with a large number of other scientists in both the United States and Great Britain, making judgments about the same topics at the same time, Lindemann's record is a bad one. Compared with, say, Vannevar Bush, Conant, A. H. Compton, Lawrence, Fermi, Tizard, E. J. Williams, Cockcroft, Bullard, Blackett – to mention only some of the more obvious names – there is no possible argument about who made the most misjudgments, both positive and negative. It would be a constructive exercise, and quite practicable now that many of the documents are available, to draw up a list of the decisions in which these men were involved, and note their scientific judgments at the time. None of them, I think, would come out with a score of 100 per cent right: but a good many judged well a remarkable percentage of the time.

Lindemann did much worse. He was concerned with three major scientific judgments (the air defence of Great Britain, strategic bombing, atomic energy). We have seen his record about the first two. The third can be left until the history is published. He also intervened in a very large number of minor judgments. I will limit myself to a few examples. In the controversy in 1944 between the continuation of mass bombing and the Tedder–Zuckerman policy of bombing communications, he was on the wrong side. In one or two cases, such as those of *Window* and centimetric radar, his inceptive judgment was correct, and he then damaged his own credit by going quite wrong in his military judgment about their actual use. In other interventions, the documents about which must still be lurking in Government departments, notably the Ministry of Supply, he was wrong throughout. One would like, for instance, to see the papers about tank design.

People have often wondered, with genuine puzzlement, why his judgment was so bad. After all, he was an exceptionally clever man. His scientific equipment was wide and deep enough for anything he tackled. One explanation is, of course, that he tackled too much. He had the opportunity to intervene more than any scientist in the world, and he took it. That in itself showed a defect in judgment. But I believe the real defect lay deeper.

He believed, as much as any man of his time, that he could solve any problem by his own a priori thought. This is the commonest delusion of clever men with bad judgment. For anything like reasonable judgment, a man has to know when to rely on others and when to think, alone and uninfluenced, for himself. It is precisely that balance which makes for what we call judgment. Without that balance, the cleverest of men are going to make the worst of guesses.

VIII

The first primary lesson, then, is banal. If you are going to have a scientist in a position of isolated power, the only scientist among nonscientists, it is dangerous when he has bad judgment.

That is a lesson which shouts at one at once. But there is a second primary lesson which doesn't shout at one quite so loud but which a lot of us feel compelled to insist upon. If you are going to have a scientist in a position of isolated power, the only scientist among non-scientists, it is dangerous *whoever he is*. This was the lesson which burnt itself in upon many during the controversies of 1939-45: whoever he is, whether he is the wisest scientist in the world, we must never tolerate a scientific overlord again.

During what I have just written, there have been examples of scientists whose scientific judgment was very good. But even a Vannevar Bush, in solitary power among nonscientists, carries a potential danger too heavy to be risked. Incidentally, Bush would have been the first to say so.

If I were writing the lectures again, I should bring out the lesson even more emphatically than I originally did. It is the essential negative lesson of what I am trying to say. The positive lessons remain as I wrote them, or at least I have not anything constructive to add. But the negative one needs, in our present nonscientific administrations, to be written up in great block letters.

Let me finish by a terse example out of the official history of strategic bombing.[41] In the autumn of 1942 the Admiralty was still bitterly concerned about the use of bombers. On 30 October the First Sea Lord proposed that 'there should be an objective scientific analysis of the effects of the bombing offensive' and that this analysis should be made by 'a committee consisting of Lord Cherwell [Lindemann], Sir Henry Tizard, Professor Bernal, Dr Cunningham, Sir Charles Darwin and Professor Blackett'.

The Chief of Air Staff reacted by saying, in an undated note, that if the Chiefs of Staff really wanted further scientific advice 'Lord Cherwell should be asked to give or obtain an authoritative opinion'.

Those are terrifying words. Not terrifying because Lindemann was Lindemann, though that gives them an added twist. They would be just as terrifying if, for Lord Cherwell as the source of authoritative opinion, we read Bush or Compton or Tizard or any scientist whose judgment has been proved unusually good. For the terrifying thing is, not who issues this authoritative opinion, but that intelligent and high placed nonscientists should believe that it exists. *That* is the danger of having one scientist in a position of power among nonscientists. Whatever we do, it must not happen again.

NOTES

1. Charles Webster and Noble Frankland, *The Strategic Air Offensive against Germany 1939–1945* (H.M. Stationery Office, 1961), vol. 1, p. 324.
2. cf. P. M. S. Blackett, 'Tizard and the Science of War', *Nature 185* (1960), pp. 647–53.
3. cf. Sir Charles Webster, *Sunday Times*, 9 April 1961; *Times Literary Supplement*, 14 April 1961.
4. The Earl of Birkenhead, *The Professor and the Prime Minister* (Houghton Mifflin, 1962), p. 202. (This book was published in England under the title *The Prof. in Two Worlds*; page references are to the American edition.)
5. cf. Sir Frederick Brundrett, *Sunday Telegraph*, 29 October 1961. See also Professor R. V. Jones (who was a close friend of Lindemann himself), *The Listener*, 30 November 1961.

6. Birkenhead, *Professor and the Prime Minister*, p. 207.
7. *Sunday Times*, 5 November 1961.
8. cf. Derek Jackson's account, Birkenhead, *Professor and the Prime Minister*, pp. 246–7.
9. J. T. Randall's letter to C.P.S., 9 January 1962.
10. 'Science and Government', p. 124.
11. cf. A. J. P. Taylor, *Observer*, 9 April 1961.
12. Birkenhead, *Professor and the Prime Minister*, pp. 203–4.
13. *Spectator*, 1 December 1961.
14. Birkenhead, *Professor and the Prime Minister*, p. 3.
15. Ibid., p. 5.
16. Ibid., pp. 46, 130.
17. cf. R. F. Harrod, *The Prof* (Macmillan, 1959), pp. 29–30.
18. Birkenhead, *Professor and the Prime Minister*, p. 360.
19. Birkenhead and Harrod.
20. Birkenhead, *Professor and the Prime Minister*, p. 11.
21. cf. 'Science and Government', p. 107.
22. Birkenhead, *Professor and the Prime Minister*, pp. 205–7.
23. Ibid., p. 209.
24. cf. Sir Charles Webster, *Sunday Times*, 9 April 1961.
25. Blackett, 'Tizard and the Science of War', *Nature 185*, pp. 647–53, and *Scientific American*, April 1961.
26. *Time and Tide*, 6 April 1961.
27. In a letter to C.P.S.
28. A. V. Hill, *The Ethical Dilemma of Science* (Rockefeller Institute Press, 1960), pp. 265–71.
29. *Daily Telegraph*, 7 April 1961, and in conversation with C.P.S.
30. *Time and Tide*, 6 April 1961.
31. Birkenhead, *Professor and the Prime Minister*, p. 217.
32. Webster and Frankland, *Strategic Air Offensive*, vol. 1, pp. 331–6.
33. S. W. Roskill, *The War at Sea 1939–1945* (H.M. Stationery Office, 1954–61), vol. 2, pp. 83–5.
34. Blackett, in *Scientific American*, April 1961.
35. Roskill, *War at Sea*, vol. 2, p. 371.
36. Birkenhead, *Professor and the Prime Minister*, p. 210.
37. Ibid., pp. 252 ff.
38. Webster and Frankland, *Strategic Air Offensive*, vol. 1, pp. 400–1.
39. Ibid., vol. 2, pp. 142–5.
40. Birkenhead, *Professor and the Prime Minister*, p. 220.
41. Webster and Frankland, *Strategic Air Offensive*, vol. 1, p. 371.

THE MORAL UN-NEUTRALITY
OF SCIENCE

SCIENTISTS are the most important occupational group in the world today. At this moment, what they do is of passionate concern to the whole of human society. At this moment, the scientists have little influence on the world effect of what they do. Yet, potentially, they can have great influence. The rest of the world is frightened both of what they do – that is, of the intellectual discoveries of science – and of its effect. The rest of the world, transferring its fears, is frightened of the scientists themselves and tends to think of them as radically different from other men.

As an ex-scientist, if I may call myself so, I know that is nonsense. I have even tried to express in fiction some kinds of scientific temperament and scientific experience. I know well enough that scientists are very much like other men. After all, we are all human, even if some of us don't give that appearance. I think I would be prepared to risk a generalization. The scientists I have known (and because of my official life I have known as many as anyone in the world) have been in certain respects at least as morally admirable as any other group of intelligent men.

That is a sweeping statement, and I mean it only in a statistical sense. But I think there is just a little in it. The moral qualities I admire in scientists are quite simple ones, but I am very suspicious of attempts to oversubtilize moral qualities. It is nearly always a sign, not of true sophistication, but of a specific kind of triviality. So I admire in scientists very simple virtues – like courage, truth-telling, kindness – in which, judged by the low standards which the rest of us manage to achieve, the scientists are not deficient. I think on the whole the scientists make slightly better husbands and fathers than most of us, and I admire them for it. I don't know the figures, and I should be curious to have them sorted out, but I am prepared to bet that the proportion of divorces among scientists is slightly but significantly less than that among other groups of similar education and income. I do not apologize for considering that a good thing.

A close friend of mine is a very distinguished scientist. He is also one of the few scientists I know who has lived what we used to call a Bohemian life. When we were both younger, he thought he would undertake historical research to see how many great scientists had been as fond of women as he was. I think he would have felt mildly supported if he could have found a precedent. I remember his reporting to me that his researches hadn't had any luck. The really great scientists seemed to vary from a few neutral characters to a large number who were depressingly 'normal'. The only gleam of comfort was to be found in the life of Jerome Cardan; and Cardan wasn't anything like enough to outweigh all the others.

So scientists are not much different from other men. They are certainly no worse than other men. But they do differ from other men in one thing. That is the point I started with. Whether they like it or not, what they do is of critical importance for the human race. Intellectually, it has transformed the climate of our time. Socially, it will decide whether we live or die, and how we live or die. It holds decisive powers for good and evil. *That* is the situation in which the scientists find themselves. They may not have asked for it, or may only have asked for it in part, but they cannot escape it. They think, many of the more sensitive of them, that they don't deserve to have this weight of responsibility heaved upon them. All they want to do is to get on with their work. I sympathize. But the scientists can't escape the responsibility – any more than they, or the rest of us, can escape the gravity of the moment in which we stand.

There is of course one way to contract out. It has been a favourite way for intellectual persons caught in the midst of water too rough for them.

It consists of the invention of categories – or, if you like, of the division of moral labour. That is, the scientists who want to contract out say, *we* produce the tools. *We* stop there. It is for *you* – the rest of the world, the politicians – to say how the tools are used. The tools may be used for purposes which most of us would regard as bad. If so, we are sorry. But as scientists, that is no concern of ours.

This is the doctrine of the ethical neutrality of science. I can't accept it for an instant. I don't believe any scientist of serious feeling can accept it. It is hard, some think, to find the precise statements which will prove it wrong. Yet we nearly all feel intuitively that the invention of comfortable categories is a moral trap. It is one of the easier methods of letting the conscience rust. It is exactly what the early nineteenth-century economists, such as Ricardo, did in the face of the facts of the first industrial revolution. We wonder now how men, intelligent men, can have been so morally blind. We realize how the exposure of that moral blindness gave Marxism its apocalyptic force. We are now, in the middle of the scientific or second industrial revolution, in something like the same position as Ricardo. Are we going to let our consciences rust? Can we ignore that intimation we nearly all have, that scientists have a unique responsibility? Can we believe it, that science is morally neutral?

To me – it would be dishonest to pretend otherwise – there is only one answer to those questions. Yet I have been brought up in the presence of the same intellectual categories as most Western scientists. It would also be dishonest to pretend that I find it easy to construct a rationale which expresses what I now believe. The best I can hope for is to fire a few sighting shots. Perhaps someone who sees more clearly than I can will come along and make a real job of it.

Let me begin with a remark which seems some way off the point. Anyone who has ever worked in any science knows how much aesthetic joy he has obtained. That is, in the actual *activity* of science, in the process of making a discovery, however humble it is, one can't help feeling an awareness of beauty. The subjective experience, the aesthetic satisfaction, seems exactly the same as the satisfaction one gets from writing a poem or a novel, or composing a piece of music. I don't think anyone has succeeded in distinguishing between them. The literature of scientific discovery is full of this aesthetic joy. The very best communication of it that I know comes in G. H. Hardy's book, *A Mathematician's Apology*. Graham Greene once said he thought that, along with Henry James's prefaces, this was the best account of the artistic experience ever written. But one meets the same thing throughout the history of science. Bolyai's great yell of triumph when he saw he could construct a self-consistent, non-Euclidean geometry; Rutherford's revelation to his colleagues that he knew what the atom was like; Darwin's slow, patient, timorous certainty that at last he had got there – all these are voices, different voices, of aesthetic ecstasy.

That is not the end of it. The *result* of the activity of science, the actual finished piece of scientific work, has an aesthetic value in itself. The judgments passed on it by other scientists will more often than not be expressed in aesthetic terms: 'That's beautiful!' or 'That really is very pretty!' (as the understating English tend to say). The aesthetics of scientific constructs, like the aesthetics of works of art, are variegated. We think some of the great syntheses, like Newton's, beautiful because of their classical simplicity, but we see a different kind of beauty in the relativistic extension of the wave equation or the interpretation of the structure of deoxyribonucleic acid, perhaps because of the touch of unexpectedness. Scientists know their kinds of beauty when they see them. They are suspicious, and scientific history shows they have always been right to have been so, when a subject is in an 'ugly' state. For example, most physicists feel in their bones that the present bizarre assembly of nuclear particles, as grotesque as a stamp collection, can't possibly be, in the long run, the last word.

We should not restrict the aesthetic values to what we call 'pure' science. Applied science has its beauties, which are, in my view, identical in nature. The magnetron has been a marvellously useful device, but it was a beautiful device, not exactly apart from its utility but because it did, with such supreme economy, precisely what it was designed to do. Right down in the field of development, the aesthetic experience is as real to engineers. When they forget it, when they begin to design heavy-power equipment about twice as heavy as it needs to be, engineers are the first to know that they are lacking virtue.

There is no doubt, then, about the aesthetic content of science, both in the activity and the result. But aesthetics has no connection with morals, say the categorizers. I don't want to waste time on peripheral issues – but are you quite sure of that? Or is it possible that these categories are inventions to make us evade the human and

social conditions in which we now exist? But let us move straight on
to something else, which is right in the grain of the activity of
science and which is at the same time quintessentially moral. I mean,
the desire to find the truth.

By *truth*, I don't intend anything complicated, once again. I am
using the word as a scientist uses it. We all know that the philosophical examination of the concept of empirical truth gets us into
some curious complexities, but most scientists really don't care. They
know that the truth, as they use the word and as the rest of us use it
in the language of common speech, is what makes science work.
That is good enough for them. On it rests the whole great edifice of
modern science. They have a sneaking sympathy for Rutherford,
who, when asked to examine the philosophical bases of science, was
inclined to reply, as he did to the metaphysician Samuel Alexander:
'Well, what have you been talking all your life, Alexander? Just hot
air! Nothing but hot air!'

Anyway, truth in their own straightforward sense is what the
scientists are trying to find. They want to find what is *there*. Without
that desire, there is no science. It is the driving force of the whole
activity. It compels the scientist to have an overriding respect for
truth, every stretch of the way. That is, if you're going to find what
is *there*, you mustn't deceive yourself or anyone else. You mustn't
lie to yourself. At the crudest level, you mustn't fake your experiments.

Curiously enough, scientists do try to behave like that. A short
time ago, I wrote a novel in which the story hinged on a case of
scientific fraud. But I made one of my characters, who was himself a
very good scientist, say that, considering the opportunities and
temptations, it is astonishing how few such cases there are. We have
all heard of perhaps half a dozen open and notorious ones, which are
on the record for anyone to read – ranging from the 'discovery' of
the L radiation to the singular episode of the Piltdown man.

We have all, if we have lived any time in the scientific world, heard
private talk of something like another dozen cases which for various
reasons are not yet public property. In some cases, we know the
motives for the cheating – sometimes, but not always, sheer personal
advantage, such as getting money or a job. But not always. A special

kind of vanity has led more than one man into scientific faking. At a lower level of research, there are presumably some more cases. There must have been occasional Ph.D. students who scraped by with the help of a bit of fraud.

But the total number of all these men is vanishingly small by the side of the total number of scientists. Incidentally, the effect on science of such frauds is also vanishingly small. Science is a self-correcting system. That is, no fraud (or honest mistake) is going to stay undetected for long. There is no need for an extrinsic scientific criticism, because criticism is inherent in the process itself. So that all that a fraud can do is waste the time of the scientists who have to clear it up.

The remarkable thing is not the handful of scientists who deviate from the search for truth but the overwhelming numbers who keep to it. That is a demonstration, absolutely clear for anyone to see, of moral behaviour on a very large scale.

We take it for granted. Yet it is very important. It differentiates science in its widest sense (which includes scholarship) from all other intellectual activities. There is a built-in moral component right in the core of the scientific activity itself. The desire to find the truth is itself a moral impulse, or at least contains a moral impulse. The way in which a scientist tries to find the truth imposes on him a constant moral discipline. We say a scientific conclusion – such as the contradiction of parity by Lee and Yang – is 'true', in the limited sense of scientific truth, just as we say that it is 'beautiful' according to the criteria of scientific aesthetics. We also know that to reach this conclusion took a set of actions which would have been useless without the moral motive. That is, all through the experiments of Wu and her colleagues, there was the constant moral exercise of seeking and telling the truth. To scientists, who are brought up in this climate, this seems as natural as breathing. Yet it is a wonderful thing. Even if the scientific activity contained only this one moral component, that alone would be enough to let us say that it was morally un-neutral.

But is this the only moral component? All scientists would agree about the beauty and the truth. In the Western world, they wouldn't agree on much more. Some will feel with me in what I am going to say. Some will not. That doesn't affect me much, except that I am worried by the growth of an attitude I think very dangerous, a kind of technological conformity disguised as cynicism. I shall say a little more about that later. As for disagreement, G. H. Hardy used to comment that a serious man ought not to waste his time stating a majority opinion – there are plenty of others to do that. That was the voice of classical scientific nonconformity. I wish that we heard it more often.

Let me cite some grounds for hope. Any of us who were working in science before 1933 can remember what the atmosphere was like. It is a terrible bore when ageing men speak about the charms of their youth. Yet I am going to irritate you – just as Talleyrand irritated his juniors – by saying that unless one was on the scene before 1933, one hasn't known the sweetness of the scientific life. The scientific world of the twenties was as near to being a full-fledged international community as we are likely to get. Don't think I'm saying that the men involved were superhuman or free from the ordinary frailties. That wouldn't come well from me, who has spent a fraction of my writing life pointing out that scientists are, first and foremost, men. But the atmosphere of the twenties in science was filled with an air of benevolence and magnanimity which transcended the people who lived in it.

Anyone who ever spent a week in Cambridge or Göttingen or Copenhagen felt it all round him. Rutherford had very human faults, but he was a great man with abounding human generosity. For him the world of science was a world that lived on a plane above the nation-state, and lived there with joy. That was at least as true of those two other great men, Niels Bohr and Franck, and some of that spirit rubbed off on to the pupils round them. The same was true of the Roman school of physics.

The personal links within this international world were very close. It is worth remembering that Peter Kapitza, who was a loyal Soviet citizen, honoured my country by working in Rutherford's laboratory for many years. He became a fellow of the Royal Society, a fellow of Trinity College, Cambridge, and the founder and kingpin of the best physics club Cambridge has known. He never gave up his Soviet citizenship and is now director of the Institute of Physical Problems in Moscow. Through him a generation of English scientists came to have personal knowledge of their Russian colleagues. These exchanges were then, and have remained, more valuable than all the diplomatic exchanges ever invented.

The Kapitza phenomenon couldn't take place now. I hope to live to see the day when a young Kapitza can once more work for sixteen years in Berkeley or Cambridge and then go back to an eminent place in his own country. When that can happen, we are all right. But after the idyllic years of world science, we passed into a tempest of history, and, by an unfortunate coincidence, we passed into a technological tempest too.

The discovery of atomic fission broke up the world of international physics. 'This has killed a beautiful subject,' said Mark Oliphant, the father figure of Australian physics, in 1945, after the bombs had dropped. In intellectual terms, he has not turned out to be right. In spiritual and moral terms, I sometimes think he was.

A good deal of the international community of science remains in other fields – in great areas of biology, for example. Many biologists are feeling the identical liberation, the identical joy at taking part in a magnanimous enterprise, that physicists felt in the twenties. It is more than likely that the moral and intellectual leadership of science will pass to biologists, and it is among them that we shall find the Einsteins, Rutherfords and Bohrs of the next generation.

Physicists have had a bitterer task. With the discovery of fission, and with some technical breakthroughs in electronics, physicists became, almost overnight, the most important military resource a nation-state could call on. A large number of physicists became soldiers not in uniform. So they have remained, in the advanced societies, ever since.

It is very difficult to see what else they could have done. All this began in the Hitler war. Most scientists thought then that Nazism was as near absolute evil as a human society can manage. I myself thought so. I still think so, without qualification. That being so, Nazism had to be fought, and since the Nazis might make fission bombs – which we thought possible until 1944, and which was a continual nightmare if one was remotely in the know – well, then, we had to make them too. Unless one was an unlimited pacifist, there was nothing else to do. And unlimited pacifism is a position which most of us cannot sustain.

Therefore I respect, and to a large extent share, the moral attitudes of those scientists who devoted themselves to making the bomb. But the trouble is, when you get on to any kind of moral escalator, to know whether you're ever going to be able to get off. When scientists became soldiers they gave up something, so imperceptibly that they didn't realize it, of the full scientific life. Not intellectually. I see no evidence that scientific work on weapons of maximum destruction has been in any intellectual respect different from other scientific work. But there is a moral difference.

It may be – scientists who are better men than I am often take this attitude, and I have tried to represent it faithfully in one of my books – that this is a moral price which, in certain circumstances, has to be paid. Nevertheless, it is no good pretending that there is not a moral price. Soldiers have to obey. That is the foundation of their morality. It is not the foundation of the scientific morality. Scientists have to question and if necessary to rebel. I don't want to be misunderstood. I am no anarchist. I am not suggesting that loyalty is not a prime virtue. I am not saying that all rebellion is good. But I am saying that loyalty can easily turn into conformity, and that conformity can often be a cloak for the timid and self-seeking. So can obedience, carried to the limit. When you think of the long and gloomy history of man, you will find that far more, and far more hideous, crimes have been committed in the name of obedience than have ever been committed in the name of rebellion. If you doubt that, read William Shirer's *Rise and Fall of the Third Reich*. The German officer corps were brought up in the most rigorous code of obedience. To themselves, no more honourable and God-fearing body of men could conceivably exist. Yet in the name of obedience, they were party to, and assisted in, the most wicked large-scale actions in the history of the world.

Scientists must not go that way. Yet the duty to question is not much of a support when you are living in the middle of an organized society. I speak with feeling here. I was an official for twenty years. I went into official life at the beginning of the war, for the reasons that prompted my scientific friends to begin to make weapons. I stayed in that life until a year ago, for the same reason that made my scientific friends turn into civilian soldiers. The official's life in England is not quite so disciplined as a soldier's, but it is very nearly so. I think I know the virtues, which are very great, of the men who live that disciplined life. I also know what for me was the moral trap. I, too, had got onto an escalator. I can put the result in a sentence: I was coming to hide behind the institution; I was losing the power to say no.

Only a very bold man, when he is a member of an organised society, can keep the power to say no. I tell you that, not being a very bold man, or one who finds it congenial to stand alone, away from his colleagues. We can't expect many scientists to do it. Is there any tougher ground for them to stand on? I suggest to you that there is. I believe that there is a spring of moral action in the scientific activity which is at least as strong as the search for truth. The name of this spring is *knowledge*. Scientists *know* certain things in a fashion more immediate and more certain than those who don't comprehend what science is. Unless we are abnormally weak or abnormally wicked men, this knowledge is bound to shape our actions. Most of us are timid, but to an extent, knowledge gives us guts. Perhaps it can give us guts strong enough for the jobs in hand.

I had better take the most obvious example. All physical scientists *know* that it is relatively easy to make plutonium. We know this, not as a journalistic fact at second hand, but as a fact in our own experience. We can work out the number of scientific and engineering personnel needed for a nation-state to equip itself with fission and fusion bombs. We *know* that, for a dozen or more states, it need only take perhaps six years, perhaps less. Even the best informed of us always exaggerate these periods.

This we know, with the certainty of – what shall I call it? – engineering truth. We also – most of us – are familiar with statistics and the nature of odds. We know, with the certainty of statistical truth, that if enough of these weapons are made, by enough different states, some of them are going to blow up, through accident, or folly, or madness – the motives don't matter. What does matter is the nature of the statistical fact.

All this we *know*. We know it in a more direct sense than any politician because it comes from our direct experience. It is part of our minds. Are we going to let it happen?

All this we *know*. It throws upon scientists a direct and personal responsibility. It is not enough to say that scientists have a responsibility as citizens. They have a much greater one than that, and one different in kind. For scientists have a moral imperative to say what they know. It is going to make them unpopular in their own nation-states. It may do worse than make them unpopular. That doesn't matter. Or at least, it does matter to you and me, but it must not count in the face of the risks.

For we genuinely know the risks. We are faced with an either-or, and we haven't much time. The *either* is acceptance of a restriction of nuclear armaments. This is going to begin, just as a token, with an agreement on the stopping of nuclear tests. The United States is not going to get the 99.9-per cent 'security' that it has been asking for. This is unobtainable, though there are other bargains that the United States could probably secure. I am not going to conceal from you that this course involves certain risks. They are quite obvious, and no honest man is going to blink them. That is the *either*. The *or* is not a risk but a certainty. It is this. There is no agreement on tests. The nuclear arms race between the United States and the U.S.S.R. not only continues but accelerates. Other countries join in. Within, at the most, six years,* China and several other states have a stock of nuclear bombs. Within, at the most, ten years, some of those bombs are going off. I am saying this as responsibly as I can. *That* is the certainty. On the one side, therefore, we have a finite risk. On the other side we have a certainty of disaster. Between a risk and a certainty, a sane man does not hesitate.

It is the plain duty of scientists to explain this either-or. It is a duty which seems to me to come from the moral nature of the scientific activity itself.

The same duty, though in a much more pleasant form, arises with respect to the benevolent powers of science. For scientists know, and again with the certainty of scientific knowledge, that we possess every scientific fact we need to transform the physical life of half the world. And transform it within the span of people now living. I

* This was not quite right. It took slightly longer, but not much (1971).

mean, we have all the resources to help half the world live as long as we do and eat enough. All that is missing is the will. We *know* that. Just as we know that you in the United States, and to a slightly lesser extent we in the United Kingdom, have been almost un-imaginably lucky. We are sitting like people in a smart and cosy restaurant and we are eating comfortably, looking out of the window into the streets. Down on the pavement are people who are looking up at us, people who by chance have different coloured skins from ours, and are rather hungry. Do you wonder that they don't like us all that much? Do you wonder that we sometimes feel ashamed of ourselves, as we look out through that plate glass?

Well, it is within our power to get started on that problem. We are morally impelled to. We all know that, if the human species does solve that one, there will be consequences which are themselves problems. For instance, the population of the world will become embarrassingly large. But that is another challenge. There are going to be challenges to our intelligence and to our moral nature as long as man remains man. After all, a challenge is not, as the word is coming to be used, an excuse for slinking off and doing nothing. A challenge is something to be picked up.

For all these reasons, I believe the world community of scientists has a final responsibility upon it – a greater responsibility than is pressing on any other body of men. I do not pretend to know how they will bear this responsibility. These may be famous last words, but I have an inextinguishable hope. For, as I have said, there is no doubt that the scientific activity is both beautiful and truthful. I cannot prove it, but I believe that, simply because scientists cannot escape their own knowledge, they also won't be able to avoid showing themselves disposed to good.

THE STATE OF SIEGE

I

LAST year, 1967, I travelled a good many thousand miles. This was partly out of duty and partly out of curiosity, but the reasons don't matter. The fact was, I came twice to North America, Canada as well as the United States. I also went twice to the Soviet Union, on one trip almost the whole length – though not the breadth – from the Baltic coast down to Georgia. On the way back, I stayed in Poland. And I paid another call, a little nearer home, to Scandinavian countries.

On all those journeys, as you would expect, I had a lot of conversations with friends and acquaintances. Many of them are people I have known for ten or twenty years. At the end of it all, when I was back in London in the autumn, just a year ago, I was left with one over-mastering impression. Nearly everyone was worried about our world and what was happening to it. Nearly everyone was uncertain about the future. There was more – I don't want to use too strong a word – uneasiness in the air than I could remember. And it was an uneasiness that I understood, that I couldn't precisely define but without question shared.

I ought to make one or two qualifications. Like anyone of my age, I had known times when people round me had been more desperately and immediately concerned. That was true in the thirties in Europe. It was true, of course, in London in 1940 and further on into the war. But then the causes of concern were not in the least mysterious, long-distance, or obscure. There was usually something for one to do, it might be tiny or ineffective, but it took one's mind away. It was possible to hope for the end of the war, and a better time afterwards. It was possible to hope, not in a utopian fashion, but as most healthy people always want to hope.

Those situations were quite unlike the present one. Those concerns were quite unlike the present uneasiness. This is harder to

shift, more impalpable, nothing like so obvious. It isn't exactly un-
happiness or dread. Many of the persons I listened to last year were
entirely happy in their private lives. Some were not, it goes without
saying: some were ill, or had illness close to them, or the other
fatalities that afflict us all. It doesn't need explanation that they
should be in distress. But it does ask for explanation that robust and
happy people, of different ages, in different societies, should feel an
uneasiness that they can't shake off. Uneasiness which seems to be
becoming part of the climate of our time. Uneasiness with an edge of
fear? Perhaps. It is a bad state. It can be a paralysing and self-
destructive state. If I had been making the same journeys this year
instead of last, I am certain that I should have felt that this uneasiness
was deepening: just as I have felt it in myself.

What is going wrong with us? Of course, we are not the first
people in history to have this kind of experience or ask this kind of
question. But we can deal only with our own time and speak only
with our own words. It does seem – and though the feeling is
subjective it is strong and one can hear it expressed by the very
young – that our world is closing in. It gives us the sensation of
contracting, not of expanding. This is very odd. It is very odd
intellectually. For, after all, ours is the time of all times when men
have performed some of their greatest triumphs. It is, or ought to be,
exciting that there will soon be the first voyage round the moon: that
is a technical triumph, and for many, I suspect, a release from some of
our day-by-day unease. What for me is more exciting are the supreme
intellectual triumphs which we are not very far from witnessing. I
can remember, in Cambridge in 1932, hearing at a private gathering
the first news of the discovery of the neutron. That doesn't sound
dramatic: but it was extremely dramatic. From it flowed all the
fantastic Alice-in-Wonderland universe of particle physics, the
extraordinary collection of tiny bits which make up what we call
matter. For a generation that collection has become more complicated
and at times it has looked intolerably untidy. Now at last the
theoretical physicists may be within touching distance of a new order
– something which is still complex, but as beautiful and as revolution-
ary for the micro-universe as Copernicus's scheme was for the solar
system. If that happens – and the betting in favour is quite heavy –

it will be one of the supreme achievements of the human mind.

I can also remember, in Cambridge about the same time, listening to some of the first discussions about a new branch of science. That new branch we have now come to know as molecular biology. Remember that the first pioneering work started only thirty-odd years ago: and think what has happened since. D.N.A. The mechanism of heredity. The genetic code. The physical structure of life itself. In the whole of scientific history, there have been perhaps half a dozen breakthroughs which signified as much. And, like all real breakthroughs, the significance is going to seep into us more deeply year after year. That was true with Darwin's revolution. So it is, and perhaps more startlingly, today. It is likely that before long we shall be told of the making, in the laboratory, of a living cell.

These wonderful things have been done, and are being done, in our own time, by people like ourselves. If you read James Watson's book *The Double Helix* you will realise that they are remarkably like ourselves. With most of our frailties and with a similar component of original sin. But they have done these things, and that ought to make us feel proud to be living at this time, and to belong to the same species. Yet are we? I think only partially. We are not very good at counting our blessings. That is a feature of our particular uneasiness. And also we suspect, and we have some right to suspect, that for these great intellectual triumphs we shall pay a price. We can't enjoy our knowledge and our understanding as unselfconsciously and innocently as once we did. Upon us all there lies the shadow of Dr Faust: or, to be concrete, the shadow of the cloud over Hiroshima.

To some extent, those suspicions (which are really a distrust of the whole human race) show a failure of nerve. To an almost equal extent, they are essential: essential, that is, if we are ever going to build a tolerable world. I shall come back to that point later. At any rate, the suspicions exist. They prevent the most supreme achievements of our time giving us the liberation that they might have done. They may alleviate, but they do not stop, the pressure of a world closing in.

The world closes in. We are bombarded with communications, but again those don't set us free. Television has probably affected the pattern of our lives more than any other technical device – including the automobile and the telephone. Television bombards us with communications about the world outside – often unpleasant, often (at least in the television of the West) horrific. We know incomparably more than any human beings before us about what is going on in other cities, in other countries. Particularly the immediate prospect of human suffering. We know it is happening. We see people starving before they have died: we know that they are going to die. We see the evening's killings in Mexico City the same evening in London. We see the victims of famine in Biafra. We know it all. We know so much: and we can do so little. We turn away. There may be an even more sinister effect, to which I shall return.

Yes, we turn away. We don't project ourselves outwards: we turn inwards. We draw what in England we call the curtains, and we try to make an enclave of our own. An enclave, a refuge, a place to shut out the noise. A group of one's own. Enclave-making: that is one of the characteristic symptoms of our unease. You can see it plain in bigger and in smaller forms. Some of the bigger forms are cropping up right round the world. The revival of nationalisms, particularly of small nationalisms which had been half-dissolved in a more outward-looking age. Take my own small island. It would have seemed very curious not long ago to be told that a large proportion of the Scotch and Welsh are going to feel intense emotion about walling themselves off in little enclaves of their own. Incidentally making things very difficult for themselves in the process by, at least in Wales, immediately encouraging a first-rate language problem. Just as is happening in Belgium, one of the most prosperous and densely populated countries on earth: if there is any possibility of shutting ourselves off behind language walls, then, in our present mood, we rush to do so.

Further, one of the bigger forms of enclave-making, again all round the world, is the behaviour of great strata of the young. They too have turned inwards: into their own customs, and often their own private language: often into a private fairyland where what some of them describe as 'structures' do not exist. In essence, they are creating privacies, even those who go out in the streets: for once you try to dismiss structures, you are dismissing society, any kind of society, including primitive, advanced, or anarchist, and you are huddling into a private refuge of your own.

One could go on with the list of enclaves that we can see being built round us, or are building for ourselves. Race and colour the most isolating of them all. But clearest of all are the smaller forms of this process. Those are the forms which so many of us are taking part in.

Let us be honest. Most of us are huddling together in our own little groups for comfort's sake. It is natural, of course, for people to like their like, and to be easier with those who have the same associations as themselves. Most people, as they grow older, get support from those few they have known for a long time. That is natural. But we often use natural feelings as an excuse. We are turning inward more than is really natural. As I said before, we draw the curtains and take care not to listen to anything which is going on in the streets outside. We are behaving as though we were in a state of siege.

II

It doesn't need saying that there are some objective reasons, as well as psychological ones, why sensible persons in the cities of the advanced world should behave as though they were in a state of siege. The modern city, the city of the last third of our century, is not an entirely reposeful place to live in. For many of us, it has a certain charm. But it is no use pretending that it is much like classical Athens or sixteenth-century Venice. It is a great deal healthier, if one's thinking of disease: on the other hand, in terms of murder and bodily harm, it is very much less physically safe. The advanced world has, we all know, become remarkably richer during the last thirty years. This is true of all industrialised countries, including the U.S.S.R. Poverty has been diminished to an extent that most of us couldn't have foreseen, and certainly didn't foresee. There is extremely little subsistence poverty, for example, in Scandinavia and Holland. Not much in my own country. Thirty years ago, it was a genial assumption that, once poverty had been effectively got rid of, so would most crime go too. Has it? In fact, even in countries where poverty is now minimal, crime is increasing by a good many per cent per year. Someone calculated, a few years ago, that at the current rate of production, the entire British population would by 2040 consist of scientists and criminals. Since that time, unfortunately, we have fallen behind in our production of scientists.

All this is hard to take. The relation between crime and poverty isn't a simple one. We don't know the Soviet crime statistics since they became more prosperous: there aren't many sets of figures which would be more interesting. But we do know the Western statistics. They are bizarre. It is true that, for several special reasons, the United States is not typical: the harsh fact is that American cities are, in criminal terms, the most lethal in the advanced world. Britain has under 200 murders a year, and the United States something like thirty times as many. But, even in comparatively non-lethal cities like London, or Stockholm, or Budapest, nevertheless there is enough crime surging round one – far more than a generation ago – to give some reason for a siege mentality. As I say, no one understands this exponential development of crime in rich countries. It may be that modern technology, on the whole, makes crime rather easier: and there are also some dark truths about human psychology, which perhaps we have been too complacent, or perhaps too kind to ourselves, to wish to see clearly.

Yet, though many of us do live in an environment with that undercurrent of anxiety, that isn't the whole story, or even an important part of it. The major unease is deeper, subtler, and perhaps less selfish. Why are we turning inwards? Many of us are lucky, luckier in material terms than any large numbers of men have ever been. Isn't it ridiculous, or plain cowardly, that we should let ourselves feel besieged? Yet, much of the time, we do.

There can't be one single unique cause for this condition. All we are inclined to do, according to our temperaments and our particular society, is pluck out from a whole complex of causes one which strikes our fancy – or more exactly one which touches a specially painful nerve. An obvious one is the increasing complicatedness and articulation of the modern industrial state. An articulation which is to a large extent independent of political systems and which has been produced inexorably as a result of the technological process itself. So that we really don't comprehend it, even those who boom most confidently about it. We feel as though we are in a motor-bus driven very fast by a probably malevolent and certainly anonymous driver; we can't stop it, all we can do is show a stiff upper lip and pretend to smile at the passing countryside. There is no doubt that, to many people, this is a genuine response. It leads – because we like to invent names which excuse ourselves and make us seem less inadequate – to all the varieties of alienation and the existential absurd. It leads a good many to wish to return to an earlier and simpler society. About that, I'd like to remark in passing that no society *when men have actually lived in it* has seemed as simple as it does looking back. The nineteenth century seemed distressingly complex to intelligent persons who were there: just read about Dickens's Mr Merdle or Trollope's Mr Melmotte. Dickens and Trollope were men of great experience: their worries were not all that dissimilar from ours, they didn't see their way through any more sharply, and they were writing a hundred years ago.

Still, the complicatedness of the 1968 society weighs upon many. That is one of many causes of our unease. Nuclear weapons, biological weapons, the power to wipe out so many human lives. That *is* novel and peculiar to our time, and it is another cause. Any of us can produce more such causes, none of them the total answer, all of them part of the truth. I am going to produce two now. They are not original, they have been said many times. Again, they are not the total answer. But they are important. They are interconnected. They are among the noises that we don't want to hear.

The first is the sheer scale of the human enterprise. In many places and for many purposes, including some of the fundamental human purposes, there are already too many people in the world. Within a generation, there will be far too many. Within two or three generations – unless we show more sense, goodwill and foresight than men have ever shown – there will be tragically too many. So many that the ordinary human hopes will have disappeared. Disappeared irreversibly, perhaps: or at least for so long that we can't imagine how they will emerge again.

This is an old story now. It has become a cliché, as Mr McNamara said in September. As he also said, the trouble about clichés is not that they are untrue: often they are too terribly true. The trouble is, we stop listening to them. Incidentally, perhaps I might be allowed to mention my admiration for Mr McNamara's statements. They are the bravest and most direct that any world statesman has made so far. He is more optimistic than I can find it within myself to be: but the President of the World Bank ought to be optimistic, while I am speaking as a private citizen.

Well, it is an old story. Everyone knows the brute facts. At the time of the first English settlements in America, there were something like half a billion human beings alive. When people still living were born, that figure, the population of the planet, would be round one billion. It is now, in 1968, well over three billion. By AD 2000 it will be over six billion, and may be nearer seven billion.

Some of our thoughtful forefathers used to have, somewhere where their eyes couldn't evade it, a human skull. *Memento mori.* A reminder that you too are going to die. I sometimes think that every politician and decision-maker in the world ought to have on his desk that graph of the human population. A reminder that they too are going to be born.

It is no use trying to comfort yourself by doubts about this kind of statistical projection. In detail, of course, such projections can go wrong. That is specifically true for advanced countries. Before 1939, for instance, the demographic curve for the U.K. was pointing down, not up, as though the population would even out at 30,000,000 by the end of the century. It is now well over 50,000,000, and looks like being 70,000,000 by AD 2000. And we all realise that the Japanese cut their birth-rate in half between 1951 and 1961. But that was the conscious effort of a whole people, one of the most educated on earth, and also the one with the most unusual social discipline and history. Those are minor ripples in the gross statistical projections, and there isn't a responsible person who doubts that in thirty years there will be nearly twice as many human beings living in our world. That is the *least* that can happen. That figure can't be lowered by any of the steps that Mr McNamara and other men of sense would wish to put into action tomorrow. So much is foredoomed. The *best* that can happen is that the increase will slow down, and that from AD 2000 on we begin to approach a limit. A limit which is low enough not to kill hope.

Doubling the world population in thirty years. That is something new in history. On a small scale, countries like the U.K., as they became industrialised, had rapid increases in population. The U.K. doubled its population between 1800 and 1850, and again between 1850 and 1900. We were relatively rich, and had the wheat fields of America to obtain food from. There has never been anything comparable on a world scale. And it is only happening because of one of those paradoxes and contradictions that keep tantalising us as we try to think about the problems of our times. It is happening, in fact, because of our partial control over nature. It is not so much that more babies are being born: the point is, we are so much better at keeping people alive. Medicine has gone round the world, the poor world as well as the rich, quicker than anything else. Not only has infantile mortality been reduced everywhere (remember, our great-grandparents, even the privileged in the most privileged countries, took the death of children as an inevitable fact of existence): not only that, but the length of life is also increasing everywhere. That is a triumph, and any decent human being rejoices in it. But it is presenting us with a situation in some ways graver than we have known before, and one that we may not be able to control.

At this point I think I ought to make something like an apology or a confession. Nearly ten years ago I gave another lecture, which I called 'The Two Cultures and the Scientific Revolution', and which produced, and in fact still continues to produce, a certain amount of discussion. But the discussion has concentrated on what to me was a secondary matter. The primary intention – at least in my own mind – was to try to depict one of the major practical crises in the world, that is the gap between the rich and the poor countries, and to suggest certain ways of thinking, practical ways of thinking, which were needed before we could meet it. As you will soon notice, I am returning to this topic here and now. And I have tried to avoid distractions or provocations, so that it is my own fault if I can't make myself understood.

In the 'Two Cultures' lecture there was a curious and culpable omission. It is that for which I can acknowledge the guilt now. I was talking about world crises: and I made only the slightest of references to the growth of population. That wasn't out of ignorance. I knew the facts. It wasn't out of carelessness. It was deliberate. I didn't want this major problem to dominate the discussion. Partly because it seemed to me then to make social hope even more difficult: partly because I didn't want to hurt other people's religious sensibilities. The religious sensibilities of people whom I knew, respected and often loved; and of others whom I didn't know. I now believe that I was dead wrong, and seriously wrong on both counts. First, any social hope that is going to be any use against the darkness ahead will have to be based upon a knowledge of the worst: the worst of the practical facts, the worst in ourselves. It will have to be a harsh and difficult hope. We have never needed it more. Second, the situation is so grave that sensibilities of any kind, any of ours, any of those we respect but disagree with, have to take their chance. We are dealing with the species-life. That responsibility has to take first place.

In smallish ways, the pattern of population is already making itself felt. Certainly it is in parts of Europe, like England or Belgium. Or in Japan. Maybe not so much in the United States, though when one flies over your gigantic conurbations,* one feels that men are happier when they have room to swing a cat round. The Soviet Union, in most of its expanse, is still a surprisingly empty country, and it is much harder for a Russian than an Englishman to get psychologically involved in the population flood, though intellectually, of course, plenty of them are.

I have a suspicion that this flood is already making us more callous about human life. As I said before, the rapidity and completeness of human communications are constantly presenting us with the sight of famine, suffering, violent death. We turn away, inside our safe drawing-rooms. It may be that these communications themselves help to make us callous. And yet, perhaps also there is the unadmitted thought that human lives are plentiful beyond belief? I don't know. There is another paradox here. For, side by side with our major callousness – which is much harsher than that of people similar to ourselves at the beginning of this century – we show, in individual instances, a concern far more extreme than they ever felt. In my own country, for example, there was a depth of emotion which swept

* This lecture, like the two preceding ones, was delivered to an American audience.

away the vestigial relics of capital punishment that still survived –
which had come down to about half a dozen executions a year. These
individual instances occupied an enormous amount of time, both
parliamentary and private; they took up energy and outward-going
feeling: much more, so far as I can estimate, than the hundreds of
thousands of deaths by starvation in Biafra. Yet let us chalk up a
point in our own favour: at times we do care.

At other times, even within our own societies, we cease to care to
an almost pathological extent. Think for a moment of the numbers of
people killed in and by automobiles. In the U.S.A. upwards of 50,000
a year. In the U.K. 6,000 or so. If that happened through a disease,
there would be outcries, foundations, research. As it is, we take it
as an act of God: without feeling: like so many schizophrenics. In my
country, there was even loud protest against the introduction of stiffer
laws to deal with drunken driving: as though driving when drunk
was one of the more sacred rights of man. If there are sane, humane
and reflective people living in a better world than ours in five hundred
years, they will look back on some of our callousness with incredulity.
Perhaps with pity too. They may understand our situation in a way
that we are incapable of. They may say that we were overwhelmed by
the population flood. Or that we were living in one of the most
violent ages in history, and so lost both our nerve and a great deal of
our human feeling.

Just one more indication of how much we are overwhelmed. There
is no single person alive who can speak on matters of simple human
decency, and be listened to by people of goodwill everywhere. To
anyone who knew him, Einstein spoke with moral authority unlike
anything that we had ever heard or will ever hear again. But he also
spoke to many men. Someone described him, about twenty years
ago, as the conscience of the world. That wasn't too much of an
exaggeration. His voice reached across the divides and confusions of
our time. Now we have no Einstein. There is no man, and no group of
men, who could conceivably be called the conscience of the world.

Maybe those smallish things I have just mentioned are pointers
along our way. But now we can't avoid any longer the fundamental
trouble we are moving into: the trouble which, in truth, we are
already in. This has certainly contributed to our state of siege. Never

mind our mental states, though. The trouble is elemental. It is the contrast between the rich countries of the world and the poor. The fact that half our fellow human beings are living at or below subsistence level. The fact that in the unlucky countries the population is growing faster than the food to keep it alive. The fact that we may be moving – perhaps in twenty years – into large-scale famine.

III

I began by saying that when one travels in many different countries, one finds people sharing the same uneasiness. I might have pointed out that I was speaking, so far as first-hand knowledge goes, of the lucky countries of the world. Take a great arc through the northern hemisphere. North America. Almost the whole of Europe. The U.S.S.R. Japan. If that was the entire world, adding in a few additional fortunate pockets like Australasia, there wouldn't be much, at least in terms of the most simple animal fatalities, to worry about. These are the rich countries: which doesn't mean anything very sumptuous, but merely that the great majority of their populations have enough to eat, a place to live in, and perhaps, as a luxury, the chance to buy a newspaper occasionally, or even a book. That does not sound magnificent: but it is more than any big society has been able to provide for all its members until quite recently. Starvation was a danger in the background for our not-so-distant ancestors. Now we have forgotten about it: we have a knack of remembering only the pretty past. In the rich countries, food has ceased to be a problem. Industrialised agriculture has had its spectacular successes in the United States and Canada. If we wanted, we could grow more food. All over the northern hemisphere, population is rising relatively slowly: too fast for many amenities, but not fast enough to cause us the most brutal concerns. The lucky countries, if there were no others, could see a way clear.

Unfortunately, there are nearly twice as many people in the poor countries as in the rich. Further, there will – nothing can stop it – be an extra billion people added to the world population in the next ten years. Of those, rather more than three-quarters will be added to the poor. All these statements, as Mr McNamara remarked with great force, are clichés. A lot of us – and most urgently of all, American demographers and food scientists – have been uttering them for years past. Here is another. The gap between the rich and poor countries is growing. Take the average daily income in a large slice of the poor countries. It is something like thirty-five cents a day. The average daily income in the U.S. is about eight dollars a day. Twenty times greater. In ten years it is likely to be thirty times greater.

Yes, those statements are clichés, all right. Some of them are dreadful clichés: and I am using dreadful in its first meaning, that is full of dread. The most dreadful of all – again, men of sober judgment have been saying it for years – is that many millions of people in the poor countries are going to starve to death before our eyes – or, to complete the domestic picture, we shall see them doing so upon our television sets.

How soon? How many deaths? Can they be prevented? Can they be miminised?

Those are the most important questions in our world today. Much more important than all the things which fret us in Western societies – student power, racial conflicts, the disaffection of the young. Though I believe there is an invisible connection between our local problems and the catastrophic world one.

To answer those questions we have to rely to an extent upon judgment – which is really informed guessing. Most of the expert demographers and the agronomists take the most pessimistic view. It is usually right, in matters of judgment, to take a pessimistic view – so long as it doesn't inhibit one totally from action, even inadequate action. That is a lesson which we have all learned who have had any experience of war. But I want to stress that neither the extent of this catastrophe, nor the time it will happen, nor whether it will go on indefinitely or be controlled, can be precisely calculated. There are too many unknowns. One of the unknowns, or half-knowns, gives a glimmer of partial hope. I shall deal with that shortly. The only contribution I can make is to give my own judgment, for what it is worth. It is worth only as much or as little as anyone else's who can read the evidence. I am neither a demographer nor an agronomist. And there are different stresses of opinion among those who know most, and some areas of disagreement.

It is common ground that in large parts of the poor world, in sections of Asia, Africa, Latin America, the collision between rising population and available food is very near. The demographers say that there is no method of curtailing the rate of population-growth within ten years. With great good fortune, and world effort, a little might just conceivably be done in twenty or thirty years. They call on the agronomists to pull something out of the bag to give the demographers enough time. The agronomists – or a large proportion of them – make exactly the same demand in reverse. Can the demographers reduce the human increase soon enough to give *them* – the people working on tropical agriculture – enough time?

Most informed opinion believes that neither step is going to happen in time: that is, the collision is going to take place. At best, this will mean local famines to begin with. At worst, the local famines will spread into a sea of hunger. The usual date predicted for the beginning of the local famines is 1975–80, though I believe that may be over-pessimistic.

The only rational ground for putting this date further into the future is the hope of increasing food production. In fact, this is the chief area of disagreement between responsible men. Here, as it happens, there is the glimmer, the ray of hope, that I mentioned. In the midst of the bleak prospect, there is one genuine piece – though in the long term it mustn't be over-estimated – of good news.

On 17 July the Indian Government issued a special postage stamp. It was a stamp to celebrate the wheat revolution. Stamps have been issued for many worse celebrations: it is very hard to think of a better. We have had some gloomy figures in this discussion. Let us have one heartening one. In the 1967–8 season, the wheat harvest in India was 17,000,000 metric tons. In 1964–5, which had better weather, the harvest was 12,000,000 metric tons. Very nearly the same increase, and the same kind of record harvest, has been grown in Pakistan. For the moment, the fear of hunger has been beaten back from the subcontinent.

This is a success story, carefully planned, and the result of many years' work. A great deal of the credit, and it is pleasant to say it here in the middle of the United States, goes to two great private foundations, the Rockefeller and the Ford. In 1942 – note how long ago –

the Rockefeller Foundation provided the finance and encouragement for the International Center for the Improvement of Wheat and Maize, set up in Mexico. The Ford Foundation now provides half this centre's funds. The budget, interestingly enough, is not very large, under a million dollars a year: but the real secret has been the scientific insight. Dwarf wheat strains have been developed which have a high degree of resistance to tropical conditions. That took getting on for twenty years. In 1962 the Indians decided their best chance was to import those wheat strains. Their own research workers have introduced other genetic characteristics into them. The Pakistanis did precisely the same two years later, and produced their own Mexipak strain. Both countries have shown great efficiency in educating their farmers. The results would have seemed impossible as recently as five years ago. The Rockefeller and Ford administrations, the scientists, their Indian and Pakistani colleagues have done more concrete good to our world than is given to most men. If I were an elector to the Nobel Peace Prize, my vote would go to them.

Something of the same nature, again supported by the two foundations, is happening to rice. There is an International Rice Research Institute in the Philippines, which started in 1962 and has been producing a high-yielding and disease-resisting strain of rice. The most promising one, called IR8, has already been exported to Asia and South America. With any luck, more hunger will be pushed back for a while.

Well, this is good news. In making one's judgment of the future, it is a factor. We mustn't lose our heads, one way or the other. The limits to food production, even when as deeply planned as this, seem to be quite sharp. The population increase has no such limits. The collision is still on. The guess I should now make – as I said, this is no more useful than that of anyone else who reads the evidence – is that large-scale famine won't happen as early as 1975–80. There will probably (it is a bitter thing to say) be serious local famines, in, for instance, Latin America and parts of Africa. The major catastrophe will happen before the end of the century. We shall, in the rich countries, be surrounded by a sea of famine, involving hundreds of millions of human beings unless three tremendous social tasks are by then in operation. Not just one alone, but all three. They are:

1. a concerted effort by the rich countries to produce food, money and technical assistance for the poor.

2. an effort by the poor countries themselves, on the lines of India and Pakistan, to revolutionise their food production.

3. an effort by the poor countries – with all the assistance that can be provided under (1) – to reduce or stop their population increase: with a corresponding reduction in the population increase in the rich countries also.

Those are the three conditions, all necessary, if we are to avoid social despair.

IV

Despair is a sin. Or, if you talk in secular terms as I do, it prevents one taking such action as one might, however small it is. I have to say that I have been nearer to despair this year, 1968, than ever in my life. With the one exception that I have just mentioned, about which we all had an intimation before this year, everything that has happened in public has pointed in the direction of anti-hope. In 1967 one could feel this in the air. This year one can see it.

I don't mean anything at all subtle. It goes without saying that to avoid major war, there has to be some sort of understanding between the U.S. and the U.S.S.R. It also goes without saying, I suggest, that to avoid the catastrophe I have just been discussing – the catastrophe a little further ahead – there has to be something more than uneasy understanding, something more positive than coexistence, between the two great power centres of the world.

As for major war, I ought to say at once that in my view the chances are very much against. These may be famous last words, or rather words not specially famous because no one is left to know them. But major war – in the sense of a thermonuclear war between the two superpowers – has in fact been most unlikely for a good many years. The agreement on nuclear tests was symbolic. Great countries don't usually commit mass suicide. The military understanding has been worked out. The balance of power has remained steady. I believe, as I shall say in a minute, that both countries will spend increasing sums on armaments. But the balance of power will still remain pretty steady. The risk of major war will be there, but it is small, and probably the least of our worries. Minor wars, and dangerous minor wars, will occur during the thirty years we are looking ahead. In some of these, nuclear weapons may be used. But even that will not produce the mutual elimination of the United States and the U.S.S.R. The minimum amount of co-existence will be preserved.

But something more positive than that? The kind of co-operation which many of us have been hoping for – hoping for, not just in terms of vague goodwill, but simply because there, and nowhere but there, seems to lie the salvation of the planet. Or a tolerable prospect for most of our fellow human beings. For a brief period – one can even put a date to it, something like 1962 to 1965– there seemed a realistic chance. Now it has become remote. It may not have disappeared: one has to go on hoping that it hasn't disappeared: but everything that has happened in this dark year has pushed it further away.

Everything, both big and little. We all know the obvious examples, the hardening of attitude in both countries. Czechoslovakia, all that we are witnessing: but let me take something which seems less relevant and more innocuous. Student riots in France. There was idealism there. Some university reforms, which ought to have been made a long time ago, have been achieved. But, on the world scale – in the light of the world crisis in which these students are going to live their middle age – they did harm. There is no need to exaggerate the harm, but it is perceptible. Most of the population of France has been thrown back, like the rest of us, to this contemporary state of siege. That was predictable to anyone with the political intelligence of a newt. The forces which hold our advanced society together are very strong. Only people whose vision of the future is limited to about a week underestimate those forces. But the cost of bringing the forces into play can be very great. You know that in the United States. It tends to make the whole society look inwards. The French society is now looking inwards. And that was the last thing that we – if we have any concern about the world – wanted to happen.

Contemporary France hasn't, of course, made things easy for my country: they tend to regard us as a minor and displeasing extension of an even more displeasing United States. Incidentally I wish

General de Gaulle wouldn't insist on referring to us collectively as Anglo-Saxons. I happen to be one: but, purely on grounds of anthropological accuracy, he ought to recollect that he himself is far more likely to be of similar origin – from some related tribe which emerged from the German forests – than are about 60 or 70 per cent of the present population of the United States. Where does he think the northern French came from? But still that doesn't matter. It is a local quarrel. In the broader sense, we need France very badly. As an independent voice which can talk to the Soviet Union. And in particular which can talk to the East European associates of the Soviet Union. Warsaw, Bucharest, Prague and to some extent Budapest still look to Paris with greater cultural sympathy than they do to New York and London. If ever we can imagine positive colla-boration between the superpowers, it will need the kind of mediation which France could help supply. But France has been forced inwards. The independent voice won't be valid for some time. Positive colla-boration is that much less likely. Even small things, like the Sorbonne riots, have made their own contribution this year – in the wrong direction. It has never been more important to be tough-minded. There are a lot of gestures, protests, sacrificial actions, which aim at good things, which are in spirit progressive – and which in the result, objectively, end up by being the opposite of progressive.

Sensible persons may very well observe that this positive colla-boration between the U.S.A. and the U.S.S.R. is unimaginable any way. To cope with this catastrophe that everyone is predicting needs three separate quantum-jumps in human endeavour – each of them different in kind from anything that men have had the will to do before. The effort that the poor countries have to make on their own account – in particular the major effort to limit population in-crease. It must come from within the poor countries themselves: it must be matched by a similar restraint in rich countries (that is a psychological necessity): it must have the unqualified support of world opinion, including organised religion, everywhere. Can anyone, sensible persons will ask, believe that *that* will happen?

The first primary agreement between the superpowers to agree to collaborate for humane ends. Wouldn't it take some immediate hostile threat from elsewhere in the galaxy to make that even

remotely practicable? Even then, the suspicion, the to-ings and fro-
ings, the possibility that hostile intelligences from outer space might
perceive the superior virtues of American-type capitalism or Soviet-
type communism respectively? For any lesser danger, and a danger
ten or twenty years ahead, there is not even the language of discourse
in which the superpowers could collaborate. Can anyone believe that
that will happen?

The third quantum-jump is perhaps even more unlikely than the
other two, if that is possible. Assume the wildly improbable, that
some sort of collaboration is set going. Then consider the sheer
magnitude of the endeavour. To avert the crisis is going to mean
sacrifices such as rich countries have never contemplated, except in
major war. Much greater than the United States has ever had to bear
in any war. There are various estimates of what is required. The
most drastic I have seen doesn't come from an American source,
though many Americans have told us the size of the problem. This
extreme estimate is that, to make the world safe while there is time,
the rich countries would have to devote up to 20 per cent of their
G.N.P. for a period of ten to fifteen years. Obviously that would mean
a radical decrease in military expenditure: it would mean that the
standard of living would stay still, and then decrease. It sounds a
fantastic estimate: any amount of that order couldn't be absorbed by
the poor countries. But it is an error in the right direction. In the
whole of this exercise of seeing our dangers, most of us – and this is
certainly true of me – have been complacent. We have been playing
at it.

Anyway, the effort needed, both in money and human resources,
is immense. Even the United States – granted total benevolence –
couldn't do it alone. The U.S.S.R. certainly couldn't. The United
States and Western Europe together could make some sort of impact:
but that couldn't and wouldn't happen – since it would mean major
curbs in military spending – without the U.S.S.R. coming into
partnership. Even then, the cost would be very great. Not just in the
fairy arithmetic of governments, but in the ordinary lives of ordinary
citizens.

Does anyone believe that *that* will happen? We are all selfish.
Political memory lasts about a week, the professionals say. Political

foresight stretches about another week ahead. To stint ourselves to avoid a disaster in twenty years – what body of people would ever do it? Right. When sensible persons ask me any of those three questions – does anyone believe that that will happen? – the answer is, of course not. For myself, I wish I could: of course I can't.

Now I want you to consider the alternatives, that is, what will probably happen. I am going to suggest three models for the next thirty years. They are all projections, in slightly different directions, from the first part of this discussion.

Model A is the gloomiest. It is, I am afraid, the most likely. The relations between the superpowers will not alter much. They will still coexist, in the sense of avoiding major war. They will spend increasing sums on armaments, anti-ballistic missiles and so on: there will be no greater security for either, and probably not much less. Internally, they will change less than many who live in other countries would expect. This will disappoint both their friends and their enemies. The U.S.S.R. is a very stable society. So, despite all surface appearances, is the U.S.A. Incidentally I know no country where the surface appearance is more misleading. You will go on talking about collective nervous breakdowns: and remain, except for technological irruptions, not so dissimilar to the present state. You will still be burdened with the horrible legacy from the past, for which the ancestors of my countrymen were as much or more to blame as the ancestors of yours. A great many English fortunes were made out of the Negro slave trade – which, in the miscellaneous sordidness of human history, was one of the more sordid passages. And the sins of the fathers have been visited not only on the children, but on someone else's children.

Both the American and Soviet societies will get richer. In many ways, the U.S.A. will get richer faster than the U.S.S.R.: in places the U.S.S.R. will concentrate its priorities effectively, and will keep up. The rest of the advanced world will polarise, as now, towards one or the other of the superpowers. The increase of population all over the rich world may get a little less. In the poor world it won't, except in one or two pockets. Despite local successes, as in India, the food–population collision will duly occur. The attempts to prevent it, or meliorate it, will be too feeble. Famine will take charge in many countries. It may become, by the end of the period, endemic famine. There will be suffering and desperation on a scale as yet unknown. This suffering will be witnessed – since our communications will be even better – by the advanced countries, whose populations will be living better than they are today. It is hard to imagine the psychological and political conditions which will be created by such a gap. Some of us are lucky who won't have to live in them. Without question, the rich populations will feel they are in a state of siege, sometimes in a literal sense: and it may be that our present unease is a shadow thrown backwards from the future.

Model B is a shade more cheerful version of Model A. It depends on several things all going right simultaneously: some, though not dramatic, relaxation between the superpowers: the success of initiatives like Mr McNamara's: the extension of the Indian agricultural triumph. Some sanguine observers believe that, with immense good fortune, this might conceivably be enough: not enough to avert serious suffering, but enough to tide it over, and give mankind a generation's breathing-space to think and plan. I find it hard to believe that they are being realistic. But I respect them for saying, in effect, that in times of trouble it is better to do something rather than nothing. The worst doesn't always happen. That is an old stoical maxim that has taken us all through grim times. The trouble is, it may not be adequate for these.

Model C. This is by far the most unlikely of the three: and yet we have to act as though it is more likely than it is. The only decent way to respond to a state of siege is to break out of it. Or at least to try to. Most of us are private citizens, who can only do little things. But the whole world is made up of private citizens, and if they can see the situation, then the situation may be changed. Most of the time, human beings are rapacious and selfish. Some are capable of great nobility, but we can't build on that. Many in rich countries are so selfish that they would – and maybe will – be willing to get richer and use the technological superiority which their riches give them to fight off the hungry millions outside. I for one shouldn't like to live in such a world: and in purely material terms it couldn't be long maintained. But we have to take selfishness for granted. We can also, however, take human intelligence for granted. For all our faults, that has been the strength of the species. It is our best hope now.

We have to tell the facts. We have to make sure that people understand those ominous curves – the curve of population, the curve of food supply. We have to tell what the collision means. And this must be done, not only by high officials like Mr McNamara, but by private citizens like ourselves. Scientists will have to do it: people in universities are in a strong position to do so: it is the plain duty of churchmen of all kinds.

It is going to need great sacrifices. Including one of the most difficult sacrifices of all, the sacrifice of our rigidities. For, in some ways, a state of siege is comfortable. If we break out, we are going into the harshness of the streets outside. American citizens and Soviet citizens are called upon to face an unfamiliar harshness: the harsh but active assumption that the opposite society is not going to collapse, within foreseeable time. It is no use waiting until the U.S.S.R. becomes capitalist or the U.S.A. communist. If we wait that long, the world population will have doubled, redoubled, re-redoubled, 7 billions, 14 billions, 28 billions. . . . That is the fate which we have to drive home. By the side of that fate, our similarities as human beings ought to be stronger than our differences. Is there any hope that it will prove so?

One hears young people asking for a cause. The cause is here. It is the biggest single cause in history: simply because history has never before presented us with such a danger. It is a very difficult cause to fight, because it will be long-drawn-out, it is going to need using political means for distant ends. We have to stop being trivial. Many of our protests are absurd, judged by the seriousness of the moment in which we stand. We have to be humble and learn the nature of politics. Politics is bound to be in essence short-term. That is no one's fault. Politicians have to cope with the day's tasks. American governments have to try to keep their country safe, in the short term as well as the long. Soviet governments have to do exactly the same. But it is in the nature of politics that the short-term duties come first. It is the duty of all the rest of us, and perhaps most of all the generations which are going to live in what is now the future, to keep before the world its long-term fate. Peace. Food. No more people than the earth can take. That is the cause.

I should be less than honest if I told you that I thought it was likely to succeed. Yet we should be less than human if we didn't try to make it. We live in our time. This is the responsibility of our time, and it is our own. Sometimes I console myself with a piece of rabbinical wisdom:

> If I am not for myself, who am I?
> If I am for myself alone, what am I?
> If not now, when?

EPILOGUE

I⊤ will be obvious to anyone reading these pieces with an eye on the dates that I have become more pessimistic. The mood of 1968 and 1970 has altered, not grossly but perceptibly, from anything written ten years before. I am moderately certain that this is due to objective reasons – that is, that the state of the world, and the outlook for its future, have become manifestly more ominous over this period of time. As I said in the Prologue, hundreds of people have been uttering these warnings: it has made no effect, and of course it could have made no effect unless the tide were flowing with us. The tide has continued to flow in the opposite direction.

Perhaps there has been some tiny impact on education. The Prime Minister of Sweden, Mr Olf Palme, has told me that I have had a personal influence on the Swedish educational system: in a more impalpable fashion, it is possible that some of our statements – particularly those given with more professional authority than I could claim – have filtered into educational thinking in parts of the Western world.

When one's said that, one's said all. But what matters is not the failure of self-appointed spokesmen, but the objective reality we have been trying to face, and its direction in the future.

One danger has receded, that of thermonuclear war, or at least of thermonuclear war between the superpowers. It was always the least of the three major dangers, and has now diminished further. Blackett's* analysis – which in 1949 plunged him into deep trouble – seems likely to have been right. We can take some comfort from that.

But the other two dangers have not receded, but become more acute. The gap between the rich and the poor countries hasn't lessened. It is becoming wider every year. Nothing has stopped, or

---

*P. M. S. Blackett, now Lord Blackett, O.M., recently President of the Royal Society. Cf. pp. 113–28. He and I have thought on similar lines since we were young men, and his judgment has been better than mine.

even slowed down, this process. The United Nations agencies have done what they can, there has been goodwill in governments: but none of that has been able to break through the confines of the political and financial machinery. The poor countries are becoming relatively poorer each decade, and, certainly in some cases, absolutely poorer also. By the end of the century, the average income of a North American will be forty times the average income of his neighbour in Central or South America. It is hard to imagine such a world.

Even that, though, is not the worst of it. The menace – closely related to the disparity between rich and poor, but throwing a darker shadow – of over-population, the growing flood of human lives, hangs over all. If I were giving the Fulton lectures again, I couldn't be any more sanguine. There are now one or two positive factors, but the situation is not changed: except that time is going on, two years have passed, and we have no time to play with.

Early in 1971, I took the opportunity to introduce a debate on this subject in the House of Lords.* The House of Lords is a dispassionate body for such a debate, and there was no substantial difference on any side. I made an attempt to bring out the positive factors. Yes, the Green Revolution – to which I had referred at Fulton – has been a success, though a qualified one. It is proving possible to grow more food in Asia: but it is unrealistic to believe that that food-growing can be increased indefinitely. Dr Norman Borlaug's statement must be treated with full attention. He has been the pioneer of the Green Revolution, and in 1970 was awarded the Nobel Peace Prize. No one has ever deserved this prize more. In his first press conference after the award was known, he said that the work of his institute, and any similar work, could only win us all perhaps twenty years' breathing-space. The potential resources of food were limited. Unless the growth of population could be controlled, then we should destroy the species.

That was even more gloomy than I find myself. I don't believe that we shall destroy the species. The human species is extraordinarily tough. But it may very well find itself living in conditions which, to most contemporary Americans or Englishmen, would seem intolerable. The prospect which I foresee is similar to what I

* See House of Lords *Hansard*, 10 February 1971.

suggested at the end of 'The State of Siege': a prolonged period of hardship, sporadic famine rather than widespread, commotion rather than major war. To avoid worse will require more foresight and will than men have shown themselves capable of up to now.

In this same debate, while there weren't any major differences, there were some of stress. Blackett agreed with me in principle, but offered some grounds for qualified hope. A few countries had not only reduced their rate of growth, but actually stabilised their population. That is true of Japan, Hungary, Yugoslavia (incidentally, it is very nearly true of the United Kingdom). It was possible to envisage the world population stabilising at something like fifteen billion, four times its present size. With immense efforts we could provide for such a population.

I remained, and remain, unconvinced. At the end of the debate the Government spokesman asked me – with the friendliness and seriousness which had been evident all those hours – if I couldn't bring myself to be more cheerful. The question was too well-disposed to duck. I had to say that intellectually I couldn't. Emotionally I preserved a kind of irrational hope.

Intellectually I still can't, and I am afraid that I am unlikely to be able to. That means that I can't add anything helpful, which is a compelling reason for not adding anything at all. That is why I have decided to publish this collection now.

One last word. It is others, much younger than I am, who will have to cope with these problems in their own lives. Emotionally, I gain some courage from the attitude of the educated young – the educated young, that is, all over the West. They are far better prepared for their future than we ever were. They know more, often at first hand, about the poor world. They feel for it, with an unsentimental but brotherly feeling. They have thrown the prejudices of race away. They are more genuinely international in spirit than any generation before them. Of course, the political and economic barbed wire opposes them, just as it has opposed us. The objective difficulties are as harsh. Yet, for myself, if I can find any source of hope at all, it lies in them.